Motherloss

Motherloss

Lynn Davidman

UNIVERSITY OF CALIFORNIA PRESS
BERKELEY LOS ANGELES LONDON

University of California Press
Berkeley and Los Angeles, California

University of California Press, Ltd.
London, England

© 2000 by the Regents of the University of California

Library of Congress Cataloging-in-Publication Data

Davidman, Lynn
    Motherloss / Lynn Davidman.
       p. cm.
    Includes bibliographical references and index.
    ISBN 0-520-22319-5 (hardcover : alk. paper).
    1. Grief.   2. Bereavement—Psychological
aspects.   3. Mothers—Death—Psychological
aspects.   4. Loss (Psychology)   I. Title.
    BF575.G7 D37 2000
    155.9'37—dc21
                                                99-053072

Manufactured in the United States of America

09 08 07 06 05 04 03 02 01 00

10 9 8 7 6 5 4 3 2 1

The paper used in this publication meets the minimum
requirements of ANSI/NISO Z39.48-1992 (R 1997) (*Per-
manence of Paper*).

Writing this book brought my
mother, Shirley Zuckerman
Davidman, closer to me. For
her blessed presence in my
life, I dedicate this book to her
loving memory.

And to my husband, Arthur
Abrams, whose steady love
and nurturing enabled me to
dive deep into the past and
emerge into a happier present.

They are not dead who live in lives they leave behind. In those whom they have blessed, they live a life again.

Eleanor Roosevelt

Contents

Acknowledgments

It has been said that it takes a village to raise a child. The same could be said about writing a book. In the five years I have worked on *Motherloss*, I have been blessed with respondents, assistants, friends, and colleagues who have helped, guided, and nurtured me on this journey. The trip has always been challenging and occasionally quite painful, but I was lucky to be accompanied on it by warm and loyal supporters.

My largest debt of gratitude is to the sixty women and men who so courageously broke their own and the larger society's silences about death and shared their experiences with me. Constructing their narratives of motherloss brought back painful memories and feelings for them and for me. I am deeply grateful to them for their willingness to push through their grief and reflect upon it. Many interviewees told me that they volunteered for this study in the hope that others might be helped to avoid some of the pain they themselves had suffered. To the extent that this book can help to break the legacy of silences and serve to alleviate others' distress, I will have repaid my respondents' generosity, at least to a small extent.

At each stage of my work on this book, I was lucky to have an extremely bright, dedicated, and creative research assistant. I am grateful to Lila Corwin, Betsy Hurd, Liz Mackie, Susan Meagher, Kaitlin O'Shea, Samantha Coren Spitzer, and Maia Weinstock. Each performed a yeowoman's task of helping me to keep the thousands of pages of transcripts in order as well as subdivided by theme, to be on top of the recent literature in the field, and to think through various approaches to organizing the manuscript. Desiree Ciambrone, Kay Jenkins, and Lisa Welch provided inspired assistance at critical moments and I thank them.

In my final eight months on this project, Miriam Ryvicker became involved in every detail of the book's writing and completion. She came to know my interview transcripts thoroughly, read drafts of emerging chapters, and discussed with me—back and forth and round and round—the best form in which to represent the stories of motherloss. In the process we moved beyond the standard professor–student-assistant relationship to become friends and confidantes.

During the period in which I worked on this project, I was fortunate to have two fellowship years at two marvelously stimulating intellectual centers. In 1994–95 I was a visiting scholar at the Center for the Study of American Religion at Princeton University, where I participated in the weekly seminars on religion and culture. The invigorating environment there provided a context in which I had time and support to conduct many of my interviews and share my emerging ideas. I owe particular thanks to Robert Wuthnow, the director of the center, for his ongoing collegiality, advocacy, and enthusiasm for my work.

During the 1997–98 academic year I was privileged to be a fellow at the Bunting Institute of Radcliffe College. There, among a community of thirty-five amazingly talented women, I worked through the major themes and arguments of my book. Several of my "sister fellows" engaged with me deeply on my work: Marion Bethel, Anne Fleche, Mary Favret, Renny Harrigan (the associate director), and Ruchama Marton. My friend Anita Garey and I were lucky to be at the Bunting, working on our books, at the same time. During that year we talked through our emerging ideas, provided each other with steadfast encouragement and helpful suggestions, and shared the joys and struggles of writing as we sipped tea, took long walks, and ate great food.

I can honestly say that this book might not have been completed were it not for Shelly Tenenbaum's overriding belief in its importance, not only for a wide group of potential readers but also in my own life. Shelly and I have been intellectual partners as well as close friends for twenty years now. When, in the middle of this project, I was feeling sad and overwhelmed by the painful memories it was evoking, she insisted I had to go on and see this work through to its end, reminding me of how resolved and satisfied I would feel when it was finished. She knows me well and her judgment was, as it often is, right on target.

Mary Jo Neitz was my sounding board for various emerging insights, large and small. Over the five years I worked on this book we had numerous conversations about central themes, theories, and approaches. Her insights always inspired me while her friendship, tact, and humor provided me with strength, confidence, and perspective.

Shelly and Mary Jo, as well as Phil Brown, Lila Corwin, Anita Garey, Larry Greil, Maud Mandel, Ida Mann, Miriam Ryvicker, and Susan Sered all read the entire manuscript, and sometimes several drafts of the chapters. In addition, Karen McCarthy Brown, Ruchama Marton, Saul Olyan, Bonnie Ryvicker, Joyce Starr, and Alan Zuckerman read parts of the manuscript. All of their comments, as well as my numerous conversations with them during the years I worked on this project, pushed me to be my best—to think and write clearly and to take my analyses to their furthest limits. Each stimulated my thinking, strengthened my resolve, and encouraged me to follow my instincts and write a book that pushes beyond traditional boundaries and weaves together the social with the personal, the social sciences with the humanities.

This book owes its title to Jenna Joselit, whose tongue it rolled off when I told her I was casting about for a title.

Naomi Schneider, at the University of California Press, has shared this journey with me. She deeply believed in this project from its inception and she not only provided skillful assistance but also shared with me her own personal insights on premature maternal death, a common experience that made our working together on this book a gratifying venture. Sue Heinemann, my production editor, graciously oversaw the book from manuscript to published version.

To these and all the other people in my "village," my gratitude for stimulating as well as sustaining me while I probed deeply into others' and my own consciousness for insights into motherloss and for a life-affirming way to write about its meanings.

PART I

Introduction

I

The Researcher and the Researched

On Sunday morning, November 7, 1993, my father died. I was thirty-eight, he seventy-one. To say we were not close would be an understatement; he and I had hardly spoken for twenty years. But that night I accompanied my brothers to Jerusalem, to bury him there, next to the new grave to which my mother's remains had been transferred four years earlier. I had not seen this grave before; I had been opposed when my father and brothers had moved my mother's grave. Yet that night, at the cemetery where my mom and now my dad were buried, I was transformed into the thirteen-year-old girl whose mother had died. "I want my mom," I repeatedly sobbed, mourning the lost opportunity to have known my mother over the course of my life, to have her know me now as a woman. And I wondered about the many ways in which my life would have been different—and easier in significant respects—if my mother had not died when my brothers and I were young.

While I was crying for my mom, women in my extended family surrounded me, held and comforted me. My older and younger brothers were there, crying for our father, but they did not react to the expression of my long-held grief for our mother. We were together, but alone in our experience of loss. We had never talked about our mother before and were not about to talk about her then. Yet later, in replaying that cemetery scene in my mind and trying to fathom my brothers' reactions, I began to wonder not only about myself but about how their lives would have been different if our mom had not died of cancer at the age of thirty-six.

For more than thirty years I have pondered the ways in which the loss of my mother at a young age shaped me as a woman. But after my father's funeral another question struck me: How did the early loss of our mother affect my brothers' lives? How did our experiences, which were clearly shaped by gender as well as by our particular family constellation, social class, and religious and ethnic affiliations, compare with those of other adults whose mothers died when they were children? My passion to answer these questions has led me to research and write this book, *Motherloss*.

This book, at least in some ways, has been in the making for over twenty years. I began my career as a sociologist, exploring people, places, and issues that have great resonance for me personally. Throughout my academic life, beginning with my undergraduate coursework, I have engaged in intellectual work at least partly as a way to understand my own life. I pursued the fields of psychology and religious studies before coming upon the sociological lens, which provided me with the most satisfying ways of asking questions and seeking answers. By placing individual experience within larger contexts and by tracing the linkages between self and society, biography and history, sociology offers a broad perspective in which to understand individuals' lives and the factors that shape them.

The issues that have been most central to me, given the facts of my biography, revolve around the themes of meaning, identity, and gender. While I was growing up, I experienced two major biographical disruptions. The first was that my mother died of cancer when I was thirteen years old, leaving me in a patriarchal Orthodox Jewish home with my father and two brothers. The religious certainties with which I had been brought up immediately dissolved: I reasoned that if the rabbis my parents had consulted had assured them that everything would be fine, then the religion made no sense and there must be no God. Six years later my lack of religious beliefs led my father to disown me, and I was thrust into the world on my own to build a new life. These two experiences produced in me an ongoing passion for studying issues of gender equity, the quest for meaning, the construction of identity, and the intersection of all three.

As a sociologist, I am aware that the various ways individuals create a sense of self and build their lives are shaped by numerous social factors, such as gender, race, ethnicity, social class, religion, education, and the general cultural norms and values of the time. I was drawn to this discipline precisely because I found that highlighting these broader influences helped me to understand my own life and the lives of the people around me. For example, one source of the conflict between my father and me had to do with his upbringing in an immigrant Eastern European family and my coming of age and being educated at a time when the ideas of the contemporary U.S. feminist movement were widely available. His family had warm memories of the shtetl; I grew up in a secular, pluralistic society in which traditional religious norms were no longer taken for granted. By seeing our individual life choices in the contexts of these larger historical patterns, I was better able to comprehend the nature and sources of our differences. Although I was still unable to resolve these differences, the application of a sociological perspective was liberating; it enlarged and transformed my own understanding of myself and of others by seeing how our lives are molded by wider social and cultural patterns.

Questions about how people make sense of their lives are best understood through the use of interpretive, qualitative sociology. As research methods, in-depth interviewing and participant observation allow the researcher to explore individual and group experiences within the context of the local, particular settings in which they are lived. The intensive conversations that produce life history narratives yield "thick," rich material offering insights into the processes through which meaning is created and transmitted.

I have sought to answer my own questions about my disrupted biography, in particular the break from Orthodox religion and the premature death of my mother, by understanding how these personal issues are reflections of and are shaped by broader social processes. My research projects have brought me into contact with people who struggle with the same issues I do, or ones that are closely related. I seek to interpret and comprehend our experiences through a continuous movement back and forth between my own memories, feelings, and responses and those of my respondents. This process of digging deep into my psyche in order to develop a subtly nuanced, rich, and empathetic understanding of their lives and simultaneously using these insights to better comprehend my own life deepens the sociological interpretations and analysis yielded by this research. As I write this book, I incorporate my own experiences where they seem appropriate. I include them not simply to reveal myself to readers but because their presence serves a larger heuristic purpose. By entering into my own feelings of pain and loss I am afforded a pathway to understanding the experiences of others and the general issue of loss in our culture.

My two major studies, *Tradition in a Rootless World: Women Turn to Orthodox Judaism* (1991) and this current book, both focus on how people make sense of and rebuild their lives after experiencing a major, unanticipated "biographical disruption."[1] In focusing my research projects on narratives of disrupted biographies, I do not assume that all other people have smooth, seamless biographies without interruptions. Many individuals experience various biographical disruptions. In fact, postmodern thought points out that the overarching metanarratives through which groups of people in Western cultures have understood their lives have come into question. People's life experiences are often in tension and interaction with the expectations and scripts of cultural metanarratives. In my research, however, I highlight those particular, major disruptions that shatter people's culturally derived expectations of their life course, requiring them to reframe their biographical narratives. In this work I focus on the predicament of premature motherloss, a phenomenon that may have been more common in preindustrial societies but is relatively rare in the contemporary United States. My earlier study highlighted the ways people who adopt a religious way of life that is quite different from their parents' attempt to create consistent narratives that incorporate these changes into their ongoing sense of self. Both studies reveal that people who live through these sorts of momentous changes are uniquely situated to engage in the narrative production of identities and the reinscription of meaning. The disruption in their expected life course must be integrated into an ongoing, consistent narrative that traces and creates a coherent sense of self.

For me, writing *Tradition in a Rootless World* was a way of coming to terms with my disrupted relationship with my father, an issue that was central to the way I understood and presented myself to others. Completing it allowed me to move on, both in my psyche and in my research. This book, on growing up motherless, forces me to probe my memories and confront my feelings about my mother's death and its impact on my life, a subject that has been deeply repressed by me and my family. The silences around my mother's sickness and death began when she became ill. I was not told what was wrong with her, and when I guessed it was cancer (what else was unnameable in the late 1960s?), my father and aunt denied it. Their responses made me terribly confused about why my mother continued to be ill, recited Psalms all day, and clutched a piece of rock from the Western Wall in Jerusalem from the time of her surgery in September until her death in March. Needless to say, I was shocked when she died. The silences surrounding her illness and death have continued until very recently; my brothers and I have almost never discussed our mother, nor was it a topic I brought up even with my closest friends.

How deeply I sought to avoid talking about this issue can be seen in my self-presentation at my first appointment with the therapist I sought out when I was struggling with the blocks I faced in my dissertation research. When I told her my life story and got to the part about my mother's dying when I was thirteen, she immediately said, "That is a very tough age at which to lose a mother." I breezily replied, "Oh, it would be tough at any age," thereby making clear that I didn't like to talk about this experience, and instead tried to normalize it, primarily through silence, as best I could.

It has taken me many more years to feel ready to deal with and probe into my experience of growing up motherless. I had known for a long time that I would eventually have to write a book on this subject, as a way of compelling myself to break the silences and better integrate this powerful piece of my biography. Nevertheless, I felt unable to take on this challenging, potentially painful task until I had a sense of stability in my life. At the age of thirty-nine I had a tenured appointment and a house of my own; I knew that the time had come. I was already three years older than my mother had been at her death.

While the particular focus of this book is the social context of mothering and its impact on the experience of early maternal loss, this study weaves in an analysis of other cultural issues as well. *Motherloss* reveals and breaks a series of overlapping silences and prohibitions in our culture, in families, in the academy—which frowns upon the use of the "personal" in scholarly work—and in our capacity for knowledge (of self, other, culture, etc.) in circumstances of rupture (a common feature of human life). I am working against the assumption that the "personal" should not be an acknowledged or explicit epistemological component of our quest for knowledge and understanding. Without exposing individual and collective taboos and assessing their sources and origins, academic research runs the risk of simply reproducing social barriers and deepening silences. This book points to one, albeit challenging, path out of this danger. In writing this book I have tried not only to place or re-place my mother in my life story and my interviewees' dead mothers in their stories, but also to reintegrate parts of our experiences that have been fractured and denied within social and academic discourse.

As I worked on this study, I was more informed than in my first project by the postmodern turn in ethnography that has led to the production of more critical, experimental forms of fieldwork narratives, particularly within the discipline of anthropology.[2] It has become less plausible to present material on others' lives that rests on the naive assumption of the authority of a researcher who goes to live among "others," discerns what manner of lives they lead, and simply reports these findings back to an audience of outsiders. Instead, contemporary ethnography rests on the assumption that all knowledge in the field is produced through the interactions between a researcher, who is a socially situated self with particular life experiences, and her respondents, who bring to the dialogue their own embedded assumptions and meanings. Analyzing the ways in which these conversations we call interviews create and shape the narratives produced is as essential to our comprehension of the subject matter as are the actual words of our interviewees. Thus I have chosen to write a more self-reflexive book this time, one that seeks to balance and mediate between the inside and the outside, self and others, individuals (including myself) and the social.

Although I represent my own experiences of mother-loss at relevant points throughout this book, the project is not primarily autobiographical. My goal is to explore the various ways that early motherloss, as it is experienced within particular social contexts, shapes the narratives people construct about their lives. My interviews for this project provided a context in which I participated with my respondents in creating narratives that make sense of their disrupted biographies and tie together the diverse parts of their lives, while doing the same for myself. Narratives, like memoirs, are constructed ways of making sense of a life. People tell stories or write memoirs to say something about who they are as individuals and the combination of personal experiences and social/cultural contexts that shaped their identities. Our stories root us, give us identity and grounding and a guideline for action. The particular linkages and connections people make in these narratives—such as "I can't nurture because I had no mother"—help them account for their life choices and constitute the primary basis for my analysis. Narratives not only render human experience meaningful and comprehensible, they also become part of human experience by enabling people to create and direct their present and their future expectations. The act of telling is as much a glance at the past as a guide for the present and future.

The interviews for this study took place over a period of three years. I engaged in intensive conversations with sixty women and men from a variety of class backgrounds whose mothers died when these adults were children between ten and fifteen years of age. I chose this particular age range because at ten a child is old enough to retain clear memories and at fifteen she is still young enough to have significant growing up to do. Also, since my own mother had died when I was thirteen, I was particularly interested in the experiences of motherloss in early adolescence. My selection of this particular life stage, however, is not meant to confine the relevance of this book to a narrow range of people. My conversations with individuals who experienced a parent's death at any age, and the reactions of individuals who have heard me talk about this work, suggest that there are many commonalities in individuals' experiences of a wide variety of losses. *The Loss That Is Forever* argues that when people under twenty-one years of age lose a parent, they never fully recover from that loss, a feeling that was expressed by many of my interviewees.[3] Similarly, Carolyn Ellis's account of her lover's death echoes many of the dimensions of loss outlined in this book.[4] So do the narratives of many individuals who lost parents as adults,[5] as well as people whose parents were present physically but emotionally absent during their childhoods.[6]

Through my research interviews, I engaged in the co-creation of narratives about motherloss, using others' experiences to illuminate my own and developing an empathic understanding of their experiences by digging deep into my own psyche for memories and feelings about my mother's death and its impact on my life.

When I began interviewing for this project, several people I know introduced me to friends, acquaintances, or relatives whose mothers had died when these adults were children. Immediately I found that people were willing to be interviewed about their memories and experiences of motherloss. I obtained my first six interviewees through these methods. In addition, two students at Brown University, where I teach, responded to an ad I placed in the student newspaper and agreed to be interviewed. After a few months, however, it became clear to me that I would not obtain a large or diverse enough sample through word of mouth, and I decided to advertise more widely for respondents.

I placed advertisements in daily newspapers in several northeastern cities and in the Sunday *New York Times*— publications that would be seen by a large and diverse population. To broaden my sample I also recruited participants through a free weekly advertising magazine that reaches people across social classes, placed an ad in a newspaper read by African Americans, and placed notices in community centers and supermarkets. Through these advertisements and the earlier word-of-mouth approach, I recruited a total of sixty interviewees, half women and half men. The large majority of the mothers of these interviewees had died of cancer or other long-term illnesses; about a third had died suddenly from such diverse causes as a heart attack, a cerebral hemorrhage, complications after surgery, and a car crash. Six were suicides.

In the first two years of interviewing, I had many more responses from women than from men. As I tried to understand why, several female respondents provided some clues. Two women told me that their husbands were amazed at their willingness to be interviewed on such a deeply personal subject. One husband had said on the morning of his wife's interview: "You're going to talk to a stranger about this?!" Over the past several decades, popular literature as well as academic research has suggested that women's sense of self is more relational than men's and that women are more likely to be emotionally attuned and expressive.[7] Perhaps this is one explanation for the fact that more women than men responded to an ad that asked them to participate in a study designed to probe their responses to a profound loss.

After I had interviewed thirty women but only thirteen men, I realized I had to be more proactive about recruiting male interviewees, since a central question I was concerned with was how gender shaped accounts of motherloss and its aftermath. An advertising manager of a newspaper suggested that I place an ad in either the auto or the sports section of the paper, and that instead of heading it "Interviewees Wanted," I should write, "Men Wanted." I followed this advice and received sufficient calls from men to complete my sample. (I also received some calls from women asking why I was only looking for men!) The ad stated that a sociology professor was looking for adults whose mothers had died when these adults were children, aged ten to fifteen, in order to interview them for a research project. I provided a phone number where I could be reached and assured readers of anonymity and confidentiality.

My interviewees ranged in age from twenty to eighty, with the large majority in their forties, fifties, and sixties. Thus they grew up in the 1940s, 1950s, and early 1960s—during the period of the postwar glorification of motherhood, the nuclear family, and the home. My respondents were spread across the range of social classes, although the majority were middle-class. In order to get a sense of their social class, I asked questions about their parents' employment and educational histories, the kind of housing they grew up in, and their sense of their families' economic situation when they were growing up. I then asked about their own (and their spouses') level of education, current employment situation, housing, and overall sense of economic standing. Five people described themselves as growing up poor; two of them remain poor today and live with the help of public assistance. Twelve interviewees described working-class backgrounds and current situations—their parents completed no more than a high school education (if that) and were employed in factories or had other low-income jobs. These respondents themselves did not have a college education, and worked at jobs that made it difficult for them always to be economically self-sufficient. A few lived with family members other than their spouses in order to make ends meet. Twelve other respondents who described working-class backgrounds had moved into the middle class, through either education, professional training, business ownership, or some combination of these. Fully half of my respondents, thirty people, had always been members of the middle class. Five individuals either had been born into or had achieved upper-middle-class status, with family incomes above $200,000 a year.

All of the interviews took place in the Northeast, in several cities and towns. The large majority of my interviewees were white and of European descent. Six respondents were people of color: a Mexican American man; one male and two female Asian Americans, all of them middle-class; one African American woman who grew up quite poor but was comfortably working-class now; and a biracial man who had a working-class background and was still working-class. Thus this book is based more on the experiences of white middle-class Euro-Americans than on those of any other group, and includes analyses of the impact of their social class and gender on their experiences of motherloss and its consequences. In the chapter that follows, and throughout the book, I discuss how motherloss affects the type of family that policy makers, social scientists, and often ordinary folk deemed "normative" when these people were growing up—that is, the nuclear family, with a wage-earning husband and a stay-at-home wife.[8] It is this hegemonic model of the family embedded in our social institutions and idealized in our culture that is missed and lamented by my interviewees.

In families that live in extended kin networks or other varieties of household and family structures, more people than the mother may be involved in the intense emotional and physical work of caring for young children. Maternal death is thus likely to be experienced differently within

these families.[9] This study of motherloss cannot gener-
alize to make claims about families that are arranged differently from the nuclear family model. I look forward to
the work of scholars who will enlarge the perspective offered here by conducting new studies of the various forms
and meanings of motherloss among people whose family
structures and roles may yield narratives that vary in significant ways from those represented here.

Interviewing people about such an emotionally
charged subject is quite challenging, especially since it is
an issue about which I have my own (not always conscious) emotions. During the interviews, many of my respondents—over half of the women and a third of the
men—cried as they told their stories of pain and loss. At
those moments I paused and sat with them while they
cried. To me this was the most appropriate response, especially in view of the fact that when their mothers were
ill, when they died, and even afterward, most respondents
were encouraged not to cry but to be strong and move
on. Several people apologized for crying; some said, "I did
not expect to do this." I assured them that this was a perfectly understandable response, given the depth of pain
and loss involved in losing a mother at a young age.
Sometimes the person's account touched on themes that
were central in my story and my own eyes filled with
tears; on occasion my eyes filled with tears of empathy
even if it was not a subject that struck home personally.
When the person was ready, we continued with the interview.

The silences and taboos surrounding early maternal
death make it difficult to construct a coherent life story
that weaves in the significance of this event. This became
apparent during the interviewing process. When I began
talking with people about motherloss and its aftermath

in their lives, my intention was to ask a bare minimum of questions so that they would be free to tell their stories in any way they chose, including the order of the narrative, the relevant details, and the special emphases. I soon found, however, that this was not an easy subject for people to simply expound upon. Respondents asked me to prompt them with questions to help them focus, remember, and articulate. After four interviews it became clear that I should prepare an interview guide that would help jog people's memories and provide a framework for our discussions. Drawing on insights from the first few interviews, from my own life, and from a diverse body of literature on families, on mothering, and on loss, I developed a set of specific albeit open-ended questions that helped to draw people out.

Ethnographers are emotion workers. In order to do this work with integrity we need to seek actively to create a safe space for our interviewees as well as for ourselves. We have to rely on our instincts and on our general socialization as members of the society, knowing the norms of what to say and when. But sometimes we need to rethink our instincts in order to carry out our work. Because in our culture death is a taboo subject and we are surrounded by advertisements and elements of popular culture telling us that we should be happy, members of our society often instinctually try to smooth over others' expressions of sadness and loss; "Don't cry," they say, or "It will be OK." Ethnographers have these same conditioned reactions. During my interviews, however, that would have been an inappropriate response: it would have put me in the role of deepening and furthering the silences that nearly all of my respondents have faced throughout their lives. That would have constituted a violation of their feelings and their freedom to express them. I worked hard to establish an atmosphere of openness and acceptance, finding ways to validate and affirm the sentiments that emerged in the interviews.

Sometimes, when an interviewee was describing a situation or reaction we had in common, I interjected a brief comment about the parallels with my own experience. In general, though, I avoided talking about myself or my findings, unless the person specifically asked. Although I clearly recognize that interviews are conversations, I thought it would dishonor the person's focus on her story by intruding my own. The interview was meant to be a context in which my respondents could pull together and articulate what were usually buried and long-hidden reactions; to shift the focus to myself seemed disrespectful and potentially distracting. I know that feminist and other forms of progressive research aim to break down the subject-object hierarchy of the standard research situation, in which the interviewer retains power by asking questions and the interviewee becomes vulnerable by revealing personal information.[10] When I began this project I thought I would try to minimize those distinctions, and that one way to do so would be to share information about myself. But early on I came to realize that the subject of the research was one that had caused great disruption in people's identities and their biographies. Through the interview, respondents had an opportunity to revisit this disruption and reweave a coherent life story. Interjecting myself into the construction of these narratives would have taken attention and focus away from the respondent and further disrupted the person's attempt to mend his disrupted biography. Many interviewees, however, inquired about my general findings at the end of our conversations; they were eager to know whether their own experiences made sense and could be understood as "normal," given the circumstances. At that point I responded to their questions in a general way, not offering information about any particular people.

While most of my respondents articulated the profound pain that accompanies early motherloss and were open in their emotional expressions of this pain, I also sometimes noticed someone controlling the amount of pain she allowed in during the interview. For example, an expressive fifty-two-year-old professional woman became tearful at the beginning of the interview, as she began to immerse herself in the details of her early experiences of motherloss. At that point she sat up, blew her nose, and said, "I did not think this would be so hard." I could see her pulling herself together and resolving then that she would not let in so much intense pain during the remainder of the interview. She sat up in her seat, arranged her face, and seemed to take on an air of resolve. She did not cry again during the three-hour interview.

Conducting such interviews—or doing research on any kind of trauma—is a very demanding process. Although I worked out my own reactions and solutions, I believe there are common dilemmas that arise for many researchers who focus on painful, deeply troubling experiences in others'—and perhaps their own—lives. It is my hope that as we and our respondents break the silences that keep these traumatic experiences invisible, social scientists will more explicitly develop an ethic of care—of ourselves and others—that we may apply to our research.

During several phases of the research, I did an interview nearly every day. At one point I was traveling by public transportation up to two hours each way to meet my interviewee, often in her or his home. (All respondents were interviewed in the place of their choice; a few selected my office in order to ensure their privacy.) The interviews themselves typically lasted for two hours; sometimes they went on for several hours more. Needless to say, the process was quite draining. After I wrote up notes from the interview, I found myself unable to do much else for the rest of the day; I frequently found myself sitting still, staring off into space. I felt like a rag doll, limp and exhausted. I was aware that these reactions stemmed not only from the rigors of the research process but also from the gut responses I had to so many of the stories. The themes of silences, loss of caring, and attempts to replace that lost caring were emerging loud and clear. People often spoke of fathers who simply could not cope with their own pain and loss, let alone their children's emotional (and sometimes physical) suffering. These themes struck deep chords in me, bringing up buried feelings of sadness and loss for my own similar experiences. And so with the help of a therapist I worked to become conscious of my own repressed memories and responses. Having a clearer grasp of my own sensibilities and sensitivities helped me focus on the similarities as well as the important distinctions between my story and those of my interviewees.

While this research has taught me a great deal about numerous dimensions of social life, it has also engaged my whole being: my conscious actions, such as having my mother's picture on my desk as I write; my conversations, in which I now am more likely to talk about my mother, what she was like, and what her death meant to me; and my subconscious life as well. Repeatedly while working on this project my dreams have given voice and image to my suppressed memories. In the middle of my research, I found myself quite depressed by all the pain and emotional devastation revealed by my respondents and the ways these feelings echoed in my own psyche. I felt paralyzed, unable to proceed any further. I discussed these feelings with some of my closest friends, and most felt I should drop the project, that it was too deeply painful to stay with for the remaining two to three years that it would take to complete the book. And yet just when I thought I had reached a clear decision to stop, my mother began to appear in my dreams, something that had happened only rarely before. I knew then that I could not give up; my mother had come to help guide the way.

There was a pattern to my dreams about my mother. In some, she would reappear after being gone (dead?) for a while, and would once again be living with me and my father and brothers in my childhood home. Yet she was somehow not properly fulfilling her old roles, especially the task of feeding us, one of the key functions of women in families.[11] In all of these dreams I and sometimes my older brother were quite concerned about planning meals, purchasing food, and putting it on the table. In some of these dreams I would confront my mother or complain to my father about her failure to feed us properly. These dreams continued over a period of three years as I worked on this project. At some points they would be repeated four or five nights a week. These dreams not only revealed to me how tough it had been for me, as a young adolescent, to take on a maternal role, but also provided insights that shaped parts of my interviews. In fact, nearly all of my respondents described the disruption in daily meals that resulted from their mother's illness and death. These conversations helped me understand how critical the mother's feeding her family is, not only for its nutritional value but as a symbolic manifestation of her caring. And indeed, the social organization of gender, with its assignment of the caretaking role largely to women, is the key structural and cultural factor that shapes individuals' experiences of motherloss and its consequences.

During my analysis of my interview transcripts I hit another roadblock. I found that the process of sitting in solitude at my desk and lingering over the interview material so that I could develop my analysis was quite painful. For a few weeks I found myself leaving my office every afternoon and treating myself to an ice cream cone, whose symbolic significance as a search for sustenance was suggested by a friend. At one point I came to a standstill. I was trying to read the transcript of an interview with a man who was in a deep depression and expressed his despair about making a satisfactory life for himself. The fact that this man had been disinherited by his father compounded his feelings of abandonment caused by the death of his mother—an event that can be perceived as a loss of something our society regards as a birthright. His narrative was a story of painful loss, of betrayal by his father, who allowed his new wife to take over the family property; she was currently residing there with her children, excluding my interviewee. For about two weeks I found myself barely able to work—I felt that I had to get through that particular transcript in order to go on, and I just could not make my way through that interview material. Again a friend stepped in to help, by pointing out to me the connections between that narrative and my own life story of being (unintentionally) abandoned by my mother and being rejected and disinherited by my father. Although I saw the connection, it did not ease the process right away.

At that time I was blessed with two undergraduate research assistants who were helping me with various aspects of the research process. I asked them if they would be willing to read some transcripts aloud to me, explaining to them what I was going through. They immediately said yes and so one of them read aloud that particularly painful transcript while I took notes. Somehow, by removing the isolation of working on it all alone, I found it much easier to make my way through this transcript. For the next month my students took turns reading one transcript to me each working day. Motherloss, as many of my interviewees reported it, often produces a deep sense of isolation and aloneness. My students' presence with me as we made our way through these painful narratives helped create a more comfortable environment in which I could continue to work. As I worked on the interview transcripts and the feelings they evoked, I understood that my task required my ability to function on several levels. In order to do the analytic work with the interview texts, I had to recognize the grief they brought up in me. During this stage, one key aspect of my work was grieving. As I came to a better comprehension of the meaning of my own loss and integrated it into my life, I was able to think through the wider theoretical implications of this study.

Two years ago I began to dream about being afflicted with some form of paralysis. In some dreams I was walking and suddenly found myself unable to move my legs; in others, my vision was impaired, and I could no longer see. To me these dreams revealed my anxiety about making my way through my own and others' repressed memories and feelings about motherloss, developing an analytic interpretation, and writing my book. But I also knew that I could and would complete this task and emerge more informed about the subject matter, the nature of ethnographic research and writing, and, of course, myself. The discipline of sociology, with its practice of breaking silences by probing deep beneath the surface of taken-for-granted assumptions and its emphasis on the interplay between the personal and the intellectual, the self and society, has both prepared me for this task and provided me with a way to do it.

2

Narrating Motherloss as Biographical Disruption

People live by stories; they attempt to give shape to their lives by placing them within the available narrative frameworks of their culture and society. The preceding chapter represents a significant part of my story; it forms a narrative of biographical disruption and repair. Circumstances—whether social, such as a revolution, a war, or an epidemic, or personal, such as facing a major illness or the death of a loved one—that shatter a person's culturally derived expectations about her life course pose challenges to her ongoing sense of self. In chapter 1 I showed how I attempted to create a coherent sense of identity by taking those events that challenged my earlier self-understandings—my mother's premature death and my break from traditional religion and family—and weaving them into a continuous narrative of identity.

Our sense of self is shaped not only by the events in our own individual lives but by the larger social and cultural contexts in which they occur and through which we develop language to express our lives and experiences.

These contexts establish a set of expectations about the normative life course and provide a framework for understanding oneself in relation to one's society. Major disruptive events, however, disorient a person's sense of rightness in the world and thus establish a need for her to refashion her biography, thereby realigning her sense of self with her social world.

Within U.S. culture, the normative mother is one who is intensely and exclusively devoted to her children. Yet no one has asked how this particular social construction of motherhood affects families in which the mother is absent.[1] Nuclear family ideology prescribes that women should be the emotional foundation of the family, and the ones who do the largely invisible, innumerable tasks that make nuclear family life possible. If families conform to this model, what happens to its members when the mother is no longer able to fulfill her role? Although, theoretically, many of the particular tasks a mother does can be taken care of by other people—fathers as well as other women and men—her death undermines her family's ability to maintain the form and functions of the dominant nuclear family model. Given the deep belief, embedded in our social institutions and ideologies, that children are best reared through the intensive devotion of their mothers,[2] what light can we shed on motherhood and the family as institutions—and as sets of practices—by listening to the stories of those whose mothers died prematurely?

As a sociologist, I am especially interested in how the particular social and historical context in which this loss occurs shapes individuals' representations of and evolving relationships to their experience of motherloss and its consequences. In order to analyze the narratives I co-created with my interviewees not only as individual sto-

ries—a more psychological approach—but sociologically, in terms of how social structures and culture shape
these stories as a group—I will situate them in the context
of three broader conversations. The first addresses the
social constructions of motherhood in twentieth-century
U.S. society that have shaped our conceptions of motherhood and thus of what is lost when one's mother dies.
The second is about American attitudes toward death and
the impact of what Ernest Becker has called the denial of
death[3] on the formation and articulation of these narratives of motherloss. The third is the discourse on narratives as a form of identity construction.

Social Constructions of Motherhood and the Nuclear Family in the Twentieth-Century United States

In the twentieth-century United States, the dominant
model of the family was the nuclear one, based on a division of labor between a breadwinning husband and a
stay-at-home wife, who was responsible for the physical
and emotional well-being of her children and husband.
By saying "dominant" I do not mean to imply that all or
even the majority of families in this country fitted this
model throughout the twentieth century, or that they fit
it today; rather it has been institutionalized as the normative form. The nuclear pattern has been reified and
typified as "the family" in social policy, in the organization of our major social institutions (work, government,
education, religion), and in the majority of our cultural
representations. At least until the 1970s, when sweeping
social changes—such as women's increased participation
in the labor force, the rise of the divorce rate, and the
increased visibility of alternative family forms—raised

questions about what a "family" is,[4] deviations from this pattern were publicly criticized as threatening to children and to the larger society.

The social, economic, and political circumstances that shaped the emergence of this family form during the period of industrialization have been the subjects of intensive scrutiny and analysis.[5] Here I present a brief and necessarily simplified overview of this social history in order to situate my analysis of motherloss in the context of the dominant social constructions of motherhood and family in United States society.

The nuclear family form became firmly established at the time of industrialization, which brought with it the differentiation of social spheres, new forms of specialization, and a growing separation between work and family life. As factories replaced family farms, one result was a growing separation between such institutional realms as work and home, public and private, production and consumption. Men became associated with the public, productive world of work and women with the home, the private realm, and consumption. With the advances of industrial capitalism, the man's sphere of operation widened while the woman's became increasingly confined to the domestic world of hearth and home, which was less and less conceived of as a domain of economic production. Women's roles in economic activity were obscured while those of men were solidified and enlarged.

These social structural changes were accompanied by newly articulated ideologies that typified the personal meanings of the doctrine of separate spheres. Men's role was not seen as terribly problematic; it was assumed (by the men who ran industry and formulated social policy) that men were to be the movers and shakers in this emerging world order. But, as the historian Mary P. Ryan has written, within the first three decades of the nineteenth century, and for the first time in American history, "the topic of womanhood was among the central preoccupations of the national culture."[6] During this period of massive social change, the "woman question" arose as a serious social problem. As the social critics Barbara Ehrenreich and Deirdre English phrased it, "in the new world of the nineteenth century, what was a woman to do?"[7] Of all the possible solutions to this question, two opposing versions highlight the parameters of the discussion. According to one version, women would be equal to men and could enter the world of industrial labor in the same manner and with the same status as men. Alternatively, women's lives could be defined by a new ideology, the "cult of true womanhood," according to which women were to cultivate their "natural" gentility, piety, and purity in order to establish and protect the home as a domestic haven away from the harsh world of industrial capitalism.[8] It was this solution that was trumpeted by the industrialists—women would have the time to consume the new goods of the market—and by the cultural ideologues who glorified the virtues of feminine domesticity. The broadening distinctions between female and male roles in society were legitimated by pronouncements about their essentially differing personality traits and characteristics. Woman's peaceful and moral nature and her domestic virtues were presented as the opposite of, and the solace for, the aggression, competitiveness, and harshness that men needed to cultivate in order to survive in an increasingly impersonal marketplace.

It is critical to note, however, that this ideology was generally limited to white middle-class women; poor women of all racial and ethnic groups, who could ill afford to cultivate those idealized feminine virtues, struggled to earn a living. Nevertheless, the dominant ideas of any age are typically the ideas of the ruling classes. As Sharon Hays wrote in *The Cultural Contradictions of Motherhood*, the child-rearing model of "the white, native-born middle class has long been, and continues to be, the most powerful, visible, and self-consciously articulated."[9] Thus the ideology of the nuclear family, with its gendered spheres of labor and personalities, emerged as the dominant social and cultural ideal. It became the hegemonic family form, enshrined in social institutions (such as the workplace, government, education, and religion) and even supported by "domestic feminists" at the end of the nineteenth century. Deviations from this family form were seen as inferior and in need of correction.

Even as women's and men's roles were being reconfigured and redefined, children's place in society and in the family underwent similar transformations. Before industrialization, children were productive workers within the household economy. When production was separated from the home, however, middle-class children's economic contributions to their households declined. So, too, did infant mortality, at least partly as a result of the spread of knowledge of the germ theory of disease and the growing field of public health. Childhood thus emerged as a special and distinct stage of life, characterized by innocence and requiring special types of dress, play, and activities. The needs of the increasingly precious child meshed with the structures and ideologies of the new womanhood. Although the household's economically productive activities were significantly reduced, women's work there was still essential. In fact, middle-class women could best fulfill themselves by focusing full-time on what became defined as their most important and critical task—motherhood. Women were encouraged to make motherhood their primary if not exclusive function during their children's formative years. Women and children would thrive under these conditions of mutual involvement: mothers would devote all their energy to rearing their children, who required great amounts of unconditional nurturing and caring in order to flourish.

Over the twentieth century, as women's participation in the labor force has fluctuated, so, too, have the social ideologies concerning motherhood and appropriate gender roles. In the first three decades of the twentieth century women were discouraged—by workplace policies as well as prevailing ideologies—from working in paid employment. During the 1940s, however, women were encouraged to do their patriotic duty by responding to the job vacancies created when men were called to war service and by the increased production needs of a society at war. Although many women remained in the workforce after the war, women's primary duty was still defined by their roles at home. In fact, in order to ensure jobs for the returning soldiers and encourage families to produce babies who would repopulate the society after the losses of war, the government instituted a variety of policies that would provide jobs and education for men and create housing for their growing families. Correspondingly, the late 1940s and 1950s saw a renewed emphasis on domesticity and a heavy-handed reassertion of a gendered division of labor. As the sociologist Talcott Parsons prescribed, men were to be the "instrumental" members of the household: they would represent the family to the outside world and earn a living sufficient to support their "dependents." Women's function, in contrast, was to be "expressive": they would tend to the emotional needs of their families, provide countless daily support services, and manage the interrelationships between family members.[10] This renewed emphasis on domesticity, combined with the institutional support available to returning soldiers and their families, contributed to the rise in child-birth rates known as the "postwar baby boom."

The large majority of my interviewees, who were between forty and sixty years of age when I met them in the mid-1990s, were born in the 1930s, 1940s, and 1950s. Their upbringing was shaped by the ideological dominance of the separate-sphere division of labor and emotional traits. In those years, popular culture—as expressed through the media of magazines, film, radio, and eventually television—represented and reproduced this model of nuclear family life. Many of my respondents—and their parents—imbibed images of gender and family life through watching TV shows such as *I Love Lucy*, *Leave It to Beaver*, and *Father Knows Best*, which glorified the nuclear family. It is these cultural representations, with their solid social structural foundations, that were the bases for my respondents' childhood conceptions of gender, motherhood, and family and that—many years later—became incorporated into their constructions of the meaning of motherloss.

"My Whole World Disappeared"

The intensity and exclusivity of motherhood as it has been constructed in our society means that children who have lost their mothers feel they no longer have a stable foundation for their lives. They feel like the sixty-five-year-old interviewee, a man, who said, "My whole world disappeared." Central to our definition of the maternal role is that the mother should simply "be there" for her children and husband.[11] "Being there" is a way of talking about the numerous tasks (such as cooking and serving meals, giving baths, organizing appointments for family members, going on school trips) a mother performs that actually constitute the social group as *family* on a daily basis.[12] Therefore, mothers cannot simply be replaced; my research indicates that individuals and families often feel that they have fallen apart when the mother dies. A nurturing, caring, unconditionally loving mother is so central to our idea of family that it is virtually impossible to have a family without her.

Several friends and acquaintances have described themselves to me as "unmothered" or even "wildly un-mothered," although their mothers were still alive. Their perceptions of their mother's lack of complete emotional availability to them led them to experience themselves as growing up motherless. Even people who felt that their mothers were generally good and available to them nev-ertheless expressed disappointment over the mothering they received: it never met the standards of our society's idealized constructions of mothering and motherhood. These conversations suggest that one of the key reasons mothers cannot be replaced when they are gone is that there is a confluence and confusion as to who is missed— the ideal mother or the real one. For children, their par-ents generally loom larger than life; if a parent dies during one's childhood, then, it is hard ever to develop a realistic view of her or him as a person. As Mary Gordon writes in her memoir of her search for her long-dead father, "Perhaps that is what it is to grow up: to understand that the parent of your childhood is an invention, that if such a person ever lived, he or she is no longer living. That the living parent of adulthood is not the reconstituted giant of the child's mind and heart."[13]

Many of my interviewees described their family before their mother's death as involving a mixture of feelings and emotions; mothers may have had nasty tempers, slapped them, been strict disciplinarians or profligate with the limited family resources. Nevertheless, when they talked about the caring they lost, they did so in superlative terms, echoing our cultural ideals of maternal perfection and unconditional love. Clearly, it is easier to idolize someone who is no longer present to remind you of her human fallibilities. The mythology of the beatific mother promotes great strain in our society and culture, a tension that is starkly visible in the stories of those whose mothers died prematurely. By closely analyzing these particular cases, we are afforded insights into the more general issue of constructions of motherhood in white middle-class U.S. culture.

Given that the nuclear family, with the mother at its center, has been the primary model of family in our society for so long, people often react strongly to deviations from this pattern. When confronted with events or experiences that threaten their maintenance of this ideal, those affected, as well as those around them, often react with feelings of discomfort and shame. To counteract this sense of embarrassment, people often devise strategies, such as silencing and minimizing the sense of disruption, in order to retain a sense of normality. For example, in situations other than motherloss that threaten the image of the ideal nuclear family—incest, family violence, divorce when it was less common, and child abuse—people often try to hide the "deviance" through a process of normalizing. My respondents' narratives of motherloss illustrate these same strategies. It is so challenging to conceive of a family without the mother that we have no vocabulary with which to discuss the issue, no guidelines for how to cope. Therefore fathers and other adults usually concealed the severity of my interviewees' mothers' illnesses from the children and pretended that nothing was wrong, that they were still a normal family. The denial of illness became a silence that continued after the mother's death and often throughout respondents' lives.

Attitudes toward Death in the United States

The Denial of Death

Although death is a natural process and an inevitable concomitant of life, the denial, avoidance, and stigmatization of death and serious illnesses characterized American society throughout most of the twentieth century. Even when it intrudes on their immediate worlds, Americans have characteristically avoided discussions of and direct confrontation with death.[14] Modern U.S. culture has promoted a particular "etiquette of death" in which "conventional words and meanings suggest three major themes: *neutralizing, euphemizing* and *ridiculing* death."[15] The process of dying has—at least until recently, with the rise of the hospice movement—been removed from the home and placed in institutions, where it has been rendered invisible, sanitary, and neutral. Avoidance and denial hamper our ability to comprehend and come to terms with death.[16] The noted social historian Philippe Ariès has commented on the great silence that settled on the subject of death in the twentieth century.[17] The British social scientist Geoffrey Gorer argued that death is treated today much as sexuality was in Victorian times.[18] In the twentieth century, death replaced sex as the major prohibition. As Ariès writes, "Death has become a taboo, an unnamable thing . . . and, as formerly with sex, it must not be mentioned in public."[19]

Denial of death is not a universal phenomenon; rather, our silences surrounding death are culturally specific and stem from social conditions that are particular to Western societies. Studies have highlighted the cross-cultural variation in attitudes toward death.[20] Even in Western societies the taboos surrounding death are a relatively recent phenomenon. Ariès observed that in earlier times in Europe, an individual's illness and death were a public matter and all members of the family and friends of the dying person were exposed to this process. The dying person's bedchamber was a public space for people to accompany the dying person, children included. The common notion that children ought to be protected from issues surrounding death is a relatively recent phenomenon. "Children were brought in [to the dying person's bedchamber]; until the eighteenth century no portrayal of a deathbed scene failed to include children. And to think of how carefully people today keep children away from anything having to do with death!"[21]

The American denial of death and grief has been influenced by various cultural conditions. Kathy Charmaz suggested that "the fear of death is most noticeable in western cultures characterized by industrialism and individualism."[22] John Stephenson suggested the same interpretation: "Death is . . . contrary to many of our values. . . . Indeed, a great many people find the subject an intolerable one to deal with, and try to avoid any mention of it. Part of this avoidance of death lies in the fact that death is, in a sense, un-American."[23] The Protestant ethic of hard work and achievement has been translated into the American ethos of getting ahead and staying in control of one's feelings and actions. Death is seen as the opposite of progress and as the ultimate loss of control. In a society "where we overvalue competition, success, achievement and perfection . . . anyone who falls short of the mark" may be seen as deficient.[24] The failure represented by death is therefore "excluded from daily life to the highest possible degree. The dead are not allowed to show that they are dead; they are transformed [by funerary practices] into the mask of the living"[25]

The Medicalization of Death and Mourning

The denial and invisibility of death in everyday life are shaped not only by our cultural values of achievement and progress but also by the institutionalization of medicine as the primary arbiter of health, sickness, and death in contemporary American society. In the modern world, medicine has taken charge of life and death, replacing the more traditional institutions of the family and religion.[26] Doctors have become the new priests who are expected to fight sickness, cure patients, and vanquish death as the enemy in a moral battle for the preservation of life.[27] Therefore, a patient's death is conceived as a failure. Media images reinforce the notion of doctors' control over life and death: in the many popular medical TV shows, doctors often make such comments as "I lost him," suggesting that in this particular skirmish, death was the victor, death defeated the doctor's best efforts.

Philippe Ariès has traced the origins of the contemporary denial of death to the medicalization of health and illness:

> One dies in the hospital because the doctor did not succeed in healing. . . . Death is a technical phenomenon obtained by a cessation of care, a cessation determined in a more or less avowed way by a decision of the doctor and the hospital team. . . . Death has been dissected, cut to bits by a series of little steps, which finally makes it impossible to know which step was the real death, the one in which consciousness was lost, or the one in which breathing

stopped. All these little silent deaths have replaced and erased the great dramatic act of death.[28]

Just as death is stigmatized, so, too, are the illnesses that are associated with it. In *Illness as Metaphor* Susan Sontag outlined how the stigma of such deadly diseases as tuberculosis and cancer have become attached to those individuals afflicted with them. This stigma is a major factor in the silencing of those people: "A disease widely considered a synonym for death is experienced as something to hide." In treating cancer patients, doctors sometimes lie to them, concealing the seriousness of their condition. Similarly, sick people and their families hide the disease not only because it is associated with death but because that very association renders it "obscene—in the original meaning of that word: ill-omened, abominable, repugnant to the senses."[29] Although cancer is no longer necessarily a death sentence, it was perceived as such in the mid–twentieth century, the period in which most of my respondents' mothers died. Consequently, in an effort to avoid the shame associated with cancer, families kept the mother's illness a secret as long as possible.

The stigma associated with cancer is not confined, however, to death from this or any other deadly disease. All forms of death, whether sudden and unexpected or long anticipated, are subjected to the same stigma and silences. Mental health professionals and some social scientists have seen suicide as a particularly shameful way to end a life. Kathy Charmaz has suggested that survivors of persons who have committed suicide often experience self-doubt and wonder about the "real" reasons their relative or friend took her own life. "The negative effects of suicide" are most likely to be felt by those closest to the dead person—spouse, parent, lover, child—"whose lives are closely intertwined and whose identities are directly linked with the suicide."[30] The lack of clarity about the nature and causes of the death may lead to rumors, gossip, and the deeper stigmatization of survivors.

Just as attitudes toward death vary over time and across cultures, so, too, do conventions of grief and mourning. In contemporary U.S. society medical and mental health practitioners, to a certain extent, have taken over the role of religion and family in regulating death and grief. We have delegated the management of grief to doctors, psychologists, and social workers, who set the standards for appropriate grieving behavior by establishing certain expectations about the expression and duration of grief. The notion that grief is a finite process that can be resolved through clinical treatment exacerbates the cultural denial of mourning by keeping grief, like death, out of the realm of everyday experience. These assumptions reinforce the notion that grief has no place in "normal" life. "The clinical view of grief . . . treats it as if it were a *disease process*. The disease imagery includes notions that grief is something one is afflicted with, something inside the person that must be gotten rid of. The feeling of loss is given negative connotations—it is something . . . that should not be experienced beyond a certain point . . . grief is something to conquer, to overcome."[31]

Our cultural attitudes toward the expression of grief, like our stance on death, bear the imprint of the internalization of values associated with the Protestant ethic. Our cultural emphasis on progress and the value of stoicism keep the bereaved silent.[32] Taking time to grieve is associated with a failure to get ahead and to "move on" with our lives; impassivity is perceived as a sign of virtue, inner strength, and competence. A public display of one's pain conflicts with the American ethos of individualism, autonomy, and privacy;[33] the inability to control one's emotions is embarrassing to the mourner and audience alike. The silences surrounding death become associated with the dead person, too. Although our culture may, to some extent, teach us to honor the dead, we are clearly not supposed to discuss them in everyday conversations.

Nuclear Family Ideology and the Denial of Death

The nuclear family, as an institution and as an ideology, further contributes to the denial and silencing of serious illness and death. The very model of the family is based on the idea that childhood is a special stage of life and that children must be protected from the harsh realities of life by their loving parents. Parents are expected to preserve children's innocence by controlling their access to potentially distressing information and painful events and circumstances. Exposure to serious illness and death has been seen as unhealthy and harmful to children's development, rather than as a natural and inevitable part of the life cycle about which they need to learn. In light of parents' desires to protect children from the idea and the reality of death, the poet Edna St. Vincent Millay called childhood "the kingdom where nobody dies." Adults' own discomfort with death and their difficulty in talking about it convey to children the taboo nature of death in our culture. "Within the family circle one . . . hesitates to let himself go for fear of upsetting the children. . . . Solitary and shameful mourning is the only recourse."[34] When there is a death in the family, adults communicate, through concealment, secrets, and lies, that the children should not ask questions but rather should deal with their feelings privately. Like Eve's eating of the apple, children's experience of death catapults them into another world—from the sheltered realm of childhood into an adult awareness of finitude.

The death of a parent is also silenced because it produces a family that in form and function deviates from the normative nuclear model. Silences around death are greatly influenced by the ideology of the nuclear family, whose existence depends upon two parents performing their appropriate roles. When a family does not look or function like this model, members may be stigmatized. In the mid–twentieth century, divorce was seen as a source of shame and embarrassment, and was generally avoided as a subject for discussion. In fact, all serious disruptions to the family's ability to maintain this ideal form—such as family violence, incest, sexual abuse, and rape—have been stigmatized and silenced. Concerned about the impact of these violations of the sanctity of the family on family members, especially children, social scientists have paid a great deal of attention to violence, abuse, divorce, and father absence. The unavailability of fathers has been of concern particularly as researchers have sought explanations for poverty, social deviance, crime, and drug use. Although the mother's role in the family as emotional caretaker, maintainer of kin ties, and family communicator has been defined as crucial to the stability of the family, the impact of a mother's absence has been much less studied. Motherloss, however, clearly produces an aberrant family form in which many of the family unit's essential needs may be neglected. Thus the death of a mother, along with other threats to the stability of the idealized nuclear family, is typically silenced, minimized, and normalized by family members and those around them.

Social Change and New Approaches to Death in the Family

Since the 1960s several social movements and cultural transformations have reshaped—at least to some extent—

reactions to a death in the family. The women's movement and the increasing openness of gays, lesbians, and bisexuals as well as the rise in the number of single-parent households have reduced the stigma attached to families that deviate from the nuclear family ideal. Similarly the hospice movement and other new approaches to death and dying have created an environment in which death can be more openly discussed and confronted. Anthony Giddens has remarked favorably upon the new "institutional manifestations" of the calls for more public awareness about the process of death. He particularly refers to hospices as "environments in which death can be discussed and confronted, rather than merely shunted away from general view."[35]

Similarly, many child-rearing "experts" have attempted to challenge the silencing of death and other traumatic events in families. In the revised seventh edition of *Baby and Child Care*, Benjamin Spock and Steven Parker bemoan our culture's regulation of death and grief and the resulting silences and euphemisms. They actually advise parents that even though they may be "uncomfortable with the notion of death," they should treat death as a "natural subject to talk about" at home and with their children.[36]

To a large extent, these transformations took place many years after the majority of my respondents' mothers passed away. Although my interviewees are certainly aware of changes in the social acceptability of a variety of family forms and the increased openness about the processes of death and grieving, many aspects of their narratives are shaped by the social context in which their mothers died. Since they grew up at a time when adherence to the nuclear family form was significantly more important and death was a taboo subject, their narratives contain an interplay between this sense of motherloss as a shameful, deviant, and stigmatizing experience and more contemporary impulses to break the silence and erase the stigma surrounding death.

The Narrative Construction of Identity

This book is also about narratives; it is about individual and collective stories and the connections between them.[37] It inquires into a very particular, personal experience, motherloss, through the use of categories social scientists use to understand social life—social institutions, culture, gender, social class, and ethnicity—and shows how these factors shape individual narratives. By analyzing these narratives in terms of social structural and cultural factors, I attempt to show how larger forces shape individuals' presentation of their lives. The larger social context in which my respondents experienced maternal death produces numerous commonalities across respondents as well as some important differences.

The concept of representation is central to the narrative production of lives and identities, in interviews as well as in writing. To begin with, the accounts provided in my interviews are obviously not the *actual* experiences of maternal death and its aftermath, but rather the respondents' reconstructions of those events. Even when we describe current events and situations, we present them in terms of our own concerns and frameworks; that is, we represent them. Similarly, in describing the past, we can produce only representations, which are further circumscribed by the vagaries of memory. Although respondents may try their best to (and believe they can) reproduce the story of what happened, the passage of time erodes and changes memory, which is in any case a creation of individual consciousness. In discussing life history narratives, Nancy K. Miller wrote, "The truth of the autobiographical project is always vulnerable to the selection of emotional facts, and these so-called facts themselves hostage to the unreliable convictions of memory."[38]

Respondents' ability to construct narratives of maternal death is hampered by the silences surrounding this event. In addition, the person with whom they might check the veracity of these stories is no longer available. Mary Gordon described her inability to fully remember her father's life: "I come up against the silence of the grave. The impossibility of knowing what happened to or with the dead . . . [The dead] ensure that we will be, in relation to their lives, incapable of distinguishing fact from invention. They guarantee the falsity, the partiality, of our witness."[39] Given the gaps and selectivity in memory and the dearth of corroborating sources for their narratives, those who attempt to construct narratives of motherloss have the space for creative renderings of their experiences. These new articulations are capable of giving new and varied expression to identity and to the meaning of their childhood experiences. Finding a language, however, with which to express such a publicly and personally silenced and repressed experience and then the emotional strength to use that language can make the journey to the open and creative space of narrative construction challenging and frustrating.

The narratives created in my conversations with respondents are *representations* of the experience of motherloss as it has been shaped by memory—what individuals themselves remember and those memories that they incorporate through conversations with others who remind us of what happened—and the larger social and cultural context. Memory is bound up with the images, symbols, and rituals we see in our society. They frame the language and concepts available for thinking about social events and their consequences. Therefore, in order to theorize the overall meaning of this collection of narratives, I must ground them in explicit historical and cultural patterns. Since postindustrial U.S. society organizes its basic social institutions on assumptions of gender differences and suppresses alternatives to the nuclear family, these central cultural assumptions shape the narratives people of a particular class and generation tell of their lives and their experiences of motherloss. The connections people make in telling their stories are shaped by the norms of the society in which they live. Social discourse shapes not only public events and actions but also our personal self-understandings.[40]

I am aware that my interviewees' narratives are partial, constructed accounts. The positivist might here question the value of such life stories if we cannot guarantee their truth. "But to the investigator of psychological or cultural representation," write George Rosenwald and Richard Ochberg, "the object of the study is not the 'true' event, as it might have been recorded by some panel of disinterested observers, but the construction of that event within a personal and social history. . . . In the form a particular narrator gives to a history we read the more or less abiding concerns and constraints of the individual and his or her community."[41] Although I emphasize the constructed nature of accounts created in interviews, I nevertheless believe they yield important insights into the categories through which individuals understand their lives and the larger social and cultural realities that shape them. My goal is to seek verisimilitude, authenticity, and an experience of "Aha, that makes sense and helps me understand my own life" in my readers. As Rosenwald and Ochberg have written, "the dismantling of the realist position [in critical social science] has shattered the image of life stories as the mirror of life events."[42] At least in the spheres of psychological and social consciousness, it is the *meaning* that these stories have in individuals' lives and in the larger social order that is of interest.

Unraveling meaning, of course, is a complicated goal, and one that must be pursued with an astute awareness of and respect for the layers of meaning that may be left untouched. Storytelling, as an act of creating and representing meaning, has a "double relevancy"; narratives *"are both about the life and part of it"* because what is told and what is lived promote each other.[43] Narratives mesh the retrospective and evaluative mode with the experiential and creative level, weaving together the teller's interest in the past, her location in a constantly changing and adjusting present, and her expectations for a socially and culturally framed future.

Just as the stories my respondents tell are constructed accounts, conditioned by the vagaries of memory and the social contexts in which they aspire to remember, my rendering of their narratives is itself a constructed account. When I tell the story of my respondents' lives, I do not and cannot simply report everything I heard. Rather, my analysis is my own representation of my interviewees' representations. Within social and cultural analysis we have multiple levels of representation shaping one another. I represent myself as I seek others' stories, together with them I engage in the co-construction of narratives that give shape to their life stories, and then as a sociologist and writer I interpret and represent these emerging meanings.[44]

Nevertheless, this account of their life stories is also more than an idiosyncratic representation. The contours and meanings can extend to others, who may recognize their experiences in these stories of others' lives and thus better comprehend their own.[45] At the end of the many public talks I have given, members of the audience have stood up and reported that their experiences of motherloss (or other major losses in their or others' lives) were echoed in the narratives I had told. This helped them to situate their own biographies and reduce the sense of aloneness produced by unusual (read "deviant") life experiences.

A mother's premature death is a major disruption in a person's biography; motherless children and adults thus have no readily available narratives in which to fit the details of their life stories. This produces a sense of fractured identity and an uncomfortable state of linguistic liminality in which an individual is betwixt and between available structures for narrating experiences.[46] Rosenwald and Ochberg characterize storytelling as a "generative" moment in which characters, experiences, and thoughts are brought into existence though language.[47] Creating a story out of the fragments and pain of a disruptive life experience passes a person out of the discomfort of experiencing a fractured biographical narrative. Repairing the disruption enables that person to make sense of it through the function of ordering and categorizing inherent in language. An individual can now reexperience and revisit the disruptive event, armed with an approximating language and metaphor to describe and contextualize that experience and integrate the narrative of it into a working and mutable life story. Story finding is not a single event; rather new and revised stories constantly struggle to reintegrate the liminal disruptive experience into new structures of knowledge and experience.

By telling their life stories individuals reconstruct their biographies, thereby establishing a continuous sense of identity. "Self-understandings are not only revealed," say Rosenwald and Ochberg, "but fashioned and enlarged in conversation." In the very narration of their lives, individuals make claims about their coherence and impose upon them a sense of connection and order that is rare in actual lived experience. Stories hang together through the work of story makers; in effect, the storyteller says, "This person I am today is the one I have spent years becoming." By articulating a coherent life story we are able to figure out who we are and how we got to be this way. Articulating and, in a sense, reexperiencing motherloss are ways of repairing the rupture caused by loss, mending our disrupted biographies, and normalizing our identities. "The subjective conviction of autobiographic coherence is intrinsic to a sense of identity."[48]

The representations produced through this process must be understood in an active sense. By *doing* something, talking and engaging with me in this narrative production of identity, my respondents challenge the taboos that further removed their mothers from them. Accounts are essential to composing a life; so are our daily practices. Life is not simply the words that we use to describe it, but rather is made up of the countless acts we perform every day. Although the data I have collected are in verbal form, my respondents enlarged their accounts with descriptions of practices—actions—and with visual representations. People often showed me photos of their mothers and artifacts of her life and told me about the specific practices through which they maintain a sense of their mother's ongoing presence. My goal here is to discern not only how social and cultural forces shape people's narratives but how these stories themselves are constructed through practices and rituals.

In collecting and representing respondents' life stories, I seek to fashion a way out of the silences—personal, professional, and cultural—that throughout our lives have been our typical ways of dealing with motherloss. As we break the long silences and find new forms in which to tell our particular stories, we create alternative narrative frameworks that may help others give shape to their distinctive life patterns.[49]

The production of life history narratives, like the writing of memoirs, involves a quest for self-knowledge and psychic integration, for cultural and social demystification. The process can reveal how our deepest, most personal selves are shaped by or resist being shaped by the structural organization and cultural assumptions of our society. This, of course, is also the task of sociology. This project combines methods and insights from social science—systematic gathering of data and development of theory—with those from the humanities and blends them together in a search for a broader and deeper understanding of the forces that have carved the patterns of our lives. Within this work I push at and cross over the boundaries between these two modes of understanding human social life: my explication of my research findings is woven together with my own autobiographical reflections on the topic, each deepening and illuminating the other.

The memoir has become a popular form of literature. A wide range of people—government and literary figures, psychiatrists, popular actors and actresses, artists and ordinary folks—have been reproducing their life stories and the significant events that shaped their lives. As Mary

Gordon wryly observed in her own memoir, "I entered the cave of memory, which nowadays seems like a tourist trap in high season."[50] There are a variety of explanations for the current prevalence of memoir. Postmodern thought suggests that memoirs are quite fashionable now because they blur the modernist boundaries between private and public, subject and object.[51] In addition, postmodern theory has asserted that our culture now lacks those overarching metanarratives through which whole groups of people can frame and make sense of their lives. Individuals are thus left to construct their own stories in an effort to establish a sense of meaning and order in their lives. Alternatively, Vivian Gornick, the author of several volumes of memoir, suggests that our age of mass culture, under the influence of modernism, elevates the idea of the self to a degree unparalleled in history. "Today, millions of people consider themselves possessed of the right to a serious life. A serious life, by definition, is a reflective life; a life to which one pays attention; a life one tries to make sense of and bear witness to."[52] The therapeutic has triumphantly taken over, legitimating intensive self-reflection and testimonials.[53] For some, the personal details are satisfying in their own right; for others, it is in the larger sense that is made of them that their lasting value lies.

A writer, as James Baldwin once observed, "writes out of one thing only: himself."[54] While this basic insight poses few problems for autobiographers, since the telling of their lives is their explicit task, it poses certain challenges to the sociologist. In writing about a subject that is so close to home (literally as well as metaphorically) and using my own inner life as a key to understanding others' similar experiences, I am in danger of hearing and representing only those stories that are closest to my own.

Of course, I am drawn to those narratives that resonate with my own experiences. In recounting her search for literary precedents about parental death, Nancy Miller described this tension: "As a reader of autobiography, I perform an awkward dance of embrace and rejection: He's just like me, she's not like me at all."[55] Stories that parallel our own are validating, affirming, and help us to normalize our lives and life choices. My interviewees were eager to know if my other respondents were like them, whether others' narratives of motherloss resembled their own, thereby ensuring their own "normality," despite a life that differed from the dominant cultural scripts.

Nevertheless, I have taken great care to pay close attention to opposite cases, to locate and identify those experiences that differed from mine. While I am keenly aware that my reflections on my own life are a major source of my insights about motherloss and its consequences, I have purposely sought out people whose narratives contrast with my own. Some interviewees told stories that challenge some of my most basic assumptions, such as the man who told me that he experienced his mother's death as a relief rather than a loss. Not only do people have different experiences, they also have diverse ways of recounting their experiences that draw upon their own backgrounds and circumstances. In a work that relies primarily on narratives, it is important to give the reader a sense of how people themselves package their stories. Obviously my own voice, as researcher, organizer, and narrator, is dominant. But it is consistently in conversation with—and held in check by—the voices of the diverse people who chose to talk to me, all of whom articulate and represent their lives in their own distinct terms.

People frequently organize their life stories around a particular event or a primary sequence of events. Since premature parental death is such a significant loss and disruption, respondents generally spoke of their lives as divided into two major periods—before their mothers' death and everything thereafter. Mary Gordon described the death of her father when she was seven as follows: "It was then that my life split in two, into the part when my father was alive and the part when he was not."[56] The death of a parent is usually described as a trauma that causes an invisible tear in a person's self-identity. This narrative pattern, emphasizing the radical rupture of a mother's death, creating a clear sense of before and after, is reminiscent of a primary story line in our culture, which describes the person who, despite great odds, overcomes obstacles and goes on to live a good life. It is not surprising that this pattern emerged in the overwhelming majority of my respondents' accounts. Their mother's death is named as the obstacle they had to overcome; her loss was the most significant event in their lives.

Constructing a linear narrative, partially driven by the Western paradigm of progress and forward movement, is certainly central to the project of articulating a coherent life story. The basic model of "lost, then found" or "chaotic and then ordered" provides the underlying structure for most narratives of disrupted biographies.[57] The narrative patterns of my motherless respondents echoed, in some basic ways, the core cultural script of the individual who faces major obstacles and traumas and nevertheless succeeds in overcoming them and henceforth lives a good life. This smooth progression from there to here may be a way of attempting to normalize biographical disruptions, but it also must be regarded as a formula that represents how we may *want* our lives to be or to sound. I am fascinated by the points of disjunction between this available story line and the variety of contesting structures and tools that are used in the telling of narratives. Forward movement is not always possible and a smooth path from past to present becomes more complicated as the disrupted event resurfaces and pokes out from the boundaries of the past. Nevertheless, nearly all of my respondents' narratives illustrate the ways they have coped and persevered and gone on to lead satisfying lives.

As I listened to the tapes of my interviews and read and reread the transcripts, I was struck by the prominence of certain key elements that appeared, albeit in different forms, in nearly all of the stories. The sheer frequency of their occurrence was a powerful indicator that although these were individual accounts of loss, they also reflected broader social patterns. The following themes surfaced in nearly every account: the childhood loss of caring, the silences and denial of grief that surrounded it, the search to replace lost caring in childhood and later in adulthood, respondents' attempts to integrate the loss into their lives by breaking silence and retaining their mother's symbolic presence, and a desire throughout to normalize the severely disruptive experience. Nevertheless, although these key themes defined nearly every interview, they were manifested and described in a variety of ways, reflecting the differences in respondents' age, social class, and gender.

As I attempted to represent in writing the narratives I heard, I, like many other contemporary ethnographers, struggled with the basic issues of form and content. I sought a way to represent these gripping stories as vividly as they had been told to me, retaining the force of their emotional impact. But I also wanted to analyze them sociologically, by showing how personal experiences are nevertheless conditioned by the kinds of ascribed and achieved characteristics that sociologists and anthropologists characteristically highlight. The precise voice in which I could achieve both these goals eluded me and I tried several styles, moving back and forth between them in frustration.

Many ethnographies, including some in which the researcher inserts herself into the field, are divided, in standard social science fashion, into chapters organized according to key themes. I initially attempted to write *Motherloss* in this more standard style, but despite my repeated attempts, I found myself unable to work within this form. In contrast, when I attempted to write sections that reproduced individuals' narratives, my writing flowed easily. When I then tried to force myself away from that form, back toward chapters guided by themes, I felt stuck and frustrated. I finally decided that I needed to write this book in the form in which it kept trying to emerge—that the more standard sociological form of organizing data by dividing it into thematic chapters could not capture the sheer emotional impact of the stories I was working with. I could not chop these powerful accounts into bite-size quotations that I used to reinforce the many themes and subthemes I had generated in my analysis. Like Lila Abu-Lughod when she set out to write her self-reflexive ethnography, *Writing Women's Worlds,* I wanted to write in a way that reflected the wonderfully complex stories of the people I had come to know.[58] Had I tried to represent my interviewees' narratives by splitting them into chapters reflecting my own analytic categories, I would have diminished their overall emotional power and their potential to overflow social scientific categories. I have tried to preserve the integrity of my respondents' experiences by representing their narratives with narratives of my own that echo their words and forms of expression.

PART II

Narrating Motherloss

3

An Archetypal Narrative

Sheryl Smith

When Sheryl Smith,[1] a forty-four-year-old executive director of an international media institute, with an office in Philadelphia and five employees, greeted me at the door to her modest duplex, she was surrounded by at least a dozen dogs, all hovering close to her. Raising and showing these dogs, upon which she showers lots of affection, is a major passion in her life. Sheryl's mother died of cancer at the age of thirty-six, when Sheryl was twelve years of age.

Sheryl's story is that of a woman who until recently put all of her energy into her work. Shortly after she graduated from college, she began working in the news media. As she explained, "I was always a high achiever, a hard worker. I got a job as a producer with a network news agency in Madrid, and I moved there for a couple of years. I had stints in Brazil, Argentina, and the Middle East. Lots of it was great, though it was really demanding and hard work.

"One of the things I covered in the Middle East was the

Israeli invasion of Beirut. On September fifteenth the Lebanese president, Bashir Gamael, was killed by a bomb. And on September seventeenth, in revenge, there was a massacre of Palestinians. That night I was nearby when that happened. My driver and I were caught and held prisoner throughout the night while the massacre was happening. I didn't know it was happening. I was just terrified that I was going to get killed. Then we were released, and when we went back, we found out that this massacre had taken place. We went through the streets of Shatila, this Palestinian camp, and it was horrible with all these bodies. When you're a producer, you really have to experience things intensely because you go there yourself and you see it, and you work with the photographer and crew. We had to put the story on the air. So for the next week, all week long, I was looking again and again and again and again at these bodies.

"The Palestinian women wear these flowing black robes. I was fascinated by how they breathed. They breathed in such a noisy, outward way. I don't think I made the connection right then with my mother and the silence in that room and everyone saying, 'It'll be OK. Everything's going to be OK,' and you know she's dead and it won't be OK. The Palestinians' grief is—first of all, they wail, this rhythmic wailing. They throw their bodies around. They grieve with their entire body. They throw their bodies. You feel their grief. You can *really* feel their grief. There were a lot of funerals, mass funerals. So I was watching this, and I was also editing it for the show and constantly watching it. I know that at the time I made myself numb to it. It was a horrible thing and I had to just get through it. I got back to the States in September and in December I started to feel sick all the time, like I had the flu, all the time. Sick. I was getting depressed, and I just got more and more depressed. Eventually, what happened was that into my depression came twelve Palestinian women. I would just be lying in bed feeling sick, and I would see these women, and they would look like the way you look as a person, sitting and real. Not like you have your eyes closed and you imagine it. You have your eyes open, and one's sitting there, one's sitting there, one's sitting there, there, there. And they would always be really close to me. They'd always be around me. And I would be in bed with my sheets wrapped around me, terrified. I didn't know what to do, so I looked up the number of a psychologist, and in her little blurb it said that she worked with women. I went to see her, and it was still a couple of months before I even told her about these visions, which continued, and terrified me. I was really sick a lot, seeing doctors all the time. Finally, months into this therapy, I finally told this woman, Sandy, about these visions.

"And she said, 'I think it's a gift.' "

"And that turned it around, that I could then see it from that angle. She pointed out that they haven't hurt me, there hasn't been any hurt. Then she helped me understand what these Palestinian women meant to me. What they meant was this grief, the wailing and the throwing of your body, every little cell in your body just having this huge, outward grief. So I just started to feel that maybe it wasn't quite so frightening. And suddenly they just seemed to be there to grieve. And what were they grieving? They were grieving for my mother, just grieving for my mother. I didn't cry much at all when my mother died. Neither did my father. Now I think that a lot has to do with the American denial of grief. Be brave. Be strong. Everything will be OK. That's what I keep remembering I was told.

"In fact, I was not even told that my mother was ill. I turned twelve in June, and I guess she was sick that summer, I don't have any memory of it. But in the fall, she was supposed to be the speaker at a fashion show that I was in, with a lot of other people, small fashions, and I remember her best friend got up and said, 'Evelyn's voice is not working today, so we all hope she'll be back soon,' because she was always the MC. She had this vibrant personality. 'And we hope she'll do the next fashion show,' for the Ladies' Auxiliary. I was so surprised! I had no idea there was anything wrong with her. She sounded fine to me. Apparently by the time they found the lump in her breast, she already had fully engaged cancer in many areas of her body. It spread quickly from wherever it started.

"She died shortly thereafter, in May, May twenty-third. Through the whole winter I just remember people saying, 'Don't worry. Your mother will be fine. Don't be upset. Say your prayers. Don't worry.' Being a child, I didn't worry. [Here she gave a bitter chuckle.] I took them literally. I guess that as a result I just felt *so* betrayed later. Because when people would tell me not to worry, I didn't worry. I didn't know that actually that's a signal you're supposed to worry. I now feel just the opposite. If you can't cry with every cell of your body, you can't grieve. How can you feel? How can you feel this horrible thing that happened to you? You need these heart feelings in your body. I wish that when my mother died I had screamed like a Palestinian woman. Screamed and shook my body and beat against the wall, threw myself on the floor, beat against the floor. Because that's what I observed, and I think that's better for life. Not crying is the death response. You kill something in you. You shut it down. Screaming, crying, and beating—these are all things that aren't part of my heritage, but if something terrible happens to me I hope I can do that.

"My father, too, could not cry or grieve. He threw himself into his work as a surgeon. I just don't remember him being around in my early teenage years. He was at the hospital. I was afraid of my father. He's of German descent, and he saw his paternal duties as being to yell at you, and that's what he did. 'That skirt's too short.' 'Comb your hair.' I was pretty much a straight-A student, but he goes, 'Why aren't these A-plusses? Why did you get this B?' He never gave any of what I can think of as feminine nurturing. He was a frightening figure to me in those years."

Sheryl's narrative is structured around two significant life-changing events. The first is the disruption caused by the death of her mother, a focal event in nearly all the narratives I heard. The second is the moment of epiphany she had in therapy, when she suddenly came to understand the pain and impact of this loss in a radically new way. These two events define the shape of the narrative as well as its basic elements. I have chosen to place Sheryl's account first, as an archetypal story, because it articulates and represents the major themes that emerged in nearly every narrative in this study: the silences that surround the mother's illness and death, and the profound impact of the loss of a mother's caring. Sheryl poignantly articulated her perceptions of her family's secrecy concerning her mother's illness, the denial of grief, and the messages she received to "be strong and move on." In addition, her narrative, like the others, reflected the ways the gendered organization of caring labor in the United States and the centrality of the mother in the emotional maintenance of the family make motherloss a devastating experience.

Cancer caused the deaths of more than half of my respondents' mothers; as we have seen, it was generally unnameable at the time they died and carried with it an aura of shame and stigma. Nearly all of my interviewees described the silences that surrounded their mothers' illness and death, and their own attempts to integrate this experience into their lives.

I remember that when my own mother became ill, I was told that she was sick, but whenever I'd ask what was the matter, the response was simply "She's sick." And when I guessed she had cancer, it was denied. One morning my aunt, with whom my brothers and I were staying while my mother was in the hospital for surgery, called me aside and asked me why I had told my school friend that my mother had cancer and had a breast removed. I said, "Well, I said she has cancer, but I did not say she had a breast removed." My aunt asked, "Well, why did you say she has cancer?" I responded, "Because she does." My aunt then told me, "Your mother does not have cancer." "Well, then, what does she have" She replied, "Your mother had thoracic surgery." I later looked up "thoracic" in the dictionary and learned it meant chest. I understood that my aunt had told me nothing and that I was tangled up in a web of secrets and lies.

My interviewees related the devastating consequences of the gendered division of labor in the family on their experiences of motherloss. Sheryl emphasized that her father, like the fathers of most of my other respondents, was unable to find a way to deal with his own loss and pain, let alone to help his children deal with theirs. As Sheryl said, her voice wavering, "It's a little hard for me to say anything mean about him or something, although when I think back I feel angry for the lack of support. I look back on that little girl and I just kind of feel sorry for her that nobody—for years—gave her a hug or a kiss or said, 'I love you.' I just don't remember it. I don't want to be mean and say that it was my father's fault. I'm sure he was doing the best he could. I just don't think he had any idea of what children, especially a little girl, needs." By throwing himself into his work, he provided a model, which Sheryl assiduously followed, of using intense, consuming work as a way of avoiding emotional pain and engagement.

The silence that began with her mother's illness has continued throughout Sheryl's life. I asked, "Did you ever talk about your mother?" and she said, "Never. Never, her name was never mentioned again." I probed, "Was that made explicit to you with a set of instructions or did that evolve?" She replied, "My father said we had to move to get out of that house, because it reminded him of my mother. We were kind of excited about that and happy to move, and it seemed like it would be an exciting thing to do. We went to the new house, and it was like she's not there. She never was in that kitchen. She never put something away in this cupboard. She never had those plants. So she just was gone. She was never mentioned. It sort of became like she had never existed. It was our way of dealing with it, I guess. I think to contemplate such a loss would be painful on an ongoing basis, so we just never talked about or thought about it. Now I like talking about it. It's not something, though, that I've shared my thoughts on, because your friends don't ask you, 'How does it feel to lose your mother?' If you want to talk about it, you have to go to therapy, which I have done. It feels good now in this interview to organize these thoughts in kind of a linear way."

In describing her mother, Sheryl presented an image of the perfect, most wonderful mother, who baked cookies and had them ready for her kids when they came home from school, and made them Halloween costumes by hand; a devout, pious woman who was beloved by all her friends. Her mom was active in many things, was the head of the Women's Auxiliary of the hospital, the Junior League, and the PTA. Sheryl said, "She was an absolutely wonderful mother. She was a perfect mother. I'm the oldest of four. She was always there. She was the totally involved mother. We went home for lunch every day. Had four plates on the kitchen counter, with the tuna fish sandwiches. Daily life with my mother was so unbelievably good that you might think I made it up.

"When I think of her, she was a really, truly happy person. She had a sense of richness of life and the wonder of all kinds of small things. She really seemed to enjoy whatever she was doing. She liked cooking. She liked making crafts. She liked raking leaves. She loved canoeing. She used to take all the kids and put us in the canoe, go canoeing. She seemed to really get a lot out of life. That's the kind of person I remember her as."

Although Sheryl's mother may indeed have been a wonderful woman and mom, Sheryl's words also reflect the tendency, common among my interviewees, to idealize their mothers. When I asked her what she associates with the word "mother," she replied, "Sort of a beatific, removed, idealized kind of person, not like a close, human person, but as a Madonna, sort of a religious word." In the absence of a living mother with whom they would probably experience a mixture of positive and frustrating relations, those who have lost their mothers tend to idealize them as the most caring, nurturing women who ever lived. One woman, whose mother had beaten her when she was young, told me that nevertheless, now her mother would have been her best friend. When I suggested that there might be some contradictions in what she was saying, she nodded quickly, and then said, "But I am *sure* she now would be my best friend." Similarly, several of the men, in response to my question "What did you like best about your mother?" responded quite simply, "She was my mother!" assuming that the meaning of that statement was clear and broadly understood. It is striking that my interviewees' conceptions of their mothers merge with the general social construction that woman = feminine = maternal and nurturing.

The loss of this nurturing, feminine figure had particular ramifications for Sheryl's and other women interviewees' sense of their development as females. Nearly all spoke of the variety of struggles they faced in figuring out what it means for them to be female, since typically young women develop a sense of gender identity through identification with their mothers.[2] Mothers are the embodiment and representation of womanhood for their growing daughters. The lack of their mothers as models of femininity emerged as an issue for my women interviewees. Most claimed that they just did not know how to be women, as exemplified by their lack of knowledge about makeup, clothes, home decorating, and even child rearing.

As Sheryl said, "I guess that's sort of what I felt like losing my mother, that there was something important to get from a mother, something about being a woman and being feminine and nurturing, and understanding all that. It just passes over by standing side by side with your mother. Something important passes over to you and enters you through your skin and through your understanding, but it's not a lecture or one day's project. It's a particular feeling. And that is what I never had in my life, in the years when you really need to understand that concept. And by the time in my life that I was having these visions of grieving Palestinian women, not only had I lost my mother, but also I had lost all feminine parts of myself. I just didn't know them. I was a boss the way a surgeon is a surgeon. I was tough. I could give orders and demand things, but I didn't have any of that receptivity or gentleness."

Sheryl's understanding of femininity is essentialist; she states that the loss of her mother and of all "feminine presence" in her life precluded her ability to become womanly herself. She explicitly rooted her ideas in the philosophy of the psychologist Carl Jung and his disciples, who outlined the presence, in both sexes, of the feminine and masculine principles, and claimed that women were naturally dominated by the feminine principle and men by the masculine. For Sheryl, these distinctions between male and female are rather clear-cut: the masculine principle, which guides the life of males, is assertive, demanding, and sometimes harsh; the feminine principle, in contrast, is gentle, receptive, and nurturing. "I now see that one of the biggest problems I've had is that after my mother died I never had another woman in my life. No one gave me any comforting, female advice." When her mother died, her father too was left without "any feminine principle in his life," which, according to Sheryl, accounted for his closing up and being so threatening.

The essentialist view of femininity espoused by Sheryl is linked, perhaps, to her idealization of her mother as a Madonna-like woman, a standard that, in fact, no live woman could meet. Sheryl continued to express the impact of her loss of the feminine person in her life: "I can't take care of anything. I don't know how to. Some friends had sent plants to my office when I began my new job last year. But they make me feel weak and helpless. And they're just plants! [Laughing.] Because they're living things. So I have these two plants, and I just ignore them, and I secretly was hoping that they would die and then I could throw them away, because I just don't know what to do. So Rosa, the woman who cleans our offices, came in one evening, while I was still working, and she picked up the plant in her hand, and she held it up to the light in the window. And she turned the plant this way and that, and she looked at it, and she looked at the leaves and she poured a little water, and then she turned, and she poured and she turned and she poured. I never saw anything so beautiful as watering this plant. It just was the epitome of this caring, nurturing, warm attitude that this woman has. It was a natural part of her. I just looked at that, and I just thought how far that seemed from me. Now I try to be more of that. I don't feel like that was part of me, to know this nurturing attitude." It is ironic that Sheryl perceives herself as unable to take care of anything, because I watched her give care to and nurture her dogs. She was hospitable and caring toward me on both occasions I saw her, offering me coffee and a bite to eat. What is critical here, though, is her perception of herself and the way she represents herself as unable to be caring, attributing this quality to her mother's premature death. As we will see in many other narratives, respondents were likely to blame their mother's death for the qualities they liked least in themselves, although they and we have no way of knowing what they would have been like if their mothers had lived.

Sheryl's narrative, like most of the others, reflects the powerful impact of the loss of caring. As Sheryl said, echoing the words of several others I spoke with, "I felt totally at the end of my childhood when my mother died. It was totally, totally over. There was no more chance of depending on anyone to help you out. No chance of having a reliable somebody in your life. There was nobody in my life but me to help me or go to school or figure things out. It was a total plunge into nothingness. No one there for you." Although Sheryl had three siblings, she said that she and her siblings were competitive with each other and their presence did not alleviate her feelings of aloneness.

Further, although her mother's friends had promised, at the time of her mother's death, to help her out, none of them came through for her. "My mother had such wonderful friends. She did things for them all the time and they really did love her. And so many of these women came to me and said, 'I'll take care of you. I'll help you if you ever need anything. I'll help you pick out a dress. I'll take you to the store. If you have any questions I'll be with you.' I felt very reassured by all these women saying such nice things to me, that they would help me. It really gave me some strength through the funeral and the immediate time afterward that they all said that. You know what? I'm forty-two. I'm still waiting for even one of them to offer me one word of comfort or support. They *never* showed up ever again. Several of her friends lived in our neighborhood. There's one particular woman I admired so much; she was my mother's best friend. I used to go over and sit around the back door and hope that she would come out and I could talk to her, because there were so many things I needed to know and just felt so lonely for my mother. And if she came out, she would say, 'Oh, hi,' and run to her car. That is one of my biggest problems—that after my mother died I never had another woman in my life."

Sheryl's understanding of her mother's friends' abandonment of her was that these friends were uncomfortable about her mother's death and that Sheryl reminded them of a painful subject they would rather forget. The violation of our social expectations about the centrality of mothers in their children's lives is so disruptive that it becomes unspeakable—too tragic to speak about out loud. The silences that my respondents experienced at the beginning of their mother's illness thus continued long after her death; the dreadful situation of motherless children is emotionally jarring and thus family members, as well as other adults, often avoided explicitly dealing with the situation. Very often the children felt a palpable sense of waves of rejection, which began with the ultimate rejection by their mother and was replayed by other adult figures.

Sheryl's narrative traces the impact of her mother's premature death on many of her adult life choices. A central theme here, as in most narratives I heard, was the various ways she had sought to replace the caring she had lost. Many respondents, especially the women, were forced to become caretakers at a young age. Later in life, they turned their prematurely learned nurturing skills into a positive attribute by loving and caring intensely for their own children. Sheryl, however, did not choose to form a family of her own, a decision that was atypical among my respondents. Certainly, my interviewees did not choose to have children simply as a way to replace the caring they had lost; after all, most people in the world choose to have children. But many of my respondents, particularly the women, specified that having children of their own was helpful to them in replacing the caring they had lost. Sheryl's decision not to have a family was based on her fear that she might die and her children would then have the same horrible experiences that she went through. Besides, she said, "family is a painful experience."

Nor did Sheryl, like many others, try to replace the caring she lost by finding someone to take care of and nurture her. She said, "I had a few different opportunities to get married. I was going out with somebody really wonderful and great and kind. The thought that always came through, though, and made me break it off was that I thought, 'I want to be in charge of my life. I don't want anybody else to be. I just want it to be me. I don't want to have to depend on somebody else. I don't want to be waiting for somebody else to make me happy. I just want to be depending on myself. And if I'm going to be happy, I'll know I made it that way. I just want to be by myself and try and get through things by myself, because you can't count on anybody, and if you love people, they die.' "

Instead of relying on others, Sheryl sought to become a very dependable, nurturing, and caring friend. She said, "That's one thing I know that I am, I'm a really good friend. I'm there. When my friends have problems, I think that they do call me a lot, because I make sure they can count on me whenever they need to. To me that's what friendship is. Friendship is that you are there physically. It's not always possible, because I do have friends in other states and countries that I try to keep in touch with by phone, but it's the physical presence of the friend that makes such a difference. Just the being there." This is clearly the way many people spoke about their mother, describing her sheer presence in their lives as the most important aspect of their relationships. Sheryl continued: "I don't know what to say. I only know how to be there and so that's what I do. I go and I am there. That's the one thing I didn't have when I was growing up. I didn't have anybody with me. I had no physical presence at all with me. I guess that's how I learned that that was important."

For Sheryl, caring means caring for others, because depending on others to care for her is too risky. She extends this caring behavior to her dogs, as well. "You see these dogs around here. When my mother died, I really wanted a dog, and my father got me a dog. That's the one really nice thing he did for me was he let me keep a lot of dogs. I had about five or six dogs. That was my life, that I went and I spent time with my dogs. The only thing I knew about gentleness and nurturing was in my relationship with my dogs and taking care of them. And I was really happy. I can't imagine if I didn't have those dogs when my mother died, because they became my world, these beautiful animals that depend on me. And that's remained my lifelong hobby. My dogs feel real comforting to me. There's always something I need to do for them. I feed them. I brush them. I wash them. I help them raise their puppies. I have my own little world."

In Sheryl's narrative we see many of the basic elements that emerged in nearly every interview: a period of maternal illness that was shrouded in and followed by deep silences, the powerful impact of the loss of caring, the father's general inability to care emotionally for his children, the search to replace that lost caring through caring for others or being taken care of oneself, and the emerging attempts to break the silence and the walls it creates, in order to let intimacy and love flow in and out again.

Despite the cultural taboo surrounding death, and perhaps because of it, the women and men I interviewed sought, intuitively and creatively, to maintain their mothers' symbolic presence in their lives. Sheryl did this in a number of ways. For example, she told me that she regularly prays to her mom. Sheryl had been brought up in a devout Catholic family and she put particular emphasis on her mother's devotion to the church. The children in

the family were sent to Catholic schools, and a priest ad-
ministered the last rites and conducted the funeral.
Sheryl's faith, however, was shattered upon her mother's
death. "I had that feeling that there couldn't be a God
because he wouldn't let my mother die, so it must not be.
Throughout my teenage years going to church felt empty
for me, because I did not believe that if there was a God
that such horrible things can happen. Now I'm certainly
over that and think there's a God, and a benevolent God.
Things happen for a reason that have to do with a big
plan of which we're not aware. I'm totally aware of all the
traditions and rituals of my faith, but I don't practice any
of them. All of my prayers that I pray, I always pray to
my mother. Ever since she died, I've only prayed to my
mother pretty much. I have a sense of her as always with
me, she's my guardian angel."

Sheryl reacquired a sense of her mother's presence in
the process of therapy, through breaking the silences in
which her mother's death had long been buried. She further maintains her mother's presence in her daily life by
keeping in her bedroom a picture of her mother as well
as her mother's favorite skirt. She proudly showed me a
scarf a friend had brought back from London as a gift for
her—its fabric was identical to that of the shirt Sheryl's
mother wore in the photo. During the interview she
brought the picture out and showed it to me; we discussed her physical resemblance to her mother.

By keeping photographs and artifacts of her mother
present at all times, Sheryl keeps her mother with her in
her daily life. As we will see in subsequent narratives, others, too, sought ways to break silences and maintain their
mother's symbolic presence—by talking in therapy (a
very commonly sought solution by both working-class
and middle-class individuals) or having mental conver-

sations with their mothers of the sort one interviewee described to me. This woman, who is a runner, said that whenever she has a problem for which she needs guidance, she talks to her mom when she runs. Others maintain their mother's symbolic presence by displaying photographs of her and bringing them to special occasions. One woman carried her mother's picture with her in her bridal bouquet and then placed the same picture in her son's pocket during his bar mitzvah. Another man took a piece of his mother's wedding veil and sewed it into the yarmulke that he wore to his wedding. In the ways they kept their mothers symbolically present and talked to them or used their images at particularly important moments in their lives we can see some elements of sacred practice in the evolution of their responses to mother-loss.

The study of religious practices in everyday contexts, outside of those institutions that have traditionally been the primary settings for religious expression, is an emerging trend in the sociology and anthropology of religion.[3] In everyday life, people draw upon a bricolage of reclaimed, reinvented, and borrowed religious/spiritual practices to create new rituals that meet their current needs. When I did my first interviews and began to analyze my transcripts, I was surprised to find—given the reported high level of religiosity of Americans and the belief that religion is particularly helpful at moments of existential crisis—that my respondents did not feel that institutional religion offered them much comfort or guidance at the time of their mothers' deaths. Sheryl prays to her mother, certainly not a practice taught by the Catholic church, and she does so in her own way rather than in the forms the church prescribes.

An experience I had a few years ago helped me to become aware of these various noninstitutional "sacred" practices by which my interviewees maintain their mothers' symbolic presence. At that time, the man who is now my husband had moved in with me in my rather small house. There is barely enough space there for one person's things, let alone two. And so little struggles for space ensued. One day I noticed that Arthur had placed a picture of his daughters on the small desk in the living room where I have a photo of my mother when she was a child, and over which I have a wedding picture of my maternal grandparents, who filled in for her after my mother died. I removed his daughters' picture from the desk and placed it across the room, on top of a short bookcase. The next day, this scene was repeated. I asked Arthur why he kept moving the picture back when I moved it to the bookcase and he said, "Because it does not show up well in the spot where you put it." I said, "Yes, but that desk is—is—" I struggled for the right word and finally burst out: "my *shrine* to my family!"

Like Max Weber, I typically consider myself "religiously unmusical." By becoming aware of my own sacred practices, I was better able to see the many symbolic practices by which my respondents keep their mothers present in their daily lives. Erecting a memorial to one's dead parents, grandparents, and other ancestors is a religious practice in many cultures, and even in everyday settings it is a practice that is oriented to and embraces notions of the sacred.

Another way that Sheryl maintains her mother's presence is through identification with some of her mother's characteristics. For example, in describing her desire to become a writer, she expressed regret over her lack of success in completing a novel and getting it published. She said her mother had experienced the same frustration: "My mother was a writer, too. She was trying to get her children's books published. And she didn't finish it either. My new turmoil in my life is that I am not finishing things, and wondering whether it has anything to do with my mother not finishing the things she started to write." Sheryl also identified with positive characteristics of her mother—her warmth, her ability to form close friendships, her energy, and her organizational skills.

Sheryl told me that she had recently been looking through her mother's high school yearbook and found that what her friends wrote to her "are all the kinds of things people said about me. 'Evelyn, without you as a teacher, stage manager, editor, et cetera, et cetera, et cetera, this couldn't have been half the good year that it was.' That's the kind of person I've always been—doing, organizing, and managing, because I can."

By maintaining her mother's symbolic presence, Sheryl has found a way to move on and to normalize her life, as if to say, "I am a regular person; I was loved and am still loved, and therefore am capable of love and work myself." Nevertheless, the pain of her loss has remained throughout her life. As Sheryl told me, "It's been important to myself to realize that losing my mother is still an ongoing process. It's sort of never over. It's sort of an ongoing part of life." Although Sheryl's narrative takes the linear form of a profound crisis and it's gradual resolution, the story line is also a cyclical one—the emotional pain and feelings of loss re-present themselves over and over again, presenting new opportunities for integration and ongoing self-awareness.

The core themes in Sheryl's narrative emerged in some form in nearly every other narrative I was told: the silences surrounding her mother's illness that continued for years after her mother's death; the loss of caring and her difficulties finding ways to replace it in her childhood; her idealization of her late mother as the best possible mother anyone could have; and the practices by which, as an adult, she replaces that lost caring and finds ways to integrate the experience through breaking the long-held silences and maintaining her mother's symbolic presence in her daily life. Although the particular articulations of these themes vary—whether the motherless children had any available replacement caring as children, how they replaced it as adults, and the distinct ways they keep their mothers symbolically present for them—the overall contours of the other narratives resemble this one. As we listen in on other respondents' narratives, we will see their similarities as well as their differences, and we will understand how some of the particularities of their narratives are shaped by larger social factors such as gender, age, and social class.

4

The Myth of
the Perfect Mother

Ben Adler, Sid Jacoby, and Ellie Collins

Mirror, mirror on the wall,
Who is the fairest of us all?

Queen thou art the fairest in this hall,
But Snow-White's fairer than us all.

The Queen was horrified and grew yellow
and green with envy. From that hour on,
whenever she saw Snow-White, the heart
in her body would turn over, she hated the
girl so. And envy and pride, like weeds,
kept growing higher and higher in her
heart, so that day and night she had no
peace. Then she called a huntsman and
said: "Take the child out into the forest. I
don't want to lay eyes on her again. You
kill her and bring me her lung and liver as
a token."

Snow-White and the Seven Dwarfs

The beatific, capable, warm, and nurturing mother described by Sheryl was a representation that appeared in
nearly every one of my interviews, even though many of
my respondents also included in their narratives depic-

tions of some less-than-perfect characteristics of their mothers or of their relationships with them. In the absence of living mothers with whom they might quarrel, get exasperated, or simply have adult differences, respondents' representations of their mothers come to resemble our postindustrial cultural stereotypes of the pure, pious, intensely devoted, unconditionally loving mom who was featured in such TV series as *Ozzie and Harriet, The Waltons,* and *Father Knows Best.* In fact, since their mothers died when these interviewees were quite young, they often did not have the chance to get to know their mothers as separate individuals apart from their expectations about the role of the mother. Instead, respondents' depictions of their mothers were typically articulated in terms of the stereotypic features of the mother role as culturally defined.

The cultural stereotype of an exclusively and intensively devoted mother shapes most of my interviewees' accounts of motherloss. Our social image of the mother's caring as intensive suggests that her presence is critical for her children's healthy development; that her role is exclusive means that no one else can possibly take her place. Although, as we will see, some respondents told of being reasonably well nurtured and cared for by other adults—fathers, female relatives, and, in three cases, a stepmother[1]—nearly all of them emphasized that they never found an adequate substitute for their moms.

The narratives in this chapter highlight various meanings of our cultural ideals of motherhood. Ben Adler, Sid Jacoby, and Ellie Collins all emphasized that there was no way that anyone else could have satisfactorily replaced their mothers. In Ben's account the wonderful, dedicated mother whose loving devotion helped him thrive and become successful in life is presented in sharp contrast to the wicked stepmother who came into his life after his mother's death. Sid's story is dominated by his longing for a sense of affirmation and validation of his basic worth, a feeling he believes he lost and could never recover after the death of his mother. Ellie's narrative also reveals the power that cultural stereotypes and representations of motherhood have on our basic images and conceptions of "mother." Although her family never resembled the idealized nuclear family model, because her mother's early illness made her unable to fulfill her prescribed maternal roles, Ellie's narrative reveals a continuing wistful longing for that perfect mother and family.

Ben Adler: The Wicked Stepmother Story

Ben Adler, who was a seventy-seven-year-old retired physics professor when we met, was born into a Jewish immigrant family toward the end of the First World War. His father was college-educated and a self-employed professional; his mother was a nearly full-time homemaker and mother—on occasion she helped her husband at work. The family was reasonably comfortable, Ben reported, and his mother was doting, both key elements of what he considered a good childhood.

"The first ten years of my life, when my mother was alive, were, as I look back on them, very peaceful years. My mother was a very devoted mother. My father was not an active or devoted father. He was always at his business. My mother ran the household; she was the one who paid attention to my schooling and to supplementing what I got in the classroom. When I was in the third grade I was bored in school, because the teacher kept repeating the same things over and over for the slower students. Without telling me what she planned to do, my mother went to see the principal of the school. She explained that I was very bored and suggested I might be happier if I skipped a grade. The principal apparently agreed just on the basis of the interview with my mother and I was moved up into the next grade. I enjoyed school; I was reasonably studious—but never a grind—and liked reading and studying. My mother encouraged it. My father was neutral. My recollection of his role was that he was like a cipher, although he was there. He wasn't unloving, he would not rebuff me if I approached him, but he also didn't take many initiatives to interact with me."

Within the first five minutes of our interview, Ben had signaled the key elements in his narrative reconstruction of his mother. His account emphasized those maternal qualities that are consistent with the larger cultural ideals and expectations of a mother's role in her children's lives. In contrast to her husband, who was more emotionally distant, she was the main source of support, encouragement, and guidance for Ben. His mom expressed her devotion by pushing him to do well and move ahead in school, an avenue of advancement many immigrants sought for their children. His comparison between his mother's and his father's involvement in his life was explicit and reflected his assumptions about gender: "I was exceedingly loyal to my mother. She was the more caring parent; she was the one that I related to much more. As I said, my father was so neutral that even though I was secure with him and loved him as a boy loves his father, there was not the intensity, first, that boys have with mothers and second, that I had with my mother." By echoing the nuclear family model that was socially and culturally dominant during his childhood, Ben generalized his experiences, assuming they represented the typical and normal family of the day.

A mother's caring labor involves making her child's concerns her own.[2] Ben's narrative told the story of a mother who was involved with him in an all-encompassing way. He felt that her attention instilled in him a self-confidence that he was able to draw on for the rest of his life. He emphasized that after her death he became a "survivor" who grew into a man who, despite great odds, made a very successful life for himself—he became, in his terms, a "self-made man." "I think I kind of took her for granted in the sense that she was always there. This is what one does with one's mother. She was just simply my mother and I knew that she was behind me one hundred percent all the time and that I could count on her and was secure with her and all that." Ben's account of his mother's constant, steady presence in his life resonates with our social and cultural prescription that a good mother should "be there" for her children at all times and in all ways. His mother's death, then, represents a break in normality—both because a mom's dying at such a young age is not common or expected in our society and because Ben conceives of the period before his mother's death as exceptionally consistent with the culturally encoded definition of a nuclear family.

Ben's story of his mother's death began with a summer at camp. Since the age of six, he had been sent to a Jewish leftist summer camp. When he was ten, just before he and his younger sister left for camp, his mother entered the hospital for an operation that he and his sister were told was minor. Like Sheryl and me, Ben had been told not to worry; that it was a routine kind of thing. However, later in the summer his father "appeared unexpectedly at the camp, very sober, and said he was taking us back home. I said, 'Why?' and he wouldn't discuss it. Just typically wouldn't discuss it. He couldn't handle it, this degree of intimacy of discussing with a ten-year-old son and an eight-year-old daughter just what had happened. I suppose what he didn't want to confront was that we might break down crying and there would be a scene and he couldn't handle a scene, so he just said, 'You're going back home,' without any explanation.

"When we arrived back in town, we saw a number of people gathered around the house and business (which was right next door) and a little sign on the door saying 'Closed on account of death in the family.' I immediately realized my mother had died. Of course, a terrible chill went over me and I was just devastated. And I despised all the people milling around because these were not really the people who cared that much for my mother and I despised my father because I sensed that he was not that deeply upset about the death of my mother—it did not have on him the impact it had on me."

Ben's father's silence about his mother's death—his inability to tell his children what had happened and his leaving them to discover it by reading a public sign—was typical of the paternal emotional awkwardness described by most of my respondents. Ben's father informed them of the Jewish ritual obligations surrounding death but did not actually say anything about their mother's death in particular. Because of his father's inability to talk to Ben about his mother's death or to present a model for grieving that could lodge Ben's grief in a communal and supportive context, Ben experienced his bereavement alone and without any access to a wider vocabulary in which to express his feelings. The silence that began then continued throughout his life: Ben reported that his dad never wanted to discuss his wife's life or death with his children.

After his wife's death, Ben's dad asked a relative of his, a woman in her seventies, to come to live with them and look after Ben and his sister. When that arrangement did not work out, their dad found a couple who agreed to take care of the children for a year. Ben and his sister were thus forced to move out of the family home. They moved to a different neighborhood and changed schools, all within two months of their mother's death. Ben never questioned his father's sending them away; he took it for granted—in keeping with the gendered role divisions of that time—that his father was "kind of helpless, so I accepted this as an argument that was not weird or unusual." Ben also suspected that his father "wanted to go courting. He wanted to find himself a new wife, and he would have greater freedom of movement if the kids were away. My father made it clear that it was only for a year and that at the end of that year he would have found a woman to marry and then we could come home and everything would be OK."

When I asked him if he missed his mother, he said, "Of course, I missed the caring." When I asked him what, exactly, he meant by that word, he elaborated on the particular ways his mother had cared for him. "The attention she paid to my development, the concern for my well-being, her very powerful need to see that her son would become the kind of person that she had in mind, keeping in mind that my parents, my mother particularly, was like many immigrants. She was part of a transitional generation who prepared their children to go beyond themselves, although I would not have seen it that way at that time."

Despite the loss of his mother's caring, Ben reported that he did not spend the next several years feeling miserable; instead, his approach resonated with the cultural imperative of "moving on" and "keeping a stiff upper lip," regardless of his mother's death and the rejection and abandonment he experienced in its aftermath. "I was very stoical. I have always been very stoical about things that happened, especially if they happened to me without my having contributed to them. I'm always upset if I contribute to my own problems, but if a problem happens to me, I accept the fact that this is the hand that has been dealt to me and that I should do the best I can with it, that's all." Ben's father's inability to talk about his wife's death with his children, or to console them emotionally, provided a model of silent resignation in the face of life's tribulations. This attitude of stoicism and silence about death is common in American culture. Ben's father encouraged him to observe this taboo, just as Sheryl's father did with her. Ben reported that he strove to put away his pain and grief and get on with the business of living.

During the year that Ben and his sister were away, his father would periodically bring them back home to meet various women, "whom he always referred to as Aunt So-and-so. [Chuckle.] I guess he was trying to not give an impression of parading a bunch of potential stepmothers before us. There were a number of them we didn't care for at all. There was obviously one that we liked very much. She was a very motherly-type woman." Ben did not specify what that meant but assumed, as did many of my respondents, that his understanding of "motherly," like the role of the mother, was self-evident and culturally shared. "We liked her, but she didn't make the cut. Then one day he introduced us to the woman who became our stepmother, Louise. She was, at that time, about eighteen years younger than my father, who was in his mid- to late forties. She was moderately pretty, very sexy, with a very, very attractive figure and very seemingly ebullient. We thought, 'Hey, this is wonderful!' So when he asked us what we thought, we were both enthusiastic and said, " 'We like her very much.' " So he married her. That is, he would have married her anyhow but it was nice for him to have the seeming approval of his two children. So we then moved back from this couple's house into our own house and began living with Louise."

Ben was the only one of my interviewees who told of being consulted about his father's selection of a new wife. Although Ben felt that his father probably would not have rejected Louise if his children had not liked her, their positive response provided them all with hope for a successfully recreated family. Nevertheless, children do not always take well to someone who attempts to fill their mother's place. Given our social constructions of motherhood as an exclusive role, by definition a lost mother can never adequately be replaced by anyone. This idea is reinforced by many of the fairy tales we tell young children that begin with a dead or absent mother and feature a cruel and wicked stepmother—think of Cinderella and Snow White, for example. That a mother is unique and the one who can best take care of her children is embedded in our psyches from an early age. Our cultural tool kit of fairy tales reflects and reinforces this cultural notion of the role and nature of mothers. Thus, although Ben and his sister were looking forward to their young new mother substitute, the subsequent tensions were almost structured into the situation from the outset.

"Louise was childless. Things fell apart between her and us very, very quickly. By the way, I should mention now what will come up later, which is that we ended up disliking her so intensely that after a while my sister and I refused to call her—not in front of her, of course—anything but X. That was the ultimate denigration as far as we were concerned. Anyway, I think she had expected, when she married my father, that she would be marrying a very prosperous man and would live a comfortable life. My father, by the way, was not an unattractive man. She, however, became disenchanted with the relationship, with the marriage, with having two stepchildren, very quickly. She would not tolerate our having pictures of my mother in the house; she regarded it as a sign of betrayal of her. It would have enhanced our feelings about her if she would have respected our mother. But she did not have any emotional resilience so that the normal problems that come up with stepchildren she just couldn't handle at all.

"I will tell you one illustration that I think typifies the situation. One evening she and my father were entertaining guests, people that we kids knew and were curious about. We had gone to bed and the two of us crept downstairs to listen to what was being said, to be in on it. We sat on the lower stairs, which were separated by a wall from the dining room, listening in our pajamas. Louise sensed that we were there; perhaps we had made a little noise or something. So she came to the stairway and, in a rather unpleasant way, said, 'Get back upstairs. You're not supposed to be here. Go to bed.' So we went back upstairs and since we were sharing a room, we talked to each other immediately afterward. We said things like 'Well, she's not our real mother. You can't expect more from a woman who's not our real mother.' " In this scenario, Ben and his sister engaged in the comparisons between their stepmother and their "real" mother that were common among my interviewees. As was typical in such a comparison, the stepmother could never match the birth mother's wonderful qualities and presence.

"While we were talking, Louise had come upstairs and she stopped outside the door to our room and overheard what we were saying. And she burst into the room in a fury. Now, if she had tried to handle that in some warm, loving way, it would have rendered that episode meaningless. Of course we did say, 'She's not our real mother,' but she could not recognize the complexity of how kids act, having never had her own. I mean, little kids say to their own natural parents, 'I hate you. I want to leave home. I don't want to live with you anymore.' She knew nothing about how kids express themselves and she was deeply hurt and offended. From that point on, the relationship went very, very rapidly downhill to the point where she actually began to wage a war against us. She began to harass us routinely." Ben's analysis of Louise's reaction reflected the perspective of a grown person, who reflected back upon the situation in a calm, detached manner. At the time, however, neither the adult nor the children in this story were able to have any perspective on what was going on, and the tension between them escalated.

Ben's narrative specified the numerous ways in which he felt Louise unjustly made his life more difficult and less enjoyable. When he began to attend high school, he was enrolled in a good school that was some distance from their neighborhood because his dad and stepmother believed it would provide more intellectual stimulation for him than the local high school. Louise, however, forbade him to engage in after-school activities; instead he was expected to come home and do housework. Unlike the large majority of my other male interviewees, Ben was required to perform routine household cleaning and washing tasks—those that were stereotypically gendered as feminine. When I asked why his sister was not charged with those jobs, he attributed his stepmother's demands to her particular resentment of him, as the bright elder child. Later, when he went away to college, his sister was expected to take over these household tasks.

As a high school student, Ben tried to circumvent his stepmother's limiting of his activities by finding extra-curricular activities that were scheduled early in the morning, before classes officially began. One morning she caught him leaving for school quite early and she spitefully decided to yank him out of that school and send him to the local high school. Ben was shocked and dis-appointed. His disappointment was increased by his fa-ther's failure to intervene. "My father did nothing about it. I don't know if he argued with her and said it was a terrible revenge to take and that he couldn't tolerate it, but it was symptomatic of the way he behaved toward both of us children from that point on. The situation was very simple, really. He wanted to hold on to her. I think he was an older man; by this time he was around fifty and she was around thirty. She was very sexually appealing to him. I think he felt that if he staged a fight over the two children, she might leave him. So he simply decided to preserve the relationship that meant so much to him, even if it meant sacrificing his kids. I began to really de-spise him when he absolutely failed to protect me and my sister against my stepmother's attacks, and instead let her have her way. There's no question in my mind, and I'm sure my sister would share this view, that he made a de-liberate, conscious decision to sacrifice the welfare of the children in order to hold on to this woman."

Ben thus experienced himself as doubly abandoned— first by his mother, then by his father. Ben told me that these losses made him enormously protective of his sister. "The few photographs that are taken of us in those years show me with my arm around her very affectionately and protectively." As a child who had lost caring, he himself felt called upon to take on a caring role for his sister, whom he described as more sensitive and less strong than he was. This presentation of himself was noteworthy, for more than half of my interviewees reported that they and their siblings survived on their own and were too caught up in their own pain to help each other.

The loss of his mother's nurturing was made vivid in Ben's descriptions of the ways his stepmother fed him and his sister, or rather, failed to feed them. Louise spent a great deal of her time away from the house, either with her husband at his business or elsewhere. Ben reported that she never cooked dinner, except on those rare Sundays when her husband was home for dinner, too. "Then we would have a typical Sunday dinner, roast beef or something like that. Otherwise we ate out of cans. She would make us share for dinner a can of Franco-American spaghetti, which was five cents a can at the time, while she and my father would eat at the business or out, most of the time. Then, in order to make sure we didn't eat two cans, she would count the cans when she came home. She would accuse us of stealing."

At one point, their father began sneaking food to them, a sign that he knew they were not being properly fed. But his failure to confront Louise on these matters made him less of a man in the eyes of his son, since Ben's conception of masculinity equated manhood with power, vigor, and strength of character. "I felt he was not a man and that he could not fulfill a very important function. I didn't feel he should divorce her just because of the kids, but he should try harder to work things out. I could not possibly live that way as a man with a wife who would abuse my children." Ben's representation of his father as less than a man reflected his gender stereotypes—a "real" man might be unemotional, but he would certainly have the gumption to stand up to his wife and protect his children. The social structural organization of gender and our cultural models of the ideal nuclear family establish complementary roles for females and males that make one role dependent on the other—the mother is the nurturer and emotional caretaker, whereas the father represents the family to the outside world by being the breadwinner and the protector. His father's failure to fit this model made Ben resent and despise him.

Ben used the word "purgatory" to describe his sense of his life at this time. He survived these years in purgatory by planning for his future and ensuring that his future meshed with his expectations—he worked hard to graduate from high school with high grades, so he could go to college on a scholarship. Although his high school and early college years coincided with those of the Depression, he maintained his goal of escaping through education. "Given that that was my dream, I knew that the easiest way would be for me to stay at home, continue to go to high school, graduate from high school, and then get the hell out. So my attitude about what was going on was sheer endurance. It's like being three years in the army or something like that. The old expression 'This too shall pass' was my guiding motto. I would try to squeeze as much as I could out of life that was decent. I was in a good high school. I had friends."

Like my other interviewees, Ben reported that he has sought, through various strategies, to maintain his mother's presence in his life. In the years after her death, he felt "that the serenity of [his] life with her gave [him] enormous strength to confront the problems." When I asked him whether he experienced that in a direct sense, he replied, "No, I did not think of that in a concrete way, that my mother would appear to me or say to me, 'Ben, this too shall pass.' It was more the sense that I've always felt that whatever vicissitudes I faced later, that the strength with which I could survive or struggle against these things without being severely damaged was in large part due to what my mother gave to me. But it's not like I ever talked to her."

Ben described how his desire to maintain his mother's presence in his life shaped major life decisions, in particular his choice of marital partners (at the time of our interview he was in his third marriage). Within the normative nuclear family structure, the mother comes to represent "womanhood" for both her sons and daughters. Whereas for the daughter the mother's loss creates a gap in her sense of herself as a woman, the son may continue to search for the model woman represented by his mother. Ben said that he consciously sought to marry women who resembled his mother. His first two marriages had ended in divorce, because, he claimed, those women were not maternal or nurturing enough. Once again we see that no one can actually live up to the idealized mother described by my respondents.

"The nurturing I received from my mother was so important to me that I sought that quality in a woman. That is to say, I thought of my mother as a real woman, so I looked for those qualities. To me she was a very warm and loving person. She was a woman with a large bosom and a full round figure and I tend to think of her that way. There's a certain sexual content there. The fact is that there's a part of me that even in my sexual fantasies responds as a boy would to a womanly, motherly woman.

I've never liked women who didn't have some of these qualities in them, kind of nonmotherly women. My mother was my model; she was the woman I wanted to marry. In fact, my first two marriages ended because these women turned out not to be motherly at all. My first wife was not even nurturing toward our two children."

Ben's attempts to replace his mother's caring led him to search for that elusive wife who could substitute for the perfect mother of his childhood. That his sexual fantasies revolve around such a motherly woman is fascinating and perhaps is one way of accounting for his fascination with his father's sexual attraction to his second wife. In our society, mothers are not typically represented as sexual beings. His sexualization of his maternal image evokes themes that, as we will see, emerged in my interviews with Carl Diamond, another affluent Jewish man who had earlier been in Freudian psychoanalysis. Although many other respondents had worked with a therapist, no others had been through a classic psychoanalytic process. All of our life story narratives are shaped by our social and cultural experiences—the terms and concepts we have been exposed to and the frameworks available in our social contexts. Ben and Carl were the only two men who described their mothers in such explicitly sexual terms, suggesting that their narratives had been shaped by the language and thought processes they were taught during their analysis.

The sense of aloneness that Ben experienced after his mother's death has remained with him through much of his life. Although he recognized that his mother's death pushed him to become self-reliant and independent, he emphatically asserted that he would rather have had her alive, that he derived no benefits from her death. "I think she would have had a softening influence on me, a steadying influence on me, a kind of center of gravity. She would have been a focal point for me so I would have felt less alone. I think a good part of my life I have felt very alone, despite three marriages. I don't feel alone now with my current wife, but I did in both my first two marriages."

My conversations with Ben took place over several visits to his house. In each case I was invited to stay for lunch. Through these limited opportunities to observe him and his wife as a couple, I was able to discern some reasons that he found this marriage more gratifying. His wife was nurturing and protective toward him: she watched his diet, safeguarded his energy, time, and privacy, and took care of all the household duties.

Ongoing longing for the mother's nurturing presence was a central theme in my interview with Sid Jacoby, too. Sid's interview was dominated by his repeated expressions of a lack of basic confidence and self-acceptance. Although he does not represent his mother as a perfect, idealized angel, still he is certain that if his mother had not died at an early age, his self-conception would have been stronger and more firmly rooted. It is fascinating that although Ben described himself as self-confident and assured and Sid said he was forever searching for that elusive, strong sense of self, both linked their selfhood and their varying degrees of inner strength to their mothers. Throughout the interviews my respondents attributed their problems and concerns—whatever they were—to their mothers' deaths. Motherloss, represented as the critical event in their lives, became the explanation for everything that followed.

Sid Jacoby: The Search for Self-Affirmation

Like Sheryl and Ben, Sid Jacoby, a bright, accomplished fifty-year-old architect, emphasized the profound impact the loss of his mother's caring has had on his life. Sid, like nearly all of my respondents, described his mother as the caretaker in his family. His descriptions fit in perfectly with the gendered images of the 1950s, when he was a boy: "My mother was always *the* strong person in the house. She was always the person who stepped in when people needed help. My father was a problem solver, but my mother was sort of like—I guess they were both problem solvers in different ways, my father more intellectual, and my mother more emotional, by putting herself on the line all the time. If a friend got sick, my mother would go up and clean her house, make sure everything was always in order for everybody. And all of a sudden, she goes away, disappears."

Sid, like most other interviewees, emphasized that the seriousness of his mother's illness was kept away from him and his older brother. Like Ben, he (aged twelve) and his brother (aged fourteen) were at summer camp when his mother's illness was diagnosed. When they came home, they found out that their mother had gone into the hospital "for observation," their father told them, "but we learned much later that actually it was for an operation. It turned out that my father learned at that time that she had metastatic cancer and that her prognosis was very bad. So when we came back from the summer we found that our mother was in the hospital and we did not know exactly what was wrong."

Sid's words echoed in my ears as I listened to this part of his narrative. I, too, learned that my mother was not well at the end of a summer camp season when I was twelve. The first indicator that all was not well was that my mother could not carry the suitcase I had taken on the bus home with me; it was too heavy, she said. Since my mother had always carried my suitcases, I immediately wondered what was going on. In the ensuing weeks

I would learn that my mother was "sick," but I was not told the nature of her illness, even after she entered the hospital for surgery. Because of this experience, I know intimately the sense of shock when a child returns from being away and suddenly her or his world is utterly changed. A mother's illness and death place a great hole in one's life, a phrase both Sid and Ben used. To return from a vacation and find that all is not well in your world—especially with your mother, who is in many ways at the center of that world—is a major rupture in the fabric of your life.

During the ensuing year, Sid had his bar mitzvah. His mother's illness complicated his feelings about this major event in his life and his feelings about religion. "It was sort of rough in a lot of ways. Kids are supposed to be trained that religion means something, right? And here is my mother slipping away before my eyes and yet I'm going and I'm being a good boy and doing all these things. My bar mitzvah was in January. Everybody came. Hundreds and hundreds of people came because they wanted to say good-bye to her. I really wasn't aware of what was happening. My mother continued to deteriorate and she died that June. I remember so clearly, my father walked into my room at twenty to eight in the morning and said, 'Mother is gone.' And that was it. That was the story. I was not even allowed to attend the funeral; I still regret that I was never able to say good-bye. That is still so painful, so painful." The very language Sid's father used to inform him of his mother's death reflects the silences and discomfort about death in our culture. Not only was Sid not told about the severity of his mother's condition, so that he could begin to comprehend that she was going to die; his father could not even use the word "dead" in relaying this devastating news to his son.

Sid remains angry that he was kept uninformed of the major changes going on in his life. "My father should have told us; he never told us. But we saw and we didn't know. It would have been better just to know. We were not even allowed to visit her in the hospital, which was terrible, because kids grow up feeling guilty about a lot of things and it's nice to try to have a resolution of that. Because if you don't, it stays with you for a long, long time. I did not expect her to die. Although we knew she was sick, we were unprepared for what happened. I mean, even though she was not doing well and was in the hospital, who would think that that would ever happen? I remember my father talking with my uncle about my mother having gone into a coma, so I went to my biology teacher and asked her what a coma was. And she said, 'Well, you know, blah, blah, blah,' but I can remember that conversation and I can see myself in that room in Springfield High School talking with that biology teacher about this. But my father never told us; I just overheard it."

When asked to describe his mother to me, Sid highlighted her nurturing, "maternal" qualities: "The best recollections I have of my mother, actually, are when she was pregnant with my brother Samuel. We were all setting up the crib, the bassinet, I guess is what it was, and we would always be listening to little Sammy inside kicking away or whatever. We would put our ear there and she would let us do that and that was nice . . . and then I remember the baby being born and Sam coming home. It was like a big deal, we were all part of this big deal. It wasn't like 'You can't go near the baby,' it was like this was a big deal of all of ours. That is a very good recollection of doing things with her. Basically just being a little boy, hanging around."

Sid's memories emphasized the importance of his

mother's presence, her simply "being there" for her children, as a central dimension of her role as mother. Anita Garey has shown that in order to be seen as "good" moms, working mothers engage in diverse strategies that allowed them to maintain a public as well as a private sense of "being there" for their kids.[3] A mother's ongoing and constant presence in her children's life is socially defined as one of the most significant dimensions of her maternal duties, a major factor in our society's ongoing debates about women's inherent nature and the viability of employment outside the home for women who have children. Not "being there" indicates that a mother is shirking her maternal responsibilities and is not instilling a sense of consistency and stability in her children's lives.

Sid poignantly described his early loss of his mother's ongoing presence: "I felt that my world had ended. My mother was the central person in my life. It felt like, you know, how somebody pulls a chair out from under you when you're going to sit down. I remember total chaos, complete chaos. How are we going to get by? What is going to happen? I remember that we were close, that she was affectionate, she would give me a big hug and a kiss. She was also a taskmaster—she'd be like, 'I love you and now you've got to take care of that. . . . ' But even still, I always ran to my mother, never to my father. She was very affectionate and mothering."

The very word "mothering" implies a constellation of meanings, including loving, showing affection, and being caring. The caring a mother provides for her family has numerous dimensions: her ready availability—as Sid said, "She was just there; what can I say?"—as well as her provision of physical affection, guidance, and nurturance, both emotional and physical. Mothers typically perform the emotional work of maintaining kinship ties.

They are the ones who remember birthdays and anniversaries, send out cards on appropriate occasions, and maintain the nuclear family's ties with the extended family.[4] The way a mother feeds her family, in daily life as well as on special occasions, is a key dimension of her work of creating and recreating the family on an ongoing basis.[5]

Jewish life provides many opportunities for the creation of a sense of family around a table laden with special foods traditionally prepared by the mother. Significantly, these foods—such as challah (braided bread) and cholent (a stew with beef, potatoes, and beans)—are particularly time-consuming to prepare, an indication that a mother not only should feed her family but should devote considerable time and effort to doing so. Sid recalled, "On Friday night she would make these matzo balls to put in the soup. She would always make them and we were always told we couldn't take them because they were for my father. But she'd put them down and she'd know that—she'd put them down where they'd cool off within our reach, and so we'd always be eating them. So there were things like that, just little things."

The sense of family that was produced through holiday celebrations is one of the fondest memories Sid has of his youth: "We had a giant family seder on Passover, *giant*, that went from room to room to room to room, you know, that style. And a really close extended family when she was alive, a very close extended family. Everybody lived in everybody else's house. And then when she died, it kind of separated a lot." When his mother was no longer present to create those occasions that kept the family together, they began to dissolve. Sid told me that the pain of her loss was so deep that for twenty-five years he was unable to put together without stammering (something he otherwise does not do) the words " 'my mother.' It just brought up this emotional wave all the time. I just couldn't talk about it."

Sid described his mom as someone other people counted on and cared for greatly. Almost all my other respondents described their mothers in this way. Not only are their mothers described as caring, but they are also seen as the recipients of others' affection, another quality that emphasizes their caring nature. "She was always the person you went to if you had a problem in any form, shape, or size, you went to Judith and Judith did it. When she died, five or six hundred people went to her funeral. Some of her friends never recovered from her death. She was a very, very central person in a lot of people's lives."

Her friends' adoration of her has made it difficult for Sid to form a complete picture of her as a human being. "It's very hard to get a perspective on her, because when people started to talk about her, they'd start off in a rational way describing what she was like, then they would just start crying and it was all this emotional stuff again. So you could get to a point, and then it was a collapse or hagiography of Judith, as opposed to who she really was. Even talking with my aunt, who was, I guess, the person who knew her best, I would say to her, 'What is the worst thing you can remember about my mother?' She'd think for a while and start off and then all of a sudden it would slip back into how wonderful she was. So either she was totally perfect, which created this image for me that women are supposed to be completely perfect, or nobody can talk for whatever reason." The idealized mother became the template for Sid's conception of womanhood, as it had done for Ben.

Nevertheless, Sid recognized that this image of perfection upheld by everyone was at least partly an idealization. "I know otherwise, because there are things that I remember. She was a very demanding person. She had enormously high standards and it was your duty in life to have high standards and to reach for them. I try to tell my kids that they should work and try hard, but if they don't get all A's, it doesn't matter. But my mother was a perfectionist; things were supposed to be done properly. And I so wish we had had the chance to talk about that, so I could have heard her say before she died, 'Well, in spite of this or that, you're still my boy.' "

A mother's death during her children's early adolescence takes her away from them at a time when they have not yet formed an image of her as a separate person. Typically young children see their mother as "mom," a person who fills that critical role, rather than a person in her own right. And when she dies before the children have had a chance to develop an independent, mature sense of who she is, these individuals are never quite sure of who died and whom they are missing—whether it is the idealized mom of their childhood or a real person.

Sid believes that the loss of his mother's unconditional love has left him with a lifelong sense of needing affirmation of his basic value as a human being and reassurance that his difficulties in life are normal and not the result of his premature loss of maternal care. "I always feel like there's a sense that is missing. I really need that validation that I'm really OK. And so I guess when things get down, you have to have that residual feeling that you're OK, which I don't have, because I guess your mother gives you mother love and makes you feel like 'Whatever happens, I love you, so you're OK.' I don't have that. Although people tell me that I'm doing great, that I have a prestigious job, I've been successful, I've raised a family, I don't feel that. It's as if the file is missing. So when there are problems with the children [he has two adolescent daughters] or with my wife, I feel that I'm missing something as a father and as a husband, because no one taught me. There's this big hole, all the things that mothers provide you with aren't there."

Again, it is important to pause here and note the cultural expectations about mothers that do not apply to fathers. Sid does not question why his father could not provide those same things; although he regrets it, he never assumed or expected it. But that it is a mother's role to provide guidance, acceptance, and unconditional love and to instill a strong sense of self-confidence in her children is something he takes for granted. Since the mother is seen by both her male and female children as the exemplar of womanhood, both male and female respondents felt that her loss shaped them into adults who lacked clarity about some aspect of their gender roles. The women typically said that the absence of their mother as a model left them with doubts about their femininity; the men regretted the loss of their mother's advice about their emotional lives and relationships. As the emotional center of her family, the maternal figure is seen as a model as well as a ready source of advice about interpersonal, and in particular intimate, relationships.

Sid felt that his struggles with his marriage were exacerbated by his wife's similar lack of relationship skills. "My wife, too, experienced enormous early losses—her parents were both killed in an airplane crash when she was young. So neither of us can provide for the other what we both most want and need, that sense that we're OK. My reservoir is down so close to zero that I don't know if anybody could supply that. And my wife is especially bad at that because she has her own giant hurt in the same place. It would be nice if we could supply it for each other but we can't. But what we both most want is just ten minutes, you know? We'd just like five minutes to show these people [their dead parents] that we turned out OK and just to get past this, like this giant thing holding you back. So I can't tell you what my relationship with my mom was exactly like, because I just always feel that this sense of inadequacy dominates everything. We just need this validation that we really turned out OK." The validation that he seeks, however, is from a very inaccessible place in the past that is intimately and frustratingly involved in his present identity.

Because Sid was twelve when his mother became ill, it is striking that he felt that his mother's death nearly completely undermined a strong, stable sense of himself. Psychoanalytic thought suggests that a child's basic sense of security in the world is generally in place by the age of five—that the first five years are the most critical in the development of a stable self. Nevertheless, although Sid describes his mother as a loving, nurturing presence during the first twelve years of his life, he feels certain that her death during his adolescence eroded his fundamental sense of himself as a competent, adequate person. It is notable that many interviewees attributed their adult issues—whatever they were—to their mother's premature deaths. Neither Sid nor I can say for certain whether his account of the reasons for his lack of confidence is literally accurate. Perhaps he would still lack a basic sense of self even if his mother were alive. Nevertheless, his feelings about this lasting effect of his early loss were the topic we most frequently discussed.

The members of Sid's extended family tried to fill in the gaps left by his mother's premature death. Sid bitterly related that his father was unable to appreciate the depths of his children's needs; instead, he remained focused on his own grief and loss. "He is very self-absorbed. I mean, in some ways he's an enormously lovely guy. But in other ways . . . All his life he has bitterly complained about how devastating my mother's getting sick and dying was for him and never once has he acknowledged that it must have also been difficult for us to lose our mother." Sid's paternal aunt, who had no children of her own, came to live with the family to help take care of them. "She sort of took over the emotional aspects, or tried to take over the emotional aspects of things at home. My aunt was a terrible cook, so we hired a person who came to the house to clean and cook, but she also was not a very good cook." In the absence of any sisters, Sid learned some basic household skills: "Another aunt of mine was an excellent cook, so she would drive in from the city and she would take me food shopping and she would show me how to shop for the family."

I asked him whether his older brother was similarly expected to take over some of these household tasks, and mentioned that most of the men I had spoken with were not expected to do work in the home. He told me that since his older brother had had bad allergies since childhood, he had always been exempted from all household duties. Since there were no girls in the house, it fell upon Sid to learn from his aunt "how to cook, how to do the laundry, how to shop, how to run the household basically. I cooked breakfast for my father before he left in the morning. I mean, I'm a wonderful wife, if you don't mind my saying that. I had to cook, I had to clean, I had to shop, and I had to run the household. That was my job." Sid, like several other respondents, actually began to take on these tasks when his mother was ill and was unable to do them herself.

Before my own mother went to the hospital for surgery,

she took me down into the basement and said she would show me how to do the laundry. "I don't want to do the laundry," I said. "Well," she replied, "just let me show you how to do it. I'm going into the hospital and you need to know how to do the wash." "Well, you can do it after you come home from the hospital," I responded, unable and perhaps refusing to hear the underlying message. "No," she said, "I'm going into the hospital and you need to learn to do the laundry for your father and brothers." In the first batch of laundry I did, I (accidentally) put bleach in the colored wash. Perhaps that was my inarticulate way of saying that I was not prepared to take on the role I was being bequeathed—I was too young to be losing my childhood.

Sid described feeling angry about his mother's abandoning him, a feeling I understood from my own experiences and that was articulated by a majority of my respondents. "Gee, what are you doing, this is your job, and you walked out on me. And also anger that, gee, I'm entitled to certain things. I'm entitled to have a normal family life. I'm entitled to have parents." In using the term "normal family" and articulating his sense of entitlement to parents (two, not just one) Sid expressed the common view that there is indeed such a thing as a normal family and that the only form it can take is a nuclear one with two parents. He had a sense of entitlement about this definition of family—it is his birthright—and to be deprived of it is abnormal and unfair. "I'm not supposed to have to do these sorts of things. And then you feel guilty because you're angry. But there was anger and a feeling that I can't trust people, especially women. It really had a big influence on my feeling about women for a long, long time. My God, you can't count on these people, they're going to get up and walk out on you at a critical moment. When you get hurt that badly it's pretty hard to jump in again. It creates barriers to intimacy. You have all these defensive walls around yourself and women walk out on you at critical moments. I felt very weak myself."

Sid's father's remarriage a year later did little to help the situation. "He told us he was remarrying because he wanted his children to have a mother, but in fact, he wanted to have a wife. He didn't marry someone who was especially motherly. Whereas with my mother everything was 'the children this, the children that.'" Sid, like Ben, told of a woman his father had met who would have been suitable, but then the relationship ended: "Within six months people were fixing him up. He started going out with this woman who was of Italian background. Her name was Maria Venturini. That's back thirty-six years. She was a very warm, loving—You know, she would come in the house and cook these fabulous meals and she would hug and kiss us. We would all sit down, if they wanted to watch television, it was always hugging and kissing, really affectionate and stuff like that, which we needed so badly. Then all of a sudden one day my father said he wasn't going to be seeing her anymore. Perhaps her being Italian did not appeal to my grandfather, but that was that. So here's the woman who sort of looked like she could step into this role, but she was lost to us.

"Then my father went to a dinner dance or something like that and met my stepmother. I met her for the first time on Labor Day weekend. She was not friendly at all. She was enormously distant and off-putting. About a week later my father announced that he was going to marry her. So we were sort of shocked; we didn't know this person at all. They got married in November. And then my stepmother, my brother, and I had a very, very difficult decade.

"He married somebody who took care of him. She never, ever gave me any emotional support until I was fully out of the house and had a family and my own children. She was incapable of that for her own reasons. She had lost a son to cancer when he was seventeen and she had a lot of resentment against our being young and healthy, just as we resented her for being healthy and alive. And she would not let us talk about my mother in the house because she was jealous; it became a taboo subject. Though when she was not around, my father would go on about *his* deep loss and how wonderful my mother was. But he never encouraged us to talk about our feelings."

Sid, like Ben, presented an image of a stepmother who was completely the opposite of his mother. In all but three of the narratives describing a father's remarriage, the stepmother was compared unfavorably to the mother. As our cultural construction of the perfect mother suggests, no one could possibly replace this idealized mother of childhood, who was intensely present in her child's life and unconditionally loving and affectionate. The negative experiences Sid had with his stepmother—his feeling that she was not there for him—reinforced his lack of confidence about his relationships with women and exacerbated his difficulty in trusting them. Here we see how a sense of abandonment activated by a mother's premature death can create lasting barriers to intimacy by lowering her child's trust in people, thereby creating an approach-avoidance situation in which the person really wants closeness but also pushes it away out of fear of further hurt and loss.

Sid regrets that many of the memories of the period in his life when his mother was quite ill are a bit fuzzy. "It's very hard. I have sort of like a gray period in my life there. I can remember things clearly before the period of her illness, and I can remember things clearly after, when she died. But in that period it is all very gray. It's like I'm wearing dark glasses during that period and I have only small snippets out of that. It's like a period of my life that I'm not fully cognizant of. I don't know whether I've blanked it out or whether the fright and fear and pain made it impossible to register these things, but somehow they were never recorded properly. And I can't remember the sound of my mother's voice! Isn't that terrible?"

I agreed with Sid that it was sad and assured him that I, and most of my other interviewees, have the same experience—that it is very difficult to remember a voice one has not heard for decades. He was relieved. "It's good to hear that. It's nice to know other people have gone through the same experiences, because you just sort of feel like maybe this is wrong with you." Since motherloss produces a family structure that does not match the normative model of a nuclear family, those who have experienced it have lingering concerns about their "normality." Many of my respondents asked whether other people I talked with had the same experiences and feelings and were reassured when I said they had. Although our postmodern sensibilities may encourage us to be skeptical of metanarratives that purport to broadly articulate human experience, my interviewees told their narratives of motherloss not only to assert a unique and individual self but to help fit into the nebulous category of "normal." There are certain ways of talking about and placing a mother's death that can normalize that experience and begin to repair the uncomfortable and solitary sense of having been outside of the norm for so long. People tell their stories not only to integrate their past with their present and future but also to integrate their self with a larger collectivity.

Sid told me that he has a lot of friends who also lost parents as kids. "I guess we all have the same personalities in some ways, and so we gravitate to each other. It's funny. Recently I went to lunch with one of these guys and he started telling me his whole story, and I knew snippets of it, but he had never told me how he felt emotionally and psychologically. We were comparing notes on this and he has the same feeling I do that there's something wrong, something is lacking." When I asked Sid to elaborate on this feeling, he replied, "You're supposed to reach some sort of emotional level of completeness and you perceive the world as an adult. Meaning rational and secure. But I just don't have it!"

Sid's sense of the gravity of his loss and its impact on his life was not lessened by the presence during his adolescence of a few strong women who did reach out and make themselves available to him. In addition to his aunts, he mentioned that a family friend who lived nearby "knew that I needed a lot of talking and so she did that. Her name was Ann Goldberg and she was always available to talk. And when we moved to a house, another woman across the street, Sheila, also realized I needed a lot of help, and I spent thousands of hours in her house talking about my problems. My father was very resentful of all these interactions and my stepmother was very angry about her because she felt I was talking about her behind her back."

Unlike the majority of my interviewees, who felt that almost no one had stepped in to help them, Sid felt he had "all these enormously strong women who raised me and were role models for me and stuff like that." To me, this aspect of Sid's story underlines how irreplaceable one's mother as mother is. Although Sid acknowledged receiving love, support, and nurturance from other women, his narrative is nevertheless dominated by a sense that when his mother died, he lost such a crucial support that he has never recovered from it. The conception of the model nuclear family that prevailed when he was growing up suggested that only one's mother could truly fill the maternal role in a child's life—if she is gone, she cannot be replaced.

Like my other interviewees, Sid is conscious of his attempts to maintain a sense of his mother's presence in his life. "I was always taught that our parents are living on through us and that they live on in the memories that we have of them, and so these memories are very precious. Genetically, I'm half my mom, so I certainly feel her presence in that way. And I feel that in the limited time we did have, she sent me in certain directions that I'm now living with, for better or for worse. She did shape my attitudes a lot and I would love to show her that I turned out OK. I try to raise my children in ways she raised me. For example, since my children have come along, my wife and I have gotten more involved with Judaism and light candles and have Shabbat meals every Friday night. It is important to me that our children develop a Jewish identity, so that they can have a sense of a deep connection with my mother and the generations before and after. When something nice happens, either for me or for my children, I want to share it with her so she could be proud of me. Similarly, when I have problems, I sort of wish I knew what she would have told me to do under these circumstances. When I have troubles in my marriage, what advice would she have given me?" Sid concluded with the plaintive question that had dominated our entire conversation: "And I always wonder how I would I have turned out different had she not died when she did."

Ellie Collins: The Twice-Lost Mother

A portrait of the perfect, loving, nurturing mother is also central in Ellie's narrative, although for her, these images refer to the mother she wishes she had had; the kind of mother she is sure she would have had, had illness not gotten in the way. In contrast to Sheryl and Ben, who described the perfect mothering they received while their mothers were alive, Ellie told of a loss of maternal caring that began when she was three or four, when her mother became ill with a progressively degenerative illness. Ellie's narrative was replete with longing for this ideal mother who is always present for and close to her children, a representation of motherhood that Ellie held on to, despite her own mother's inability to live up to that role.

When Ellie was eleven, her mother's illness worsened and she became bedridden. Ellie's older brother was away at college, so Ellie and her dad took over the tasks of caring for her mother. Eventually her illness spread to her lungs and she died in a hospital a year later, when Ellie was twelve.

I met Ellie eight years later. She was a bright, active, and attractive college student. Our conversation was dominated by her sense of being deprived of a "normal" childhood and by the premature reversal of the caring roles and tasks between her and her mother. Ellie's love for her mother was clearly expressed. So was her sense of resentment at being asked to do chores, such as feeding her mother dinner and staying home from school to await the day nurse, that set her apart from her peers and denied her a more "normal" childhood.

Ellie's anger over this loss and over the role reversal between mother (caregiver) and child (one to be cared for) was still quite clear and palpable: "There were mornings when I was the last one left at home. My dad would go to work, and my brother was at school, and I had to wait for the nurse to come. And I'd be late for school, because the nurse was late. It didn't make any sense to me. I didn't understand why I had to take care of my mom, why I had to wait there. One time I threw a fit with her. I told her that I hated her and that I couldn't deal with taking care of her. I really flipped out. She was supposed to be doing that for me. I sat there and screamed at her. But she was an amazing person; she took it and said that she was sorry. She knew how hard it was on us. But she couldn't help it, she had no choice. Still, I was *so* angry. There were times that I just—My dad would tell me that I had to take her dinner up or I had to bring her some water or do this and I had homework to do. And I'd say, 'Dad, I'm sorry, but I'm trying to be a kid and I'm trying to do my homework and you're making me do these funny things that no one else has to do.' "

Consistent with Ellie's resentment at her inability to have a "typical" childhood was the devastation she felt because of her mother's failure to be a "normal" mother. Throughout her narrative it is evident that Ellie's sense of the archetypal and appropriate mother-child relationship was based on the dominant image of motherhood as intensive and exclusive. For Ellie, the ultimate loss of her mother to death was foreshadowed by her mother's inability to be a "traditional" mother from early on. Ellie's image and expectation of the normal happy family reflects the cultural stereotype rather than her own experience. Ellie had not lived in a stereotypical nuclear family: her father was very much involved in nurturing and caretaking for his wife and children, and her mother did not fit the ideal of the mother whose entire life is devoted to her children. Nevertheless, in her interview she made clear that this was the kind of family she still believed in and longed for.

Ellie described how as a young child she became aware of her mother's inability to simply be there with and for her. "There are always things that every other mom could do. In elementary school even, I remember every other mom could come on our class trips and she couldn't come, because she couldn't walk that well. These little things just got to me and I was so angry about them. She was in a wheelchair before she was bedridden. She had trouble, she walked with a cane before she was in a wheelchair, you know, it was every step. I remember walking with her, I always had to help her up when she sat down. People would stare. I would just be so angry. I would get so, like I just wanted—like angry at them for staring, but also angry because I wanted her to be normal. I just wanted her to be a mom."

Ellie felt that her mother's illness kept them from developing the kind of mother-daughter relationship she longed for. When I asked her if she was close to her mother as a child, she responded, "We were close. We had the initial attachment of just being a mother and daughter, but she was sick from a time when—before I could really get close to her as a person, really more than as a mom, so that I have only a few very specific memories. One is of crawling into bed with her when I was in sixth grade. An eighth-grade boy had asked me to the prom. I crawled into her bed and asked her if she thought I should go and if I should, what should I wear. I will always remember that, because it's really one of the only times that I had that with her. We didn't have time. There was too much other stuff going on for us to be close. She was too sick for us to really develop like a person-to-person relationship. From the time when I was an actual like thinking person, sort of aware of things more than when I was younger, we didn't really have much of a relationship. The times that I remember when we had those mother-daughter moments are special, because I don't have much of those and that kind of hurts. I do have those few memories, but I would love to have other stuff to fall back on, to always think, 'Well, at least we had this kind of relationship.' Maybe if she hadn't been sick, we would have, but there was really too much of taking care of her."

Ellie's idealization of motherhood reflects the cultural assumption that a mother is intensively and exclusively devoted to her children. Although her mother was incapacitated by illness early in Ellie's life, Ellie nevertheless asserted that her mom was absolutely irreplaceable. Although other women could and did fulfill some of the tasks her mother might have done, such as taking her shopping, no one else came close to being an adequate mother surrogate. "All I wanted to do was go shopping with my mom and I couldn't go shopping with her. For so long the biggest thing for me was 'All I want to do is for her to take me shopping.' All my friends get to go shopping with their moms and I couldn't. It didn't matter if my grandmother did it or my aunt did it, it wasn't my mom. It wasn't just having a woman there, it was my mom who I wanted to take me and she couldn't. Instead of going with these other women, I felt it might be easier for me to just do it on my own and learn to take care of myself than to have someone who is not supposed to be there doing it, someone who's really in the wrong place.

I appreciated their efforts; it was very nice of them, but I really didn't need it. I needed it from my mom. But I couldn't have it. She couldn't do it from when I was nine, so it was like all of my late childhood, my adolescence, like my real conscious life, the part that I really think about."

Ellie, like many of the other respondents, felt that her mother was simply irreplaceable; one of the very definitions and expectations of a mother is that she, exclusively, can properly care for her children. But unlike the large majority of my interviewees, Ellie described a father who did not fit the stereotype of the emotionally distant man who was unable to express emotions or nurture his children. In contrast to the fathers of Sheryl, Ben, and Sid, who were emotionally unavailable and unable to discuss their own and their children's grief, Ellie's dad prompted his children to express their feelings about their mother's death. Ellie told me that it was her parents' earlier experience of a profound loss that helped her father understand the importance of emotional expression.

"My parents had another child. Before my brother and I were born, they had a son who died when he was three months old, and it really taught my dad a lot about how to deal with death and sorrow. He always told us that at the time he and my mom never spoke about it. Like Philip died and that was it. They didn't talk about it. They didn't want to bring it up, because they figured it would make it harder. My dad would go out driving and just be furious. Someone would cut him off and he would say he would just chase that person on the highway, because he didn't know how to express himself, how to get any of that out, that anger. So I think from that he learned a lot about how to deal with us, that we always needed to talk about it. We needed to set aside time, even, to talk about my mom, to talk about her death and how it made us feel and what we were thinking about. The night she died, the three of us just stayed up all night talking and ended up laughing a lot, just because we were talking about her and the things she did and our childhood. And for the next six months we would maybe once a week bring out pictures and talk about her and us and just remember her. She used to write poetry, so we'd bring out her poetry and her writing. Then it sort of dwindled. I think we all still probably needed to do that, but it got to be too much. It's easier to forget than to make us all remember every week about it. It's easier to go on. It was too hard to keep bringing it up for us when we knew that we could just let it go. We would still talk about her, she would still come up in conversation, but not the way that we would deliberately set aside time to do it in the first six months." At times silence about her mother's death, in Ellie's perception, was actually comforting and "easier."

The lack of overall silences about Ellie's mother's death presents a stark contrast to the silences reported by over fifty-five of my sixty interviewees. Ellie's experiences differed from others' in this respect for several reasons. First, she reported that her father, unlike those of nearly all my other interviewees, consciously strove to fill the roles of both mother and father to his children. While many fathers either took out their anger on their children (anger that often resulted from the pain they felt at having lost their wife and their frustration that they would now be solely responsible for their children) or ignored them, Ellie's father was careful to spend time with them. "My dad is amazing. He was everything to us. He supported us through everything. He was superdad. Went to work all day, came home, cooked dinner, helped us with our homework, talked to us, did everything." Second, Ellie, who grew up in an upper-middle-class, sophisticated family in the Northeast, lost her mother in the late 1980's, an era in which serious illnesses and death were emerging from the silence and shame that had earlier prevented conversations about these subjects. The hospice movement had gained momentum, and in her community seeking help from social services was no longer stigmatized. Thus the timing of her mother's death—decades later than that of the mothers of most of my interviewees—had a major impact on her family's ability to articulate and handle their emotional reactions.

Because Ellie was so emphatic that she wanted only her own mother to perform mothering tasks for her, she was fortunate that when her dad remarried he selected a younger woman who did not try to become a replacement mother. Nevertheless, she and Ellie developed a close friendship. "I thought that it was really cool that she was sort of like an older friend, like a woman to follow. I always thought I didn't have a woman role model and I wanted one. Sandy was so neat, we had a lot in common. She never tried to sort of capture me, like I have a feeling that some stepmothers might want to do, might want to win a girl over, but she never tried to do that. It was always the three of us if we did anything, or with my brother." The distinction between friend and mom remains clear, however. "She's not my—The mom part just doesn't belong there. That's not part of her role as stepmom. I don't even call her my stepmom. She's my dad's wife and she's a friend of mine and that's it."

Despite having a father and an adult woman "friend" available as sources of support, Ellie still feels that she was deprived of the maternal guidance that she would have had if her mother had lived. More specifically, Ellie feels that not having a mother as a role model has made it hard for her to know how to be feminine and how to behave properly as a woman. This has been a particular challenge with boyfriends. "My mom died in October of sixth grade. In seventh grade I had seven boyfriends. I had started a new school and I thought that I needed to do that, like that was appropriate for my age. These boys were attracted to me and they would ask me out and I couldn't decide which one to go out with and I would go out with one for a little while and stop and then go at it with another one. Nothing really happened. Most of them were boyfriends that you were holding hands with in the hall, or something. That's the first time I ever went to parties. A lot of it, when I think back, was probably because she wasn't around and I kind of needed to get out and needed to feel female. I don't know how else to explain it. I knew I didn't have *the* female in my life anymore. She was *the* woman and I will never have her again and I needed to know that I could still be a woman without her and I could still go out with boys and be attractive and kiss boys and do all those things that women are supposed to do, even though she wasn't around." Again we hear the converse of the cultural construction of woman as mother; Ellie's words reflect her sense of her mother as representative of womanhood.

Ellie's uncertainty about 'how far' she should go with her boyfriends made her very uncomfortable. When a high school friend of hers asked her what base she had gone to, she didn't even know what a base was, and she was unsure how far she should have gone. "I didn't really have a sense of what I should be doing, you know? And I didn't feel like I could ask anyone. I sort of just went with the flow and let things happen. I think I was fine. I didn't let too much happen. My relationships with boys were never substantial. For a while they were very surfacey and I wanted to be accepted and I wanted to be liked a lot.

"I think I started out when I was much younger with the idea that OK. Male-female relationships. Male wants to fool around. That's what I'm supposed to do, right? So I'll just do that. That will make him happy and that's how it's supposed to work, right?' And I sort of dispelled that and got into a couple of serious relationships that weren't really right, but I was experimenting a lot. I was trying to figure out what exactly—'I know we're not supposed to fight all the time. I know we're supposed to have conversations and we're supposed to talk and do things together, just not exactly sure how it works.' "

Ellie's desire for the male approval and affection that would help her feel she is a woman, despite her loss of her maternal role model, still shapes her relationships. "I'm in a mildly serious relationship now where I'm really scared because I'm not sure exactly what's going to happen, because I feel like I'm at a point, now I'm twenty, where I should be getting the hang of it now. I should sort of know how I want this relationship to work and I'm not there. I feel like there's a formula almost. Like get together four times a week and each time you get together, you're going to kiss, go out to dinner, go out to a movie, come back, fool around. I feel like there's something I'm supposed to know and I don't know it. Someone was supposed to tell me something along the way and my mom didn't get to tell me and now I'm missing out on something and I don't know what it is. I always felt like my relationships with men would be really different if I had a mom. I think that's probably true. I really think that I didn't have her there to teach me about the right and wrong of relationships, the do's and don'ts and stuff like that."

Although many adolescents—perhaps most—do not, in fact, discuss their emerging sexuality with their parents, and many people feel uncertain about sexual relationships, in Ellie's image of the ideal mother and mother-daughter relationship she would have had, she and her mom would have talked about everything. Not only did the loss of her mother at an early age affect her interactions with boyfriends, it also left her feeling insecure and needy about her friendships with other women. This theme was echoed by other interviewees who said that although they had a great need to have people like them, they lacked guidance and support in developing appropriate friendships. As Ellie expressed it: "Sometimes I think I need my friends more than they need me because they have their moms. I don't know if there's that much of a connection. There may be. But that they already have the person that they can go talk to. My friends here and my friends at home, they all have very good relationships with their mothers. They all can talk to them about anything and are really close to them. I know that they sort of have another outlet that I don't have. It's like sometimes I feel like I'm very needy and I want them to like me. I want the validation of knowing that I'm an OK woman and I'm going to get a good job." Just as Ellie fantasizes about the important advice her mother would have offered about her emerging sexuality, she imagines that her friendships would be more balanced if she had her mother's guidance. In comparing herself with friends who are close to their mothers, Ellie maintains the image of the ideal mother she might have had, not acknowledging that many teenage girls actually have highly conflicted relationships with their mothers.

More than anything, Ellie emphasized that she misses having a mother-daughter relationship like the ones she sees in the "normal" world. "There are times when I just *ache* for that relationship. When you see a mother and a daughter and *all I want in the world* is to have that relationship. It's so painful when I see a mother and a daughter like that. And then especially if they're having a good time together. 'Well, I could be like that with my mom. I just know that that's what we'd be like.' Especially older mothers and daughters, because I know that relationship has lasted. It's something that's been built upon and has turned into a good—like a friendship. Every once in a while, it will just hit me. It's those times when it's so painful that it just grabs me and I just know that I will never have her again, that when she died, that was it. [Claps hands.] There's no mother and there never, ever will be. That one person, she's the only one who can ever fill that role and she's no longer there. It's just the biggest reality blow for me, because it's so easy to just go along with life [voice wavering] and know that she died and have all my friends know that she died, but to just sit down and realize that she will *never* be here.

"She won't be here when I graduate from college and she won't be here when I get married and when I have kids. That is one of the worst, when I think about getting married. I love children. I can't wait to have my own children. They won't have that grandmother. I've had all my four grandparents and it was wonderful to have them. Already my kids won't have that one grandmother that they deserve. Especially because I feel like I don't really know her well enough to tell my kids about her. I know what I know from my dad and what I remember, but I don't know her well enough as a person to ever sit down and say, 'I want to tell you about your grandma and who she was.' If I just had that." Ellie mourns not only for the mother of her childhood memories but also for the mother of her cultural ideals who will never be involved, in the ways our culture expects a mother to be involved, in her adult life. By stating that her kids will never have the grandmother they "deserve," Ellie, like Sid and many other interviewees, revealed the common assumption that growing up with an intact nuclear family is the "normal" expectation, an entitlement and a birthright in our society.

In Ellie's analysis of her current life and in her fantasies about what it would be like if her mother were still alive, Ellie relies on images of our socially constructed maternal figure rather than of her own mother, since her mother had failed to fit these stereotypes when Ellie was quite young. Rather than romanticizing the personal memories of her mother, as did Sheryl, Ben, and many of my other respondents, Ellie bases her fantasies on the idealized maternal figure prescribed by our culture. Although our conversation was replete with these images, occasionally a more realistic assessment broke through: "I've also completely idealized this in my mind since she's died, because I can. I have the opportunity to create any relationship that I wanted to with her. And I can say that if she was alive, I would tell her everything. We'd have this really close relationship and she would give me advice about whatever I wanted. I don't know if that's true, but I'd like to think it is."

The lack of this idealized mother-daughter relationship left Ellie, like Sheryl, feeling that she had failed to learn many essential elements of femininity, aside from relationship skills. Ellie talked about not knowing how to use makeup, or how to dress appropriately. Many of my female interviewees expressed that same feeling, of lacking basic knowledge about how to be a woman because their mothers did not live long enough to teach them. Sandra, a forty-five-year-old respondent, said that although she is aware that reality does not always match her fantasies, nevertheless she always imagines other women's mothers taking them shopping, and feels jealous when she sees "mother-daughter pairs" in stores and restaurants.

In discussing the caring they had lost, many respondents described the moment of their mother's death as the end of their childhood. In the model nuclear family, childhood is relational and depends upon a mother who is fulfilling a particular role in relation to her children. The loss of numerous dimensions of their mother's caring symbolized and marked their transition out of childhood. Often, having to take care of themselves was a key factor—children are taken care of; if no one is taking particular care of you, it is hard to feel like a child. Childhood carries with it a connotation of dependence; having to become independent at an early age is another marker of childhood's end.

5

A Different Script

Carl Diamond

Children's perceptions of their mother are a complex interweaving of their actual interactions with their mothers
and the assumptions and expectations about motherhood
that they derive from the culture. How well a mother fulfills her socially expected roles of nurturing, unconditionally loving, and being there for her children is a central
part of how children evaluate their mothers. Adults' as-
sessments of their mothers, however, are complicated by
their current situations and experiences, the prevailing
constructions of motherhood, and the vagaries and selectivity of memory. The accounts of adults whose mothers
died when they were children are replete with idealizations of this missing beloved figure and the sense that if
only their mothers had lived, their own lives would have
turned out much better.

In this chapter I deliberately interrupt the flow of the
narratives that highlight these idealizations, and on
which I build my argument that mothers are irreplaceable, to present an alternative account. Alternative stories

are useful because they underline the commonalities of the other accounts and also show that no story about people can be monolithic. In addition, people's narratives are shaped by the available cultural scripts and language: We construct our accounts out of the images, perspectives, and vocabulary that we learn through our participation in social and cultural institutions. In Carl Diamond's case, the frameworks, concepts, and ideas that dominate his narrative are shaped by two divergent visions. His account is a complex interweaving of dominant cultural ideals, such as the celebration of "normal," intact nuclear families, and a very different understanding of motherhood that is derived from his deep involvement with psychoanalysis, a therapeutic modality that was not typically utilized by my respondents.

Carl's narrative of motherloss was singular in his representation of his mother as a "nuisance" whom he "was glad to get rid of." Although his account actually revealed a greater ambiguity in his feelings about his mom than these words suggest, Carl, in contrast to my other interviewees, did not idealize his mother. That he expressed a strong preference for his stepmother may seem to challenge the argument that our social definition of motherhood as an intensive and exclusive relationship means that the mother simply cannot be replaced. But in his case, from the time he was quite young, his mother was subject to episodes of mental illness that eventually resulted in her suicide. As Carl told the story, these frequent interludes of emotional instability clearly marked her as inadequate in her role of mother. His account, then, does not challenge my overall thesis but rather offers an additional nuance. A mother who tangibly deviated from our culturally idealized model of someone who provides a nurturing, stable, emotional center for her family may be less likely to be represented as the wonderful, devoted mom whose place no one else can take.

Of my sixty respondents, six told of mothers who died by committing suicide. The literature suggests that such individuals may be burdened by lingering feelings of guilt and shame that hamper their attempts to make sense of their loss and integrate it into their biographies.[1] The narratives of these six interviewees, however, did not cluster together in this way. The major commonality in their accounts was a greater lack of clarity about the events surrounding their mothers' deaths than my other interviewees expressed. Although nearly all respondents told of the deep silences that controlled their access to knowledge, the adult children of mothers who committed suicide generally remained confused and ambivalent about the meaning and causes of their mothers' deaths.[2]

Carl's narrative presents a stark contrast to these other accounts of maternal suicide in at least two ways. First, he claimed to comprehend his mother's suicide and its causes, attributing it to her long-term mental illness and dysfunction. Second, Carl did not present an idealized view of his mother's life and her presence. His story differs in content as well as in structure from the other accounts I heard. Although his narrative does trace a path of chaos and disruption to biographical integration, he locates the disruption early on in his life, long before his mother's death. In addition, his narrative is framed in the language of classical Freudian analysis, a process he went through for many years during his fifties. The rhetoric and underlying assumptions of psychoanalysis provided Carl with a distinctive framework for assessing and representing his experiences. As we saw, Ben Adler, another upper-middle-class Jewish man who was roughly a contemporary of Carl's, also described a period of analysis

that clearly was influential in his self-reflection and presentation, but only in Carl's account does this perspective
and language provide a comprehensive modality for articulating his experience of motherloss. Therapy, for Carl,
became the language in which his experience could be
storied.

Carl Diamond, a seventy-year-old Jewish American,
was retired from a successful career as an agent with clients in the media. Born in Hungary, he grew up in New
Jersey, in an observant Jewish household. At the time we
met, he had been divorced for fifteen years and had two
grown children. The central focus of our conversation
was Carl's deep and long-lasting ambivalence toward his
mother. His narrative began with his childhood; he told
me that his mother was terribly ambitious for him: she
pushed him to be a child prodigy of the piano. His
mother's role in promoting his early career is the first
source of Carl's mixed feelings about her: on the one
hand, he feels she pushed him too hard; on the other, he
described his accomplishments with great joy and pride.
He expressed appreciation for the ways his mother nurtured him and cultivated his talents. As he said, "When I
was nine years old, she was my agent. I was a piano player
and she was my agent and she basked in my glory, really.
I hated it because I was nervous and didn't want to be
exposed that way, but she sort of forced me to. She lived
reflectively in my dramatic world." He described her as
cruel and demanding. Yet even as he claimed to have
hated his mother's pushing him, he also talked about this
past with pride: "In retrospect, it's very interesting because it is on her account that I can still play a musical
instrument." He felt important because of the attention
he got as a musician; as a child he performed in front of
the relatives who came to the house to hear him.

Carl's contradictory feelings about his mother extended beyond her role in his musical career. He remembered her as "a loving person who instilled great emotional warmth." He also described her as "very voluptuous, big-busted. Very beautiful. She had a Rosalind Russell–type body and I loved to sleep with her, because when I was frightened she allowed me to come in her bed. My father and mother had twin beds, so I was allowed to come in her bed. When I was about eight or nine years old I had nightmares every night and for a long period of time she let me sleep with her. She tried to wean me off it, so that she could do whatever she was going to do with my father, but I was too frightened to sleep alone two rooms away."

I was intrigued by Carl's use of fairly explicit sexual language to talk about his mother; only one other interviewee, Ben Adler, had used those terms, and that was in reference to his father's attraction to his stepmother. This sexualization of Carl's memories of his mother seemed to contradict and complicate the generally negative attitudes he expressed in our conversation. When I asked him if he had any dreams or nightmares about his mother, he said he had had dreams, "some of which were sexual. As I say, she was a voluptuous woman. I think they were pleasant dreams, let's put it that way." I suspect that the psychoanalytic framework, with its emphasis on the Oedipus complex and young boys' attraction to their mothers, shaped the narrative he constructed about his life and his relationship with his mother. The framework also provided a way for him to relate his identity to his past experience of biographical disruption. Negotiating between finding an identity and finding a language in which to express it is a continuous and dynamic process. Just as having a strong sense of self may enable a person to articulate his identity more precisely, learning an elaborated language of personal development may also enhance a person's ability to articulate and form his identity.[3] Carl's experiences in analysis also clearly shaped his narrative in other ways; his was a very well formed and eloquent story, which he narrated with dramatic flair. Clearly he had been honing this account for a long time.

Yet even though Carl described his mother's tremendous sexual appeal and the pleasure he derived from sleeping in her bed, he also described her as "nothing but a burden and troublesome" because of her serious mental illness. She was a "beautiful, dramatic individual who couldn't cope with life." Carl remembers that she threatened suicide many times when he was still young: "She was visibly disturbed to me and a threat to me and a disruption." When I asked whether he could remember any particular incidents of obvious disturbance, he recalled, "One time she sat out on the fire escape—this was in New Jersey—and she wouldn't come into the apartment. And everybody was asking her to come in. It wasn't threatening at the time, but she wanted to be away from everybody. She was a dramatic person, a would-be actress, and a would-be personality." He equates her suicide with her lack of nurturing capacities (so that she was not a "normal" mother) and as a reflection of her not caring about him.

Carl revealed complicated, mixed perceptions and feelings about his mother's actual mental condition. Clearly he perceived her as ill: "And in those days had they had antidepressants she would be alive, because she couldn't deal with the depression." But he contradicted his evaluation of the seriousness of her depression by stating, "I don't think she was mentally disturbed. I think she controlled others with her dramatic manipulations." I told him I was trying to sort through what he was saying, since I heard him saying both that she was disturbed and that she was not. He replied, "Acted disturbed but on the other hand I got to believe she wasn't. You know, from a genetic point of view I don't want her to be disturbed. I don't want any identity with that which I don't have. I cleared that out in my analysis." Again, Carl's experience in therapy helped give him the language to understand the ambiguities in his narrative and see those contradictions not as contesting his identity but actually as consistent with and formative of his sense of identity.

He described his parents' relationship as "turbulent" and said that he was always trying to be the referee between the two of them. "They didn't get along too well, which is primarily why she wasn't satisfied with her life." He said that he had to take care of his mother because his father "absconded." When I asked what he meant by that, he replied, "He had to go to work. He was never there, and frankly, he was bored with her. He couldn't take her craziness, her continual demands on him to stay home and take care of her. Well, he couldn't stay home and take care of her. We wouldn't have eaten."

When Carl was ten years old, his mother was institutionalized and his younger sister, who was five years old, went to live with an aunt. He told me that he and his dad would spend alternate Sundays visiting his sister at his aunt's and his mother in the mental hospital, a round trip that took them nearly all day. "Those were vivid, dramatic days that I would see her in the wired pen, which was protected so she wouldn't escape. She would be screaming for me not to leave and then I would feel bad that I was leaving. But it was just too much pressure for a young twelve-, thirteen-year-old to experience that."

Thinking that this must have been an awfully painful

experience for a boy so young, I asked him what his feelings were on those days. His response surprised me a bit: "It was strange, both titillation, something very different, excitement to be very honest about it. I wasn't depressed or anything, but I was excited. I think that is really the word I can use." The language of titillation is sexual; it is reminiscent of the other ways his account of his mother was sexualized. Additionally, perhaps his anger at his mother's inability to be fully available to him during her life and then her deliberate and final removal from him shaped his construction of her as a mother. Instead of seeing her as maternal, nurturing, and a warm, loving presence in his life—the more common ways my interviewees described their mothers—he substituted a view of her as sexual and bizarre. I imagine that this language and approach were fostered in his analysis and enabled him to encapsulate his reaction to his mother's severe depression in a language that conveniently meshed with his own self-construction.

This narrative pattern resonates with the narrative of motherloss told by Peter Burke, another interviewee whose mother committed suicide. His account of his immediate reaction to his mother's suicide revealed a need to encapsulate that event in a language seemingly devoid of the emotional and jarring elements of the experience and consistent with his self-construction. Peter told of returning home after having been out at a birthday dinner for his father and finding that his mother had overdosed on pills. He was fourteen at the time. "It was very normal," he told me. "The fire engines came, and they went past the house. And I went sailing out . . . I was going so fast. I got them and brought them back." Curious about his reaction, I asked him to clarify how he felt when he found his mother. Again, Peter told me, "I ran very fast after the fire engine." He was a doer, not a reactor, and he evaluated the experience as normal without delving into a complicated account of his emotional reaction. Carl focused on the sexual and strange elements of his experiences with his mother and let that explanation of his reaction suffice. At other points in their narratives, however, both Peter and Carl expressed more ambiguity and uncertainty about their responses to their mothers' suicides.

A couple of years after Carl's mother had been released from the mental hospital, she committed suicide. Carl was fourteen at the time. "And then I came home one day and everybody was in the apartment and my aunt screamed in my ear, 'Your mother is dead!' I said, 'How's she dead?' 'Well, she died of pneumonia.' I've subsequently found out that it was not the truth, the truth was much more dramatic. I was in my classroom at school, and a guy came in. 'Wow,' he said—and I even remember his name, Bianchi—'I saw a lady jump in front of the trolley. I saw her body splattered all over the sidewalk. Wow.' And that was my mother." When I asked him how he figured that out, he said, "I put two and two together. When he said he saw the body and my aunt said, 'Your mother is dead,' and subsequently it was in the newspapers, too. 'A lady jumped in front of the trolley.'"

Carl presented his feelings about his mother's death in the same way he expressed his feelings about her life—with a great deal of ambivalence. Carl described the funeral scene as "very interesting. Before the coffin was buried, the rabbi came at me with a knife." I was alarmed and obviously showed it, so he went on to explain that the rabbi wanted to cut his jacket lapel (a traditional Jewish burial ritual). "I thought he was going to stab me so I bolted, thinking he was coming after me with a knife. My father subdued me and I let him cut the lapel of my jacket. And then they buried her." The dramatic presentation of this story—so dramatic that I gasped when he told me that the rabbi came after him with a knife—and the tone of his narrative probably reflect his long career in the media. He was quite aware of the interview as a context in which to construct a life story, and he made use of his dramatic talents to do so. As he told me, "I'm putting this whole story on a slant, or that slice of the whole gestalt of things. I could come in at any point, and by putting on that slice, it will emphasize certain things that may then seem bigger than they really were in the whole."

Carl says that he was relieved and happy when his mother died because she was dangerously mentally ill and was a pain to be around. Immediately after her funeral, he told his father, "I'm not going to believe in God anymore because he took her away from me." But immediately after telling me this, he went on to say, "But I lied, because I was glad to get rid of her." I questioned whether that was his only feeling or whether his emotions at the time were more mixed. He replied, "Truthfully, that was the only feeling. I didn't miss her because all I got from her was a lot of trouble, plus a little bit of forceful, dramatic influence on me being a virtuoso. She particularly told me that she wanted me to be a successful pianist, so that I would bring her family to America. Her whole thought was that I was going to be her salvation."

Carl denied feeling anger or guilt about his mother's suicide. Nevertheless, he interpreted her actions as indicative of selfishness. "I think she was a selfish person. I don't think she gave a shit about her children or she wouldn't have taken that role. Why? I think in terms of my children or grandchildren right now. I would die for them. That's an interesting choice, isn't it? Wow. I would live for them, really." He contrasts his attitude with his mother's: "She didn't care enough to remain and nurture and develop. She wanted to fulfill herself by getting rid of the pain." When I suggested that perhaps she might have thought she was sparing him further pain, he said, "She kept saying that one day my father will remarry and then I'll have a normal house."

After his mother's death there was little talk of her in the house; the silence about his mother resonates with the other narratives we've heard. Carl said that he subsequently was very happy to live with his father. "I was his pride and joy and he was a loving father." Before his mother's hospitalization, Carl's sense of his father was that he was the absent breadwinner who was not nurturing. But in his account, his father became very caring toward him after his mother's death. Interestingly, Carl actually used some of the language in which he had earlier spoken of his mother (a loving person who took great pride in him) to represent his emergent relationship with his father. It sounded to me as if Carl had transferred to his dad the extravagant attraction he had felt toward his mother. He told me that there was a "great romantic love" between his father and himself and that his father did his best to raise him well. "I waited for him to come home at night so that we could have supper together, at some local restaurant." He described his father as "sweet, caring, lovely, good-looking, and a funny guy who found humor in everything."

Carl told me that for the rest of his father's life, Carl tried to look after him. "I loved him dearly and watched him like a tooth in my head, an eye in my head. And he depended on me totally. I think his every thought every day was me. I think that is the only love I've ever had that I felt was true love. He was doting on me. I depended on him and he fulfilled all my needs. He was a good father, a marvelous father." The construction of his father's image in this interview is noteworthy. Since earlier in our conversation Carl had emphasized his father's absence from the family, describing how he came home at 10 P.M. and rarely saw his son, it is striking that later Carl presented him as the ideal parent after his wife's death. Perhaps his father had avoided the household on account of his wife's illness. It is also possible, though, that Carl had transferred his feelings for one parent to the other. His description of his father here resembles most respondents' idealized depictions of their mothers.

Carl's sister was five years younger than he. Because of their mother's illness, he said, she lacked nurturance as she was growing up and was somewhat disturbed as an adult. She went to live with an aunt during their mother's stay in the mental hospital and went back to live there for a year after their mother's death. His father remarried a year after his wife died and Carl's younger sister was brought home to live with the nuclear family once again. His stepmother helped put the family back together: "A family life was provided. They created a healthy family relationship where I could go off and not worry that my mother was going to be there or not be there. So everything started to become normal. Up until then, my marks in school were always D. D in deportment, D in work effort, because I could never concentrate on my work, I was always worried about what would happen in the house." He describes his stepmother as a substitute mother who was "very docile, loving, and caring."

Here we can observe how the language Carl chose to describe his stepmother contrasts with the ways he generally characterized his mother. "I treated her like a mother, because she was very, very caring with me." He said that once his stepmother came into the family, they never discussed his mother or her illness, "because everything was normal, everything was lovely. Back to the family. I needed the family existence, which I didn't get as a kid." Carl's use of the term "normal" is reminiscent of Sid's and Ellie's use of the term when they bemoaned the lack of a normal family life. Although Carl described his newly formed family as the normal one, they all shared the widespread assumption that a normal family must have a nurturing mother at its center.

Carl reported that he took care of his mother during her mental illness and kept watch over her. Early on, then, he learned to become a caretaker, an approach that he claimed became useful to him in his professional dealings with his clients. Nevertheless, he felt that this strong quality also had negative consequences. He never fully developed his own personal talents, because, he said, he had spent so much energy caring about others' careers. Interestingly, in this way he actually resembled his description of his mother—someone who pushed others to succeed. In later life, however, he chose to go into therapy as a way of taking care of himself. "Having taken care of my mother in such a careful manner, I took care of my clients in the same way. I became so successful at what I did by virtue of the environment and having to take care of her. In my therapy I found out that it's the same personality, taking care of all those stupid, idiot clients of mine who were all the same nature as my mother, the same temperaments. I would nurture them all, take care of their money. Everything I did for my mother I did for them. I thought for them. They didn't have to do a thing. I catered to their wants, just as I catered to her wants." But Carl did not find complete satisfaction in nurturing others: "I was resentful of their success, so I had to get my own success. I had to have my own talents recognized."

Carl developed a sense of responsibility and self-sufficiency at a young age, and these sensibilities shaped his lifelong relationships with his father and sister. He took care of them both financially as his own career flourished. Like Ben, he described himself as a "self-made man." He told me that he had married young, had children by his mid-twenties, and set up his own business. By marrying young, Carl felt he would have a chance to create a good home life, something that had not been available to him in his younger years. Nevertheless, he had multiple extramarital affairs. "Women were always available to me in my business. I had a different romantic influence going every two or three weeks or every four weeks. Even during my marriage, which broke up fifteen years ago, I had women all over the place." I asked whether his relationship with his mother and her death might have affected his relationships with women. He replied, "I'm sure that it made me wary of women. I caught my mother coming out of the bedroom with my bar mitzvah band leader. That is why I had affairs, not because of her death, but her personality when she was alive influenced me." Like the other respondents, Carl blamed his mother for the issues in his adult life.

Carl claimed that his mother's infidelity, along with her emotional lability, resulted in his "fear of abandonment and of losing love. Consequently, I did not learn to love. For me masculinity was a matter of performing well sexually. But I chose to marry a person I was sure I could trust. My mother's craziness painted my emotional relationships with women. I married somebody I could trust, so what I got was a dutiful wife and a wonderful mother, but I wasn't interested; she was a nice dutiful wife. She was inorgasmic, which was disturbing to me because what I had with the others I did not have with her and I was continually sexually catering.

"I had a feeling in my analysis that I was getting even with all women by getting them to fall in love with me and then sort of abandoning them, because my family life was very important. I was not going to leave my wife and children, until the children were really grown up. So I stayed married all those years, not wanting to be married to my wife. And I think that I never trusted women. I think I always found it hard to fall in love. I never truly loved a female after my mother died." When I asked whether he did love his mother, he replied, "I think I loved her. It was an ambivalent relationship, loved her on a maternal level and hated her for what she did to me. But the effect it had upon me and the future of my own life was that it didn't enable me to love, because that love would be taken away. I did love my mother but that love was taken by her doing."

One way Carl entered into relationships with women was, as he said, through his sexual prowess. "I got the females to fall in love with me because I'm a sexually good partner. Like on the piano, I was always performing in bed. But I never really loved—Maybe I loved as best as I knew or there are different degrees of love. I loved my wife because she was a good mother. I loved her because she was dutiful and honorable and did not go to bed with the band leader." In listening to Carl's depictions of his sexual prowess we learn something about his self-conception as a man, a factor that may also be connected with the sexualized view of his mother in his narrative.

Despite his ambivalence toward his mother, Carl engages in rituals that periodically reinvoke her presence in his life. He has remained faithful to some of the traditional Jewish rituals of his childhood: he prays in the synagogue on holidays and visits the cemetery annually before the High Holy Days. Even now, fifty-seven years after her death, he still visits his mother's grave religiously. "I have never missed one year of going to the cemetery before Rosh Hashanah and Yom Kippur." When I asked what it meant for him to go to the cemetery, he described it as an experience of "communication, total communication. She is there watching over me. Performing these ceremonies is one way I take care of myself." What is complicated about his account of his "total communication" with her and his sense of her watching over him, just as a good mother should, is the hazy referent to this mother. Who is that mother he believes is there for him? Throughout his narrative, he emphasized his mother's lack of availability and how relieved he was to have a "normal" family life after her death. Yet he also reported that he has a watchful, doting mother whom he visits at the grave for support, nurturance, and affirmation.

"That tombstone and touching the tombstone is touching her, I totally feel her presence. I say the Kaddish when I'm there and then converse with her. For years, because she smoked, I would light a cigarette and put it in the crypt and watch it disappear, watch the ashes disappear. This was an uncompleted relationship and I was trying to continue it in a ghoulish manner, really." When I asked if he felt any response when he conversed with his mother, he replied, "Yeah, sure, otherwise I wouldn't go back. I feel an obligation, a ritual, to continue taking care of her." Her ongoing presence in his life was made clear when he affirmed that "she is a thought in my mind all the time in one form or another." He misses her at various times, in response to diverse situations. Like others I spoke with, he particularly missed her at important life transitions or special events. Like Sid Jacoby, he wished his mother had been alive to see his successes, so that her beaming claim "That's my son!' " would have affirmed his own sense of pride in his accomplishments.

6

Becoming the Mother

Tina Martinelli and Darlene Jackson

Although all of the narratives highlight the devastation involved in the loss of a mother's caring, and many interviewees felt that their childhoods had ended with their mother's death, few actually reported being required to fill all the mother's various roles in the household all the time. Since my respondents were schoolchildren when their mothers died, families devised a variety of strategies to get household tasks done. Sometimes a relative filled in; often a stepmother came in and took over the practical, if not the emotional, tasks performed by the mother; a few fathers tried to take on the dual role of father and mother. In a few instances, however, the daughter essentially became the mother, not only taking over the household duties but also playing a critical emotional role in the family.

Tina's and Darlene's stories are distinct from the others we have read in the sparcity of their descriptions and discussions of their mothers. Their clear and detailed representations of themselves as the replacement mothers in

their families seemed to preclude their ability to reconstruct many memories of their mothers, either as individuals or in their maternal roles. There is a hint here that
the family perceived the mother and daughter as inter-
changeable, at least as far as household tasks were concerned; if the mother could not fulfill her caretaking role,
the daughter would assume it. The mother's presence in
these narratives is minimized—the daughter's memories
are fuzzy and indistinct—because in at least some symbolic and actual ways, the daughter has *become* her. Tina
and Darlene *became* their mothers through taking on
their physical and emotional tasks. Not that these women
literally saw themselves as replacing their mothers, or
that their younger siblings, whose care they took over,
actually perceived them as their new mothers. Nevertheless, by taking on the maternal role, Tina and Darlene had
to become adults very quickly, thereby relinquishing their
childhood need to be taken care of themselves.

The daughter's ability to leave the "maternal" role in
her household eventually to form a life and perhaps a
family of her own was clearly shaped by her family's social class and their ways of enacting ethnic customs. Although nearly all of my female and a few male interviewees were expected to perform some routine household
tasks, in time those who were members of the middle
class typically were able to escape from that situation by
going to college, thus requiring their fathers (and siblings) to find some new ways of coping. Tina and Darlene,
however, perceived that the circumstances of their working-class lives circumscribed their choices. Both narratives reveal how the lack of material resources, coupled
with the strong sense of duty that emerged from their
families' interpretations of their ethnic communities'
standards, left these women to play the mother role well

into adulthood. I represent both of their narratives, however, in order to reveal how a situation that seems the same in two families can be experienced and represented in quite different ways.

Tina Martinelli

Tina's story, which begins when her mother became ill in the 1970s, highlights the ways her family's social class and particular understanding of their ethnicity shaped her experience of growing up motherless. The central theme in her narrative is her family's assumption that, as the eldest daughter in a family with five children, fifteen-year-old Tina would assume her mother's role after her mother died. Tina, a thirty-year-old Italian American, had two older brothers and two younger sisters. She grew up in a working-class, tightly knit Catholic community. Her mother had graduated from high school; her father had stopped his schooling after eighth grade. He worked as a delivery man for a pastry company; her mother had occasionally worked outside the home doing factory work or in sales. Tina had graduated from junior college and was employed as an office assistant.

My conversation with Tina lasted nearly an entire afternoon. She told me that when her mother first became ill, Tina learned some basic cooking and cleaning tasks. Her mother had lingered for three years. Tina vividly described her constant coughing, hacking, and choking, sounds that were hauntingly familiar to me because my own mother's cancer had spread to her lungs. The poignancy of living with such a sick mother was revealed in Tina's powerful memories of her mother's struggles to breathe. She told me that she could still visualize her mom sitting on the couch, the oxygen tank near her, gasping for breath. At the time, this clear evidence of her mother's illness got on Tina's nerves and she sought to avoid the sounds and the larger problem they indicated by hanging out with the neighborhood kids. "During the time she was sick, in my early teens, I was ignoring it, which of course I regret now. I was the type that had to laugh. I had to keep my mind off it. But if people looked at me and saw me laughing, I felt guilty about it, but that is what I needed at that time."

Tina's powerful sense of guilt, which began when she sought to avoid confronting her mother's illness directly, reappeared as a dominant feature of her account of why she was unable to leave her family home. The most unusual and striking feature of our interview was her overwhelming sense that she had no choice, she was stuck in her father's house taking care of him and her older brothers, who also still lived in the family home. Her sisters, in contrast, had long ago struck out on their own. Tina's narrative traces the various ways in which she became the "mother" in her family, taking on the mother's physical tasks as well as many of the emotional ones, to the point of sticking up for her older brother against her father, as her mother had constantly done. In fact, she described these efforts on behalf of her family in language people often ascribed to their mothers: "I try to be there for them."

In our conversation she illustrated how the unspoken assumptions about gender in her Italian American family placed a lot of stress upon her as a girl of fifteen and sixteen, pressures that continue to this day. She learned to cook, clean, and do laundry, and although her next younger sister helped a bit, the primary responsibility was Tina's because she was the eldest. One of the first stories she told me revealed the intense pressure and frustration she felt about her family's unspoken assumption that she would become the mom. Although she did laugh at the memory when she told this anecdote, her tone also betrayed intense agitation, revealing that a lot of pain and conflicted feelings remained:

"After my mother passed away, I immediately had to start cooking. I *love* to cook. It's something that didn't adversely affect me. I love to cook. But still, I remember on Sundays, and here I am—I was just fifteen when my mother died—and I had to cook. We always had a two-o'clock Sunday meal, either macaroni or roast beef or whatever. The first time I cooked a big meal was a roast beef. I retain memories. I am very sentimental about this stuff. I called my best friend's mother and I said, 'How do you cook a roast beef?' She told me the temperature and how long to leave it in. I didn't mind doing all that stuff, but I remember one Sunday. Everybody would take off on Sundays, do their own thing, hang out with their friends. My father would go off. Everybody, before they left, would say 'What time is dinner?' Now, they're asking a sixteen-year-old girl what time is dinner!

"After so many months, I don't know how long after my mother died, I just looked at it like 'They're going off while I'm standing here cooking, and I have to tell them when to be home. Now, what am I doing during the time that they're gone? I'm stuck here cooking.' And I got so mad! So I looked at my brother, I said, 'You see this bag? The chicken goes in the bag, you put the stuff in it, you shake it, and you put it in a pan, and you bake it!' And I ran off, and I cried. It was Shake 'n' Bake. It was simple things that I was cooking at the time. I went in my room, I slammed the door, and I started bawling my eyes out. I thought my father was going to come in and yell at me because, of course, I was the oldest girl. My sisters were still too young to cook. I just stayed in there for like, I don't know how many hours it was, and I came out and I started smelling chicken cooking. I started laughing because they actually did it. I think that from that instant on, my brothers learned to fend for themselves. But still, I cooked ninety-nine percent of the time. My father ended up making gravy exactly like my mother made the gravy, the red sauce for the pasta. He would basically always cook the macaroni and stuff like that, but as far as the meats go and the chicken and stuff like that, I would always do that."

In our conversation, Tina occasionally tried to normalize her situation, even though it also clearly angered her. Her statement that she loved to cook and that the assumption of this task did not "affect [her] adversely" reflected her attempt to neutralize and minimize her evident frustration. Nevertheless, the intense rage she revealed in this story and in most of our conversation belied these statements. Tina's resentment at having to do all the laundry, ironing, cleaning, cooking, and caretaking for her family came exploding out in the Shake 'n' Bake story.

At the time we met, Tina was tired of running the household. For the fifteen years since her mother's death she had had to do an enormous amount of work for her large family, and she was clearly fed up. Her father, she said, saw it as her duty to fill this role, but her prolonged stint as mother created great tension and frustration in her life. It had been bad enough to have to take on these tasks at fifteen; to still be doing them fifteen years later, with no freedom for herself, was too much for her to bear.

"It may have been a responsibility at one time, but it just gets to the point where you're sick of doing it. You know, when you're fifteen years old, other kids didn't have to do all this. Now I've been doing it for fifteen years. The things that you were responsible for at an early age that you shouldn't have been responsible to do wear on you. It's like you want to stop and I think that's why I might be bitter now because I'm home.

"Just two weeks ago I found out my father doesn't know how to iron. I'm looking at it like I can't stay here anymore. I'm the last girl in the house. I look at it like if I do leave, I'm going to feel so guilty. I'm the last person to help my father, even though my brothers are there. I just can't see my father ironing. He makes his own bed and stuff. He can handle that stuff, but I'm like, 'Dad, why do I have to iron? Why can't you iron?' I asked him seriously the other day. He's like, 'I don't know how to iron.' I'm like, 'You were in the army.' " I suggested that perhaps her dad could take his laundry to the dry cleaners. She agreed: "I know. That is what he's going to have to do because I can't feel guilty. My worst fear is feeling guilty when I leave the house. That is my worst fear. And I'm looking at it like, 'I can't stay here anymore.' "

Although her father can prepare food for himself, Tina worried that he could cook only simple things. Left to his own devices, then, he would not eat a healthy variety of foods, something Tina had been laboring to ensure for years. But Tina also acknowledged that her dad probably could manage for himself: "My father knows how to take care of himself so I shouldn't feel guilty about that. But it's just the fact that we're home and you feel guilty about leaving because we stayed home for so long, because my mother wasn't around." Unlike Peter and Carl, who had arrived at a language in which they could reconcile some of the contradictions and tensions in their lives and narratives, Tina felt trapped by her simultaneous yearning to be out on her own and her concern that her father needed and depended on her.

Although Tina was clearly angry about and tired of her role in the house, she felt that her gender, in combination with her ethnic background and financial status, shaped her life options after her mother's death. Perhaps if her family had been solidly middle-class she would have been encouraged to attend a four-year college that would have offered the educational background for a more lucrative job; thus she could have obtained the financial independence that would support an independent life. But clearly Tina felt held back by more than her lack of finances: when I asked her why she did not leave, she told me that the combination of financial and emotional issues held her back. Her role as the eldest daughter in a patriarchal Italian family shaped her current situation as much as or more than her earning capacity. Tina's reluctance to leave the family home was fed by the tremendous guilt she repeatedly expressed about "abandoning" her father. As she said, "Italians don't kick [their children] out of the house; we would have been there for a long time anyway." It was the intersection of these structural and personal factors that shaped the realities of her situation.

"Moving out—it's really awkward to move out of my house. You feel like—even right now, I'm thirty years old. My oldest brother, Louis, is a salesman. He is gone traveling much of the time, but he always comes back home. And Gino has never left the house. I left the house for a year when I was in community college [a school she was able to attend at minimal financial cost]—I moved in with some friends—and my father went ballistic. My sister Pat got married last October; she's out of the house, and I envy her. I do. And my youngest sister, Valerie, is away.

Interestingly, she is the shyest of all of us, but she was lucky enough to get a full scholarship to attend an Ivy League school and she simply stayed on after graduation. So I'm the only girl left and I feel so guilty and so stuck."

Although my ethnic and class background differ from Tina's (my father was a college graduate and a self-employed professional), as do our current situations (I had the educational opportunities that allowed me to break free and live an independent life), in many ways my narrative echoes Tina's. The traditional Jewish family in which I grew up held the same unspoken assumptions about gender—that it was the daughter's responsibility to take over the maternal role in the household—and about the need for children to remain at home until they married. My father, like the father Tina portrayed, was a gruff patriarch who was not able to communicate openly or express his feelings. Like Tina, I argued with him fiercely but was afraid to move out on account of guilt and the belief (repeated like a mantra by my father) that our family should stick together. Nevertheless, my middle-class background, together with my family's encouragement of educational accomplishment, afforded me a welcome escape hatch. As an undergraduate at an excellent women's college, I received counseling to help me negotiate my guilt. The emotional support and financial help I received from my school enabled me to leave a similarly difficult household environment.

After all those years, Tina is still struggling with this issue. "I want to leave so badly, but I really feel guilty. I really, really feel guilty. But at the same time, I yell at him all the time. I yell at him for little things. I feel like it's my house. We all feel like it's our house. We all do things to benefit the house, like painting and what not. But at the same time, he's got to yell at me for bringing in too many plants, which is my big thing. And I'm like, 'You smoke in the house. I'm bringing in plants.' Like, how can you yell at something like that? We have the stupidest arguments. We have the stupidest little, piddly arguments. They blow up into these big arguments. I'm always complaining about my brothers not picking this up, not picking that up. They leave their dishes all the time, their coats downstairs, their chairs pushed six feet away from the dining room table. I think if there was a mother there, she'd be the one doing it. I don't know; I was very close with my father when I was young. But at some point that ended and we started arguing. I really think it's because my mother died when I was at an age when I should not even have been having conversations with my father. I should have been off with my friends. But here I am having conversations with my father and arguing with him about things. If my mother were alive, she'd be the one to talk to my father. And I can avoid all this fighting by moving out, but who is that going to benefit? Right now I see it's not going to benefit him. It's not going to benefit me because I want to save to buy a house. I don't know."

In discussing what she misses about her mother, Tina mentioned that she was most acutely aware of her mother's absence at life cycle rituals and celebrations. She told me that when her sister got married last fall, they wondered what their mother would have done to help her prepare for it. "You don't know these things, and you definitely miss her guidance." In describing another major female life cycle event, her getting her first period, Tina was glad that her mother was alive at that time. "I think I have a feeling of how my family reacts, and like I said, we're not open. It's kind of weird. I remember my mother telling me, because I got my period when my mother was alive. Thank God, at least the first daughter did. So that's about it. That's the extent about being a woman, that my mother told me the basics about having your period. But as far as sex or anything like that, it wasn't even spoken in my house. I had to talk to my sister when she got her period." I asked, "Did you tell her about it in advance?" She responded, "You know something? The thing I remember about that, I was maybe sixteen when she got hers. My brother was going out with a girl at the time. It was her. I remember her *and* I telling my sister. I think I may have been awkward, that's why she sat down with me, and we both talked to Valerie about it. But it wasn't like an extensive conversation. We just told her, 'All right. You got to get pads.' And I think that my other sister and I teased her about it. [Chuckles.] Nothing was ever serious when it came to that type of conversation."

Tina remembers her mom fondly, although she does not idealize her as the best mother who ever lived. The thing she likes to remember best is that sometimes when she came home from school her mother would have bought her a shirt or sneakers or some other treat that made her feel special and loved. But she also claims that "I honestly don't remember a relationship of my mother with me. I'm the oldest girl. I just remember a motherly relationship. I just remember coming home, her cooking supper, just a basic relationship with my mother. Even though I was fifteen, I really don't remember—I'm thirty now and it's like double the amount of time. I haven't seen my mother for as long as I have known my mother."

It is interesting that Tina describes a "motherly relationship" as "just a basic relationship." She essentially portrays her mother as someone who carried out the variety of tasks involved in caring for her family—serving as the communicator, being the family "glue," preparing meals for her family and showing them that they are loved. Tina saw this as the basic maternal way of being: her mother's fulfillment of her role was just assumed to be normal and therefore taken for granted. Because Tina herself has been carrying out those tasks and obligations, her actual memories of her mother have become blurred. One force that was certainly at play in Tina's narrative was the fact that she never had a chance to construct or buy into the constructions of the image of the idealized mother. Because she stepped so quickly into the role of carrying out the duties of the mother, the process of normalizing the disruption in her biography did not include an emphasis on the mother as an archetypal, romanticized character.

Tina, like most of my interviewees, remembers her mother as a "good person" and a "beautiful woman." She said, "I remember what everybody said about my mother. That she was a wonderful person, she was a beautiful person. She could have been a movie star during the time that she was in her twenties and everything, because they always thought she was beautiful. I think a lot of what sticks in my mind is what other people thought of my mother, not what I thought of my mother." Many of us whose mothers died have had to rely, at least to some extent, on others' representations of our mothers to help fill in our incomplete memories. I, too, have spoken with my mother's friends in order to supplement my knowledge about my mother; many of my respondents described such a quest.

In many of Tina's descriptions of her mother, she emphasized those qualities she believed she shared with her mom. This was a strategy many of my interviewees used in order to keep their mothers symbolically present—she did live on, through them. Tina's mother was artistic and

Tina loves to work with plants, growing beautiful gardens and arranging flowers. "She loved animals. Friends are very important to me and I saw that with my mother, too. I saw her always with her friends. She probably really had her friends on a high priority. That means a lot to me, too. I guess I get that from her. So I'm like her in a lot of ways, with the animals and the art, friendships, even body structure is that way. My mother always told me that we're very big-boned, but we're thin." Tina's identification with her mother is so strong that for years she was convinced that she was the child who most resembled her mother, although her sister probably actually looks even more like her. "I always thought I looked like my mother. I had the hair and features and everything. My mother's chin, which I hate. [Chuckles.] If I had plastic surgery, I'd get rid of this chin; it's bulbous. I feel guilty even thinking that way. A few other people had told me in previous years, 'Oh, Pat looks more like your mother,' and I was like almost offended. I'm like, 'I'm the older daughter, I'm supposed to look like her.' But when I saw this picture, I could see that Pat definitely looked like her. And I was kind of happy. I don't know why. Maybe because I've always done what my mother was supposed to do. So let Pat take that responsibility of looking like her." Most of my interviewees expressed a desire to resemble their mothers' best qualities, but Tina's wish sprang from a different source, from her sense of having *become* her mother to a great extent rather than from a fantasy of an idealized absent figure.

When I asked Tina about her present social life, and whether she could envision a relationship that might provide her with a way out of her father's house, she made clear that her living situation made it quite difficult to form a romantic relationship. "Whenever I or my brothers or sisters had girlfriends or boyfriends, it would take a long time before we brought them home. Maybe if my mother was alive it would have been easier since there would have been a lighter atmosphere in the home. My father is the type of person that when he picks up the phone, his voice is enough to scare people. [Chuckles.] He's very gruff-sounding. Everyone's like [inhales] 'Uh!' when they first hear him; he always sounds mad. A lot of times when he talks, he sounds like he's yelling but he's not yelling, because if he was yelling you'd really hear him. He's got the high octave, like Italian men. When they're on the phone, they're very loud. It's like, 'Lower your voice. You're yelling.' 'No, I'm not yelling. I'm just talking.' But that's how he is. So to bring a guy home, for me, no, it doesn't happen."

Tina expressed regret at her lack of a social life. Nevertheless, although she clearly longs for her freedom and independence, Tina has grown up with such a compelling sense of family obligation that the very thought of leaving fills her with guilt and reluctance. And while she is aware of the many benefits she would gain if she lived on her own, in particular a stronger sense of herself as an individual, she normalized her situation by questioning whether moving out would actually benefit her. Nevertheless, she shared with me her concern that if she got married—and she does want to get married—she would move from taking care of her father and brothers to taking care of a husband and children. She would be deprived of any time or space just for herself, something that, unfortunately, she has never had.

Darlene Jackson

When Darlene, a sixty-year-old African American woman, was twelve, her mother died in a car accident at the age of twenty-nine, leaving eight children behind. Her father, who was laid off from work at the time, was driving the car in which her mother was killed. The family's and community's knowledge that he occasionally drank raised suspicions about her father's role in his wife's death and produced rumors and accusations that exacerbated the disruption of motherloss for this family. Just before her mother's death, forty-eight years ago, Darlene had had a premonition that something was profoundly wrong:

"Oh, I can remember that clearly. I think, somehow I think I'm psychic. My mother and father were going out and when she was going out the door—my sister was eight months old—she turned around and said, 'Take care of baby,' you know, that is my little sister. And it was unusual, my mother usually did not go out. With eight kids, how could you? Once in a while, but back then you always lived in this extended family; you always lived with your aunt and your grandmother. The house was always full of people. So I was the oldest one and so she went and I went to bed and I couldn't sleep, I was tossing and turning. I said, 'Something's wrong.' I'm only twelve years old and I couldn't sleep and I don't know what time it was but the telephone rang and they asked to speak to my aunt, I guess, and then I heard what she said and they said I was just screaming and hollering. My father was driving the car. . . .

"And the worst thing was they locked my father up. And it made it seem like he was a criminal. It was in the newspaper and it was awful. He never got over that. People said, 'Oh, he killed his wife. There go the kids that the father killed the mother.' They made it seem like he meant to do it but you know, my father's not gonna do that. It was an accident. We weren't there and I don't know what happened. But it took a total effect on him . . . he started to drink a lot for a while."

The rumors about her father's role in her mother's death had a deep impact on Darlene as a child, producing feelings that have continued into the present. It was a theme that came up many times during our conversation. She described how, when she went back to school after her mother's death, she had a sense that the other kids were looking at her. When she would walk down the street she could hear people whispering that she was one of the kids whose father killed their mother. She repeatedly defended her father, saying that he never neglected the children and that although he resided elsewhere for a while—actually with her mother's kin—he always took care of the children and provided them with money for the things they needed. Many of my other respondents— in fact, the majority—complained about their fathers' emotional unavailability to them and generally condemned his inability to help replace the caring they lost upon their mother's death. Although Darlene's father stopped living with the family after his wife's death, her representation of him made evident her ongoing love and respect for him.

Darlene was the oldest child. The great number of siblings had a major impact on Darlene's life both before and after her mother's death—as the eldest she had helped care for her sisters and brothers at an early age. "My mother built a strong foundation in me that I helped with the kids. I cooked, I washed . . . " Thus, when her mother died, Darlene was somewhat prepared to take on a greater portion of the responsibility for the care of her siblings.

Darlene had an extended family and community that might have supported her and helped her fill her role, but she indicated that the other adults present were not always helpful. At the time of her mother's death, the entire family was living with two of her father's sisters and his parents. Darlene explained to me that the typical extended family pattern in her community was for mothers to raise their families among their own kinfolk, but her maternal grandmother was already looking after an aunt and her seven children. Since her father's sisters had a large and relatively empty house, the growing family had moved in with them. But the best Darlene could say about these aunts was that they were "just there," meaning that Darlene and her next younger sister "had to do all the work. Like cleaning and washing and ironing and looking after the little ones." According to Darlene, the aunts not only provided limited assistance with household tasks; at their worst, they were cruel—verbally and physically abusive to the children, and sometimes skimpy with their food.

Nevertheless, she was grateful that the children were not separated after her mother's death. "When we came back home from the funeral people were whispering about what would happen with each of us; who would take care of us. I just listened because I knew you weren't supposed to say anything. But deep in my heart I knew I was going the other way. We were all going to stay together. I was only twelve years old but I said, 'No, no, no. We have to stay together.' And as each one got older they helped the other one."

Darlene became a central figure in her family's transition to a life without their mother. Many of my respondents told me that although they had siblings, each coped relatively alone and in her or his own way. In contrast, Darlene played a crucial part in replacing the caring the family had lost; by taking on the caretaker role, Darlene kept the family unit intact and functioning. In essence, when Darlene became the mother figure in her family, the new role mitigated her need to find a surrogate mother herself. Like Tina, Darlene stepped into the role of the mother without idealizing that role, but unlike Tina, Darlene described her transition as smooth and natural. Growing up in an extended kin network, in which she learned to take care of her siblings from a young age, had the unintended benefit of preparing her to alleviate the hardship for her brothers and sisters, despite the disruption of their lives. She played games with them, read to them, and organized activities they could do together. She assumed many of the roles her mother had once filled, such as helping the younger ones get ready for school and with their homework, as well as doing the washing, ironing, and starching of ribbons for Sunday school. The responsibilities she shouldered after her mother's death became a source of strength for Darlene. "I wasn't looking for self-pity because I knew that I had to look out for the rest of them. I had to make sure they were taken care of. And taken care of properly, not that they were put somewhere where somebody would treat them like orphans or something. You just have to keep going. And it made me a more mature person."

Her mother's death made Darlene assume adult responsibilities and roles in a way that is rare for twelve-year-old children. Nevertheless, her narrative—both in tone and in content—revealed little evidence of the bitterness and resentment so prominent in Tina's account. Whereas many respondents, including the majority who left their father's home and gained independence, expressed frustration and indignation at the need to take on some of their mother's tasks, Darlene seemed quite at peace with her assumption of the maternal role. Tina repeatedly emphasized the guilt she would feel if she abandoned the role of family caretaker. In contrast, Darlene was comfortably certain that this was her proper role and place in life. Although she had one long-term male friend, she never married because, as she said, "If I got married the man would have to marry seven other people, which meant my sisters and brothers. But I have no regrets because I think it was meant for me to take care of them." Nor was she able to pursue a college education, something she saw her siblings through. But she is proud of her accomplishments: "The most important thing is that I was able to take care of my sisters and brothers. I had a life of my own too, but I think I put myself in that situation. I felt that I was supposed to be there for them. I felt that they were more important than anything." Darlene's ease in adapting to this role can perhaps be attributed to several factors: the continuity of the familial role she played before her mother's death, her feeling that the role was not forced upon her but was something she comfortably adopted, and the strength she gleaned from her religious faith.

Unlike my many respondents who felt that their childhood came to an abrupt end with the death of their mothers, Darlene had already integrated a strong sense of responsibility long before her mother died. She did not have the relatively pampered childhood that was typical in white middle-class households. Rather, as a young child she had already begun to do caring work for her younger siblings—changing diapers, dressing them, and in general looking after them. Her mother relied heavily on Darlene's help with the smaller children, to the point where Darlene became almost a secondary mother figure to her siblings even before her mother's death. Each time a new child was born, Darlene knew she would have to assume additional responsibilities. She told me that the only thing she disliked about her mother was all the children she kept having. "Each time she got pregnant, I got mad and said, 'Oh, no, not another one!' You knew you couldn't say anything, you had no control over it, but that was the worst." While her mother rested after each birth, Darlene prepared the formula, washed the newborn's diapers (by hand!), and cared for the other children.

Darlene's childhood was to such a large extent defined by her motherly duties that she did not present her mother's death as a major disruption in her life. "My mother built a strong foundation in me that I helped with the kids. I wasn't angry at all [when my mother died]. Cause my life was . . . it wasn't different really because I was doing these things anyway. Taking care of, you know, a couple of things. It wasn't really any different than it would have been if she was here." Her early assumption of caretaking tasks is probably a major reason that Darlene was so comfortable with assuming the maternal role after her mother's death. Whereas in the narratives of middle-class respondents the transition from childhood to adult responsibilities was quite abrupt and left little time for adjustment, Darlene had never known any other life than that of caretaker. Her narrative was so different from Tina's because Darlene experienced a continuity of roles and attitudes rather than a sudden, dramatic change in others' expectations of her.

The normative nuclear family model depends not only on parents who properly and consistently fill their roles but also on children who are constructed as helpless and in need of intensive caretaking. Consequently, nearly all of my respondents, having grown up in nuclear families in which the mother was responsible for the physical and emotional tasks that maintain the family, experienced their mother's early death as a major disruption that produced a sense of chaos and disorder. For them, maternal death caused a dramatic break in their lives and was experienced as the end of childhood. Other family forms, however, embody diverse notions of adulthood, parenting, and childhood. Darlene grew up in a household in which the assumption of childhood as an utterly dependent and distinct stage of life did not prevail; her mother's death thus did not abruptly thrust her into a different stage of life. Alternative family forms may create less dependence on one person to hold her family together. Our society's nuclear family ideal can thus create problems for those children whose mothers suddenly become unavailable.

Darlene made clear that her religious faith was a major source of guidance and support that further eased her transition into the maternal role. In contrast to the large majority of my interviewees, such as Sheryl and Sid, who reported that their religious institutions provided little solace at the time of their mothers' deaths, Darlene emphasized the significant role the Baptist church had played in helping her and her siblings cope with motherloss. If the language of God and his mysterious but benevolent ways is meaningful to a person, religion can offer a highly explanatory structure in which to create a cohesive narrative that enables the individual to move on. Both before and after her mother's death, the family was quite involved in the church. In the summers when school was out, the children went to Bible school and to church three times a day. The support offered by the church community at the time of her mother's death was so important and meaningful that it deepened her faith.

When her mother died, "people in the church came down that morning even before church started. When they heard the news, they came to our house, and that meant a lot to me . . . which is why I now do a lot in the church. It just sort of gave you a lift to know that these people cared. It's just you needed that. It helped a whole lot." Darlene drew strength from her minister's words of comfort. "The only thing I asked the minister is 'Why? Why'd she have to die?' And he said, 'God don't pick the bad flowers. He pick the good flowers.' And then, as I get older, I say you shouldn't question why God has a purpose. There was no reason to be angry." Darlene saw her mother's death not as a senseless tragedy but as part of a divine plan that no mortal could know; by accepting her mother's death as God's will, Darlene could accept the change in her own life as equally the will of God. Her dedication to her faith alleviated much of the frustration that might otherwise have fostered resentment.

Darlene's sense of obligation to her younger siblings allowed her to care for them for the next eighteen years, until they left home. Now that they live elsewhere, Darlene continues to play the maternal role of family communicator and glue. She takes great pride in her siblings' accomplishments. Several have gone to college; one is now the CEO of an insurance company; two are teachers; another was a major-league baseball player and is now a radio sports announcer; one works with mentally disturbed children; and yet another is a counselor with a rescue mission for homeless men. With great pride she told me that they "are blessed in [their] path"; they had all helped one another and are still helping and supporting one another.

Darlene's early assumption of caretaking duties shaped her work role as well—for over thirty years she has worked cleaning the office and home of a doctor and his family. While Darlene's maternal role brought her closer to her family, it simultaneously distanced her from the rest of her social world in many ways. When I asked how important her friends were to her at the time of her mother's death, Darlene responded, "I didn't really have that many friends." She remembers that she had one friend, and that she interacted with the children from her Bible classes in the neighborhood, but she also made clear that "by the time you finished doing what you had to do," there wasn't much time for socializing. Because she was in the caretaker role, she felt that no one became a substitute mother for her—neither her extended family nor her father provided emotional support—and most of her relationships revolved around taking care of others, not being taken care of herself. Darlene grew up quickly and arduously, but instead of resenting the life she has been bequeathed, she graciously and proudly embraces it.

Darlene brought with her to the interview the only picture she has of her mother. She described her to me as she showed me the picture: "She was a strong person. Very smart. My mother was a very smart person. Even though she only went to school until the eighth grade, she liked to read. She was tall. She was a nice person. See, everybody liked her. She had a lot of friends and she never raised her voice. She was always busy; she took us to the park and to the library; she enjoyed her children." While the words Darlene used to describe her mother resemble those of my other interviewees, she did not idealize her the way most other respondents did.

Although Darlene rarely discusses her late mother with her family, she has found ways to maintain her mother's symbolic presence throughout her own life. At her mother's funeral, Darlene had a vision of her mother's father "standing there and saying, 'Here comes my child.' " She described an incident that was repeated often when she was a teenager: She came out of her house and was walking down the street when she saw a woman in an orange coat coming toward her. Her mother had had an orange coat. But as Darlene got nearer, the woman disappeared. Darlene also had powerful dreams about her mother. For example, when her youngest sister, who was an infant when her mother died, graduated from college, Darlene's mother came to her in a dream and said, "Well done. Your job is finished now." Often she has had a sense that her mother is protecting her, a feeling she does not discuss with many other people because, as she said, "If you tell some people that, they look at you like you're from outer space. But to me it's real."

Darlene believes her mother would have approved of the person she has become. Like Tina, Sheryl, and many others, Darlene outlined the similarities between herself and her mother. "Like her, I'm nice to people. I like to read. And I'm not a person that gets angry. And she didn't either. She loved the children; her whole life revolved around the children, like mine did." Her mother's early death made her a more mature person, she believes. She would not and could not wallow in self-pity, because she had to take care of her siblings. Her mother was a strong woman, dedicated to the care of her family, and Darlene has worked toward this model to satisfy both herself and her siblings. She has devoted herself to her family, and that role fulfills her and gives her life meaning.

7

Reverberating Losses

Bob McPherson, Sarah Mulligan, and Neil Roberts

The narratives we have read so far reveal the various ways in which motherless adults attempt to make sense of their loss and integrate it into their ongoing sense of selves. By telling their stories, individuals have an opportunity to frame their accounts of disruption in linear narratives showing a progression from upheaval through resolution. Our culture provides us with narrative scripts from a wide array of sources, from psychoanalysis to twelve-step programs to religious journeys. Americans often tell stories that emphasize progress and forward movement. Members of twelve-step programs, for example, learn to construct their life stories within the twelve-step framework. An individual begins his story with the experience of "hitting bottom," describing how alcohol (or drugs or gambling or eating problems) made his life unmanageable, and eventually ends with sobriety (or abstinence or whatever) found with the assistance of the support group.

My respondents' accounts of motherloss can be read as instances of the Western success story—interviewees typically described how they struggled to move beyond the chaos and desolation that followed their mother's death and integrate the loss into their life stories. A closer reading of most of the narratives, however, reveals that people's lives do not fit so neatly into a linear model. Most accounts, in fact, traced a spiraling circle in which the tellers' memories and images of the disruptive event resurfaced in old and new ways throughout their lives, presenting them with the need continually to revise their sense of their early motherloss in light of later life events. My interviewees' experience of their mothers' premature death reverberated throughout their lives, shaping narratives that circled, spun around, and included past, present, and future in any number of configurations that helped them to make sense of their experiences.

Take the narratives of twelve-step group members. Despite the seeming linearity of their narratives—"I hit rock bottom and now have been saved"—individuals who are in twelve-step programs also reveal an awareness that they are never fully "found." Instead, their conversion stories incorporate the recognition that they must struggle each day to maintain their accomplishments and not backslide. The anthropologist Gay Becker similarly argues that disruptions are a steady feature of life and thus "the integration of new knowledge is a lifelong process." Living and telling our lives involves an effort to continuously rework the disruptions to our biographies and recreate narrative coherence.[1]

All of the narratives I heard reflect this more complex pattern. They reveal that numerous occasions in respondents' lives—important life cycle events, the birth of a child, another person's death, the need to make a major decision—recreate a longing for the lost mother and a renewed sense of loss. In this chapter I present the nar-

ratives of three people in whom this pattern of reverberating losses stands out in bold relief, albeit in distinct
ways.[2] Bob McPherson's story emphasizes how his experience of motherloss has constantly and pervasively reverberated throughout his life, making it tremendously
difficult for him to establish a satisfactory sense of himself as a complete person. He represented himself as unable to create a life that worked for him—he could not
find work or love or establish a stable sense of himself.
Sarah Mulligan's account traces her search for wholeness
through her efforts to repair those particular sites of her
earlier losses. Her mother's suicide shaped her adult decision to help others avoid this dreadful and shocking loss
by volunteering as a suicide prevention counselor. She
has attempted to obliterate her earlier instability and difficulties with her family by achieving a nuclear family of
her own and becoming a steady, devoted mother. Neil
Roberts's narrative traces a full circle. His account of facing and coming to terms with his own impending death
from AIDS reveals that he draws strength from the lessons his mother's premature death taught him about the
unity of life and death. Thus he has been able to draw on
his mother's death, as well as other major early losses, to
make sense of and integrate his identity as a man with an
illness that at the time we met was all but certain to lead
to an early death.

Bob McPherson: An Unfulfilled Search

Of all the people I interviewed, Bob, an unemployed single high school graduate, stood out for the depth and con-
stancy of his depression. He had been collecting disability
insurance for about seven years, having sustained a serious back injury on his last job. He told me he was eager

to get back into steady employment, but he found few options available to him. Bob presented himself as unable to get the basic elements of his life together in a way that worked for him—he had no work, no intimate relationships, no family. He has one older sister and a younger brother. Bob described his sister as having established a successful life—she is educated and employed and has formed a family of her own. In contrast, he and his younger brother were badly damaged by their mother's illness and death and particularly by the dynamics among them, their stepmother, and her children.

Bob grew up in a working-class Catholic family in New England. Neither of his parents had graduated from high school. His mother had been a textile worker and his father was in the military. Like most of my respondents, Bob emphasized that he had adored his mother; he described his relationship with her as warm and loving. His mother was the glue that held the family together—the "foundation." He told me that they did many fun things together—"ice skating, swimming, going for walks, and going to the store for root beer floats." Unfortunately, when Bob was eight she was diagnosed with stomach cancer, a condition that was kept secret from Bob and his siblings. Nevertheless, his mother "had a great sense of humor, even after she got sick. She'd forget about her pain and try to do as much as she could with us, she would never show it, even though she was really in terrible pain. She had a very good sense of humor and she kept the family on the right course. She did a lot of things with the church, she was very involved in the church. Neighbors liked her, she got along very well with the neighbors."

Bob felt that it was his mother's devotion to her family that made her refuse to go to the hospital when her condition worsened. She preferred to remain with her family as long as possible, and so she spent most of her illness at home, being taken care of by friends and relatives. In order to make their mother's life easier when she was obviously in pain, Bob's older sister took over the cooking and cleaning, and made sure all three children got to school. Bob tried to be as helpful as he could, cleaning up after himself and trying to cook some things. His mother was not hospitalized until the very end.

Bob remembered being shocked when he first saw his mother at the hospital. "I went to see her about three or four days after she went in and she, she was a good-sized woman but she had lost so much—I never realized that— She was down to ninety pounds at that point. The last thing that I remember is that I went in her room and I guess I was holding on to her hand. Then, after I left, we went to my father's sister's house and that is when she passed on. I was told the following day." Bob was eleven years old at the time.

The secrets and silences through which the details of his mother's illness were hidden from him exacerbated the shock and pain of her death. While she was sick, it became evident to Bob that she was unwell, yet both of Bob's parents reassured him that she would be fine. Her eventual death challenged his sense of reality and his trust that people could take care of him. "I don't know how to say this, but when she was sick, my mom looked horrible, and as a child at that time I didn't know what was wrong. I'd ask her what was wrong and she would just nod but when you have cancer you have a lot of things that—She was very, very sick. But she wouldn't tell me what was wrong, she said she was going to take care of me; she'll take care of me, she'll take care of me. My father at that time did not say too much. He said, 'Don't worry about it, she's going to get better.' And at the same time he would be breaking down crying. He would go to work and come home, he'd starve himself and cry and cry and I didn't know how to handle it. I'd be asking questions but I think today, you're not kept in the dark as much. That's all I was told, she'd be OK, he said, 'don't worry she'll be fine,' but I was home with her a lot and so when I went to school, I'd come back and I knew something wasn't right. Sometimes I blame my father for not being up front with us about how deeply ill she was."

As we have seen, the silence and denials Bob faced were common among my interviewees: Sheryl, Sid, Tina, and nearly all other respondents described how painful it was for them to see their mother's illness and suffering and to have no idea what was happening. All felt helpless as children in this situation. Several of them, such as Sheryl, described how this denial of their experience and their need to stifle their emotions led to a serious depression later in their lives.

When he returned to school, Bob's sense of alienation and social isolation deepened. The death of his mother made him different from all the other children, different and less fortunate. "I felt out of place because we're at recess, and the kids would be saying, 'My mother made this for me today, we're going to do this tomorrow,' and all this family stuff. I felt outcasted. Like I'd be with my friends but I wasn't really with them because they had the family and I am the one who . . . I felt alone and isolated. And it was difficult and I got through it but school was never the same after that. My mind was always elsewhere. I knew I was coming home to an empty house. Because right after she died my dad was still working and he wasn't married, my sister was at school . . . it was very difficult. I went from, when I'd come home my mom would be there and I'd have a snack and have her talk to me about how my day went." In the 1960s, when Bob was going to school, air raid drills were common. "If I had an air raid—I used to get a lot of air raids as a child—and I'd come home and I'd be crying and she'd start rocking me. I guess all these things would be on my mind all the time and I didn't know how to deal with it or talk about it. And I've just never been able to put it behind me. I think about her all the time and I, I just never dealt with it."

Bob's feeling of a lack of affirmation and support after his mother's death worsened after his father's remarriage a year later, a situation about which he still seethes with hurt and resentment. During Bob's mother's illness, his father had befriended a widowed friend of his wife's who was trying to raise three children. The two of them married and Bob's father "had the intention of putting two families together and making them one. But it never turned out that way." The most serious grievance Bob expressed against his stepfamily was his perception that all of his family's resources went to his father's new wife and her children. "Everything that belonged to this family went to them. For instance, today I'm living in an apartment and they are living in my home that my mother left to my sister. I feel that this woman was so strong-willed and my father wasn't a fighter—the only thing I can say is that by going to war [in World War II] he came home unable to fight."

Bob's older sister responded to the situation by staying away from the house as much as possible. "This woman tried to make a slave of her and take advantage of my father, who was working such long hours at this point. And my sister would just never come home and stayed at school where she did well and my younger brother went to stay with an aunt at that time because this woman didn't want to be bothered raising somebody else's three children. And when I could get my father alone I used to try to tell him that she was doing this, that she was taking over and she was mean and taking everything away from us and she would browbeat my father. She would bring him to the point where he would just give in and let her go. I could see it because I was more on the outside looking in at her instead of being married to her and not being able to see."

Bob repeatedly referred to the sense of dislocation that accompanied his father's remarriage and to the stepfamily's appropriation of his family's resources as causal factors in his ongoing depression. He told me that his father's new wife and her children strove to maximize their own benefits from the blended family at the expense of Bob and his siblings. "Before they met my father, they had nothing. I don't know if you would call it slums where they lived, but they didn't live in a pretty area. I didn't know what cockroaches were till we met these people and they were living with them! So I went from trying to deal with my mother's death to this other situation where I had nobody at that point, my father was giving them everything. And not just material things but love and you know, I needed my father at that time and I had nobody, I was just somebody to yell at, to do all the dirty work there, and she never let me leave the yard. I've just never been able to put this behind me and it affects me today. Whereas my sister was able to let the pain out and find a way where she got so caught up with everything in school that she was never home that much and my brother went to my aunt's house at age eight because of all the abuse. My dad's wife would hit and yell and scream all the time. She was the kind of person who, at one moment she could

be the nicest person and the next minute she would just
go out of control, breaking things, punching us, picking
up something and whacking us with it. My younger
brother [who was four years old when their mother died]
had a bed-wetting problem. And when he wet his bed she
would punish him for it, making him kneel in corners in
wet pajamas and beating on him. Finally my aunt found
out and she made my father let him stay with her." To
Bob these long-ago events were still so vivid that it was as
though he were experiencing them now. In particular, his
stepmother's takeover of his family's resources, even their
home, continually tormented him, leading to his ongoing
sense of himself as rejected, abandoned, and alienated.

The insecurity and lack of safety that Bob said he felt
living with his stepmother was highlighted in his account.
Although a primary concern of most parents is to ensure
their children's safety and to keep them out of harm's
way,[3] Bob, like Ben and Sid, felt that his father was so
much more committed to his new wife than to his kids
that he failed to protect them from her anger and greed.
Bob bitterly contrasted the instability of his life after his
dad's remarriage with the safety and warmth he had enjoyed when his mother was alive. In his new situation, he
could never predict when violence would erupt, so that
much of the time he felt frightened, alone, and sad.

"That is my problem pretty much today, I mean I get
by, I survive, but I've just never been able to put that all
behind me. I think about it at night, I think about it when
I wake up. I went to counseling. He would talk to me and
I guess it goes in one ear and out the other. I guess I just
never dealt with it very well. I feel that if the events never
happened, my life would have been different. You don't
know how to go through this. And like my sister's differ-

ent, she's been able to put it together, she's made a family of her own. But when we were young, with my sister and brother not being there, I took a lot of the brunt. And there were jealousies because my sister is the type of person who excels at everything they do. She played piano, she plays clarinet, she is very talented and her children have it and then I bore the brunt of the awful stuff. "I know I have an ax to grind and I shouldn't feel this way. I'm not able to move ahead because I'm living in the past. This never stops. And I'm stuck. Just so stuck."

Psychological and psychiatric research has found a significantly higher incidence of depression among adults who lost a parent when they were young than in the general population. Camille Lloyd, a psychologist in the United States, reported: "Of studies that compared the incidence of childhood bereavement or other childhood loss among depressed patients and controls, the majority found an increased incidence among the depressives. . . . The childhood loss of a parent by death generally increases depressive risk by a factor of about two or three."[4] The death of the mother, in particular, has been implicated in several of these studies. Research by the British psychologists Antonia Bifulco, Tirrill Harris, and George Brown found that "the loss of the mother before the age of 17 years, either by death or separation for a year or more, doubles the risk of depressive and anxiety disorders among adult women."[5] Although not all adults with depression suffered such an early loss, reviews of the research literature consistently indicate "some evidence for an association between early death of the mother and severe forms of depression in adulthood."[6] Although many of my respondents, like Sheryl, reported struggling with depression in their adult lives, Bob's story represents an extreme case; he consistently presented himself as completely immobilized by his mother's death and the events that followed.

Bob explicitly stated that of all the people who might have died in his family, his mother was the worst possible one to lose. As we have seen, the normative nuclear family model charges the mother with the emotional care of her family, whereas the father's primary responsibilities are financial. Those mothers who try to fulfill this ideal of intensive and exclusive nurturing are often experienced by their children as the family's foundation or glue; without them the family as a unit would come apart. Bob said, "I just wonder sometimes if it would have been my father that went on and not my mother, because I know I've met other people in my situation and when the mother either leaves the family or passes on, the family just comes apart. *When she left there was no longer a family* even before he went and married this woman. As far as the nurturing and the support—that wasn't what men were supposed to do back then. And my father and my uncles, they are not that type of hugging and crying and I love you. He tried in his own way, assuring me he'd take care of me, but it was difficult. He had a hard life, aside from everything that happened afterward with them, he lost a job and you know, men like my father go to war and they're never the same either. So between all that and trying to take over being two people, I think he did not want that task. And it just went from bad to worse. He should have wound up in counseling at that point. If he had done that and also not cut himself off from the rest of his family members like his sisters and brothers who tried to talk with him, I don't think he would have made some of the decisions he made. He went from crying and shutting himself off to getting himself involved with my stepfamily and doing things with them and he was never home with me and my sister and brother, he was always off with them. He just didn't care very much about us, just himself and that was it."

The deep misery into which Bob's mother's death plunged him led him to question and abandon the church in which he had been raised. He felt that religion and God had let him down. Several other respondents expressed this feeling, one that resonated with my own, as I described in Chapter 1. Bob never went back to the church: "And I blame the religion, because I didn't think it was supposed to be this way, I thought that these things don't happen and like I say, I walked away from it." Bob's early recognition that his life looked and felt different from what his church had led him to expect created cognitive dissonance. Since he knew his life was full of pain and tragedy, it seemed apparent that religion could not provide a framework or the language that would help him to integrate a sense of the meaning of motherloss.

Bob's depression had a catch-22 effect on his ability to form relationships. Since it is often difficult for people to become close to depressed individuals, his depression weakened the likelihood of his making close friends or a romantic attachment. In turn, his loneliness exacerbated his depression. "Every relationship I've had has been a complete failure, so I've given up on that pretty much at this point and I'm just trying to get by on my own as best as I could. What that situation did to me is I fear commitment. I don't think I'll ever get married. Thankfully my sister at least has been able to have a family. She has a good family and they've done well. But me, I've just never been able to and my brother is worse than I am at this point. I mean, he works, but he and I have the same problems. We can't make any commitments and our personal lives are a disaster."

Bob understood his fear of commitment as a reflection of his fear that he might unintentionally do to others what had been done to him. More important, however, was his fear of never finding a woman who could match his idealized view of his mother: "I don't know if there is a woman out there who can replace my mother. I get close and as soon as I get close, there I go . . . I break it off." Bob's words echo the central point in nearly all of my interviews—the mother, as the central emotional figure in a family, is simply not replaceable. Even if her tasks are taken over, she herself, as the *mother,* is always missed. Like Ben, Bob was in search of his lost mother.

I understood Bob's words here to mean that he had not had any serious committed relationships. But after we had been talking for over an hour and half, he offered: "I don't know if I said this in our conversation, but I was married." I replied that no, he had not. "That's interesting," I said. "You forgot it?" "It was forgettable," he said. I asked for more details. "I was twenty-one. Living on my own. I met this girl through a friend. We were married less than one year. I think I did it because of the loneliness, the feeling in me that I had to be close to somebody. But then one day I went to work, came home, and everything was packed and gone. She went back home to her parents, she said she didn't want to be married, she didn't want to have children, she made a mistake and so on. I think a lot of it was my doing. I didn't make it easy for her."

The failure of his marriage was linked, in Bob's mind, to his early losses, which made him unable to become deeply involved with others. "How can I put this. I have a limitation and I feel that if I go beyond, then I fall apart. At that point, I was like a child. I was twenty-one. I wasn't a grownup, I was a child. Once she left, I didn't even try to make it work after that. But that's probably been my way my whole life. I get my toe in the water and as soon as it gets up to my waist, I just hurry up and run out. Maybe I took on too much when I was a younger child, disciplining myself, bringing myself up." The early end of his childhood left him feeling, as an adult, that he was still somewhat of a child. His mother's death and his father's choice of a new wife left him without the caring, nurturing, and support that might have built his self-confidence and esteem, and might have made him more willing to risk intimacy as an adult.

Bob's struggles to maintain steady employment reflected and exacerbated his depression. He told how in his early twenties he had had a good job: he was promoted to supervisor and earned a decent salary. But then he had a freak accident at work that seriously damaged his back and necessitated surgery. He had been living on worker's compensation for seven years. During that time, Bob struggled with alcohol and substance abuse. Eventually he was able to break those habits but he still had not found a satisfying work situation; his story is replete with circumstances and mishaps that repeatedly got in his way.

A few years after his accident, he tried to go to a small local school for a business degree, but left a few credits short of completion. The aunt who had cared for his brother—and for him, some—after their mother's death had gotten ill and Bob felt it was appropriate to leave school to take care of her. A couple of years later he and a friend tried to operate a car salvage business, but a bicycle accident in which he broke his ankle ended that career. At the time of the interview he was trying to find a job and make a life for himself, but he was often too depressed to act—an emotional condition, he acknowledged, that had plagued him for years.

As our conversation went on, punctuated by his tears, I could feel how deep his depression was. My heart went out to him. While I did not feel that it was my place to suggest a course of action, I was so struck by his pain that I asked him if I could share some information about depression that I had learned from my other interviews and from my reading.[7] When he eagerly said yes, I told him about the psychological and psychiatric research indicating the higher prevalence of depression among people who suffer early and serious deprivations, such as the death of a parent, as compared with a "normal population." I explained the theory outlined in *Listening to Prozac,* that the mind-body connection ensures that premature losses not only affect people on the emotional level but are inscribed on the body as well. Such experiences may permanently alter the brain chemicals that control mood.[8] Bob responded that his therapists had also told him this and had suggested that he try antidepressant medication. He resisted the idea, however, because of his earlier drug and alcohol abuse and because, although he was painfully aware of his deep depression, he felt that it was something he "should" be able to get over without the assistance of chemical substances. In retrospect, I realize that my intentions were to make this man more aware of the broader context of his own personal and severe pain, but I also wanted him to feel "normal" about his depression and to know that he fits into a recognizable group pattern. The tendency to normalize is, indeed, deeply carved into our patterns of interaction.

About the only time Bob feels a sense of peace and

comfort is when he visits his mother's grave, as he does regularly. He maintains and affirms a sense of connection with his mother there. "I ask for her help sometimes. I feel like there were a few times when I was going to make a decision to perhaps end my life but after I felt her presence I didn't go through with it. Sometimes I go there and ask her, 'When are you going to come get me?' And that's how I feel a lot of the times, I feel like the love that I got from her, I don't have it here on earth. I feel alone. I am alone." Although he acknowledges that some people, such as his sister, care a great deal about him, he recognizes that her primary concern is her own family. Bob told me that he dreamed that his mother was waiting for him in a happier place.

When I asked him if he truly wants to die, he said that he saw death as peaceful and as a way to reunite with his mother. He quickly claimed, however, that he would never actually kill himself. "I'm not saying that death isn't sad but in my case I'd be going back to see the ones that meant so much in my life, my mother, my aunt, and some of the other relatives I cared deeply for. Yes, that's how I look at it. It's terrible but sometimes I look forward to it."

The deep pain that Bob expressed throughout the interview made me wonder whether our conversation was too difficult for him and whether he regretted being asked to dredge up numerous painful memories and experiences. I asked him directly how he felt about being interviewed about such a profoundly sad experience. He told me that he felt positive about the interview and that he was pleased he had answered my ad: "I didn't think I could open up as much as I have. I mean, I've talked about it sporadically, but never this deeply. And it feels better, I feel better than I did when I walked in. I kind of dreaded this. I thought that I would lose it and that maybe this time the tears would gush forth. Sometimes I wish I could really cry about it. Maybe that is what I need to cleanse myself of the whole thing. You know it's unfortunate that I had to resurrect the other side with the stepfamily but it comes as a whole package and unfortunately I can't leave them out of it. They've become part of the picture." He acknowledged that talking about motherloss is quite painful and speculated that the interview might have been quite difficult for other respondents. He had wanted to go through with it, despite his fear of further pain, because he thought, "Hopefully in time this would help families so that others would not have to go through what I did. I thought, if this can benefit somebody down the road, somebody picks it up, reads it, that the family would be looked at differently. The family situation is so crucial. Somebody has to start addressing this problem and hopefully this book is going to do that."

Sarah Mulligan: Completing Her Mother's Story

Sarah's narrative was distinguished by the remarkable frequency of painful disruptions in the first twenty-five years of her life. The most striking theme throughout was her ongoing difficulties in locating a family context that would provide a safe space in which she could grow up and thrive. Her story, punctuated by repeated losses, nevertheless ends with her reporting that she had, at last, created a stable family of her own and was finishing her mother's story in a more positive way. Sarah now presents herself as a full-time mother who does some part-time work at home and plans never to move again.

Sarah, who was forty at the time of our interview, was born into an Irish American family in Oklahoma in the mid-1950s. Her dad was a minister when she was young and the family moved frequently, following her father's ministry. Sarah felt that her dad was remote and uncaring, but she described a wonderful relationship with her mother, highlighting her mother's goodness, warmth, and caring qualities. "She was very sensitive. She was caring toward other people. She would take time to explain things to me. She would sit down and tell me stories. When I was young I was a swimmer and often I would wake up in the middle of the night with charley horses in my legs. I would wake up with these horrible, horrible cramps and she would sit on my bed and she would rub my legs and talk with me." Sarah elaborated on her mother's beauty and the special ways she took care of herself and others. "She was always kind to everybody. She loved everybody. She was bubbly. At church, she'd be chatting with everybody and everybody knew who she was. I loved her and liked her a whole lot." Not only was Sarah's mother good, kind, and helpful to others, she was also much loved by them, a quality described by many of my respondents.

"I was proud of my mom. I was in the Girl Scouts and she would get very involved in our activities. I remember being in a Girl Scout meeting one time and she walked in, carrying brownies or cupcakes or something like that. One of the other girls leaned over to whisper to her friend, 'Whose mom is that? She's really pretty.' One day my mother organized a really special event for the Girl Scouts—we went to some hospital, some ward in a hospital that our little troop went in and we had made—It must have been Washington's birthday. 'Cause out of paper towel tubes and foil and cardboard we made little hatchets. And we filled them full of goodies for whoever it was who was in the hospital and we went around and handed them out and we all just felt so special. And I was just so proud. I remember so many good things about her. She used to make little projects, which I do with my own little boy now. Arts and crafts things; it's a lot of fun. In the summers she would go to the pool with me. She would hang out with me and do mom-kid things."

Sarah's account so far resembles those of my other respondents: she depicted a warm loving mother who was there for her, took care of her, and shared time and activities. By the time Sarah was ten, however, her mother was hospitalized, in a coma that resulted from an overdose of sleeping pills. Like most of my interviewees, Sarah was not informed about the actual nature and seriousness of her mother's illness. In fact, as an adult she remains less clear about the details of her mother's illness and death than my other interviewees—a result, perhaps, of the shame and stigma that attaches to suicide.[9] Six of my interviewees had lost their mothers to suicide. Although their accounts diverge in important ways, three of these respondents reported that they had been kept in the dark for many years about their mother's depression and the actual cause of her death. Two brothers I spoke with did not learn that their mother had committed suicide until many years later when, as college students, they each had sought the counsel of a therapist.

Sarah related relatively few stories from the time when her mother was depressed and in the hospital and she is unsure about the details of that period. "Mommy would go to the hospital once in a while. Um . . . and hospitals were places where people were sick and I didn't really . . . It was, it was normal to me that she would be there. You know, I didn't picture her suffering because some of the places we would visit her were nice and she looked fine to me. Sometimes the ambulance would be at our house in the middle of the night. Mom would have fallen down the stairs. She had a lot of concussions. Recently my brother told me she had a drug problem. I know nothing of any drug problem. But it could have been something like that. I know she was on medications for diabetes. But she could have had a drug problem. She could have. I don't know. She died of a drug overdose. I don't know.

"The actual day she died was March 5, 1967. I had just come home from a church retreat weekend and my dad told me in the parking lot when he picked me up that my mother had died. Now, she had been in the hospital since Halloween of the previous year [for sixteen months]. She had attempted suicide then and there was so much brain damage that they put her in the state hospital and she was in a coma and that was just . . . She took an overdose of sleeping pills. The whole story behind what actually happened, I'm unclear. No one ever explained it to me. I know she was very sick, but my mom was sick a lot. My mom had, I believe she had emotional problems. She spent some time in and out of hospitals and she was depressed. She spent time in a hospital for depression, I think. I think, again, you know, I'm just assuming a lot of these things 'cause I was a kid. They didn't, they didn't talk about that stuff with kids. Um, but she had taken an overdose. I don't have any idea why, to this day."

Sarah's repeated assertions that she did not understand or have any real knowledge of her mother's illness and death set her apart from the other interviewees, whose narratives depicted how they eventually put together a sense of what had happened. Also, after her mother's death, Sarah's life became so complicated and so full of rejection and abandonment that it seems possible that she never really focused on working out a coherent story about her mother's death. Sarah remained mystified; her mother's overdose and death came to her as a great shock and a puzzle she still could not solve, since it clashes with the image she has maintained of her mother as a "responsible person. She went to work. She had a, you know, a wonderful job and she was steady in it."

Carl had reacted to his mother's suicide with an angry denunciation of her; her mental illness made her such a "nuisance and bother" that he "was glad to get rid of her." In contrast, Sarah presented her mother's suicide as a completely unanticipated and terrible event, since her mother was a regular, responsible person. The pain and shame of a parent's suicide can lead to a variety of reactions. Carl's vociferous denunciation of his mother might be one way of coping with and minimizing his hurt; Sarah's normalization of her mother's life and her lack of memories of her mother's depression can function in the same way.

Sarah's idealized image of her mother and of their relationship glossed over the possibility that her mom might have struggled with depression for years before she ended up in the hospital. Her strategy resembled that of Phil and Tommy Greene, the brothers I mentioned earlier who had been unaware of their mother's suicide until many years later. Their narratives, too, emphasized the warm, wonderful, loving, ideal family in which they grew up. When I asked Phil whether he saw any inconsistencies in his account, since his mother had attempted suicide seven years before she actually died and therefore clearly had struggled with depression, Phil nodded. He then shrugged and said, "But I really mean it when I say my parents were very much in love and our family was your average normal, happy family."

Both Sarah's and Phil's reactions to their mother's suicides are reflected in their attempts to normalize what must have been a very disruptive event, and one they probably experienced as shameful and stigmatizing. A mother's taking of her own life is such a radical negation of her role as nurturer and protector of her children that by minimizing their mothers' unhappiness and their differences from "normal" moms, these respondents may have been seeking to reduce some of the pain and anger they felt. Even if the end of their mother's life made her stand out from others, until that unexpected moment, they had the same kind of normal happy families that the cultural ideal prescribed.

Sarah's lack of information about her mother's illness, suicide attempt, and death and her subsequent difficulties in her relationship with her father led her to wonder whether anyone, particularly her dad, could be held accountable for her mother's death. Midway into our conversation, she revealed that her mother was left on her own for two days after taking an excessive amount of sleeping pills. When I asked if she had any thoughts about that, she replied, "Oh, oh, major thoughts. Then I wondered if this was why he didn't talk to me about it. These thoughts had gone all the way to maybe he hasn't talked to me about this because he killed her. Could he have killed my mother? And that's a terrible thing to think about your own father. But I would never say that to him because I don't want to be hurtful to him. He's getting to be an old man now. I want to keep things on an even keel with him. But I've wondered that. You know, why didn't he take her to the hospital for two days? Well, maybe he thought it was one of her depressions, one of her things, you know, and I'm just not gonna do this anymore. Or maybe it was just the point where he was fed up and didn't care anymore or maybe there's something that I don't even know about. The whole thing's like a soap opera. And one time I said to him, 'Seventy-five sleeping pills, Dad, two days—she'd be dead. I'm sorry, she'd be dead.' So I played this scenario out in my head where she took the pills, they weren't enough to really worry him. She took a few more. They weren't enough to really worry him. And so it was just like on and on to keep taking more and more. 'Come on. Help me. Help me. Help me.' That's what I think may have happened, I don't know. And by the time he got her to the hospital there was enough brain damage that . . . that . . . I guess they told him she wasn't gonna recover. The stomach pumping showed she had taken seventy-five pills. But when I think about her I don't think about that. I think about her, you know, the pretty picture I have of her."

After her mother died, Sarah's relationship with her father quickly degenerated. Instead of being supportive of her as she mourned the loss of her mother, Sarah's father was angry and silent, insensitive to her needs. Unfortunately, many interviewees described similar experiences. One example of Sarah's father's inability to support her emotionally is seen in her account of trying to hide in her room during her mother's wake rather than join a bunch of people she didn't know who "seemed to be having a big party." Sarah's father repeatedly came into her room to say, "You will be out there and you will be civilized." So eventually she joined the group. Sarah said, "Well, he was not emotionally close with me. He was articulate, but he was a very stern father, very domineering, very outspoken about what he wanted done. But we weren't close. And he, he didn't know how to handle things, he really didn't. Everything fell apart pretty quickly after she died."

Sarah and her father never talked about her mother. "We never talked about my mother ever again. I . . . I could tell any time I was . . . 'Well, my mom,' my dad

didn't want to hear it. Even after I was grown up. Even
. . . I could go over there tomorrow and if I could say, 'Oh,
look. This is something that Mom gave me before she . . . '
he would not want to hear it. We never talked about it."

The impact of those silences and her longing for her
mother was exacerbated by Sarah's feelings of aloneness
after her death, a painful situation that was common in
the narratives I heard. In those first few months after her
mother died, Sarah began to spend a lot of time at home
by herself. "He started going out at night. I would come
home to an empty house and sometimes go to sleep in an
empty house. He was gone more frequently. I don't know
about eating. I know the church ladies continued to bring
us food. But it was nothing for him not to be home. And
that was probably when I stopped going to school. 'Cause
I was in a lot of pain. I was in a real lot of pain. I didn't
have anybody to talk to. And I wanted to withdraw. I really wanted to withdraw into myself. And Dad wasn't
home. He went to work. I stayed home. I just sat in the
house all day. I would watch TV. I would watch game
shows. I would cook, which was a big mistake because I
set the oven on fire one time. So I had to run next door
and get a neighbor real quick. By the time she came in,
the fire had put itself out. It was just an oven fire. Nevertheless, I considered myself to be grown up. I knew I
was really supposed to be in school but I didn't want anybody to see me." Being at school with her peers would
highlight her sense of difference from them and deepen
her sense of stigma.

Sarah's father had gotten involved with other women
during his wife's illness. "He was seeing other women
while my mother was sick. Uh . . . openly. He used to tell
me about the women he would bring home and then . . .
that he was a man and he had his needs. And you know,

I was just twelve years old but I knew what was going on. I just, 'Yeah, Dad. Yeah, Dad.' And I just put a lot of trust in him because this man, this man was a preacher. He was a Bible-toting, rabble-rousing, fire-and-brimstone . . . and he was cheating on his wife, lying to his children."

Sarah's father remarried shortly after his wife's death—a common pattern in the accounts of motherloss I heard. "He got married again very, very quickly. That, that was just . . . that's the stuff soap operas are made of. I'm serious. She died in March. He married in July. He married a woman who had been a friend of my mother's. And in fact, my mother was her boss. He married my stepmother very shortly after my mom died and I took a lot of my anger and hurt out on her."

In many of the interviews I conducted, interviewees described the disruptions of their childhood caused by their mothers' deaths as reinforced by a series of aftershocks—more isolation, abandonment, and loss of family connections and intimacy. All those disruptions, although sometimes very separate events, became implicated in the motherloss event. Eventually, three years after her mother's death, when Sarah was fifteen years old, her father asked her to leave the house, exacerbating her feelings of loss, isolation, and abandonment. "My father's wife had three children of her own in addition to me and my younger brother and very quickly there was a baby on the way. As far as I was concerned, I didn't want anything to do with it, and I started getting into trouble. Just minor trouble. I smoked cigarettes, got caught smoking cigarettes. Things like that. And my dad said, 'Well, that's it. That's it. We don't want you here anymore. I can't deal with this.' "

As though the disruption caused by her mother's death and being kicked out of her father's house were not enough, yet another traumatic family situation followed. "My aunt offered to put me up out in Los Angeles, which sounded great to me. Uh . . . so I moved in with my aunt and uncle out in California. I lived with them for a year, about a year. That was a nightmare. That was an absolute nightmare. My uncle was an aerospace engineer. So we had a beautiful home and I went to a good school, had everything I could want. I never hurted for anything, you know, I always had what I wanted, but he drank. He drank at least a fifth of vodka every other day, at least. And this was during the work week. The man would not walk out of his house without . . . If he would go . . . if we would go on a drive to the ocean, he'd pack a cooler with beer. The man was a drunk." Aside from being an alcoholic, he also tried to molest her sexually. "It got to the point where I got in an argument with him one night and he threatened me. . . . I locked myself in the bathroom and he started pounding on the door and I got really, really scared. And I . . . My aunt got him away from the door and he left. I ran out of the house and I never went back. Never went back in his house. The next morning he put a bullet hole through my bedroom window. Sick man, really sick man."

I was quite moved by Sarah's description of the difficulties she faced in finding a warm, loving family situation, not to speak of a safe one, after her mother's death. At the age of fifteen, a very vulnerable age, in need of a sense of security after her mother's death and love and affirmation after her father's rejection of her, Sarah was hurt again by someone close to her. Many other respondents also spoke of their family's inability to provide a safe haven for them after their mother's premature death. Ben, we recall, vividly described his stepmother's abusive behavior toward him and his sister. Many others told sim-

ilar stories of their lives with their stepmothers. Carl was
the only interviewee who emphasized the improvement
in his family life after his mother's death, attributing it to
the order and "normality" that his stepmother brought to
the family.

Fleeing from her uncle, Sarah went straight to a
friend's house. "I spent the night with a girlfriend who
lived down the street and I went to school the next day. I
didn't know where else to go. [Chuckles.] I went to school.
And I talked it over with another one of my other friends
and she said, 'Well, you can come to my house.' We got
to her house and as it worked out, her parents let me
move in with them. I was very, very fortunate. I stayed
with her until I graduated from high school. That was
another three years I stayed with her family. My father
never sent them a penny. They didn't need it, but he never
did. I was angry at him about that."

Although Sarah was living with a family, she nevertheless felt that she had to grow up on her own. "I had very
little supervision from the time my mother died on up. I
basically raised myself. I went to a big school. The people
at school didn't have time. I kept my grades up. That's all
they cared about. I went to school two, maybe three days
a week, or I went to the beach and hung out at the beach.
I got through high school, I don't know how but I got
through high school. I got a couple of C's, but if you're
going to school two, three days a week, I thought that was
pretty good." She laughed. Many of the other people I
spoke with similarly felt that they had to grow up when
their mothers died because they suddenly had to care for
themselves and sometimes their families, too.

After high school, Sarah was still unable to create a
stable family situation. She moved to another city, where

she met her first husband, a military officer. Together they moved twice, once clear across the country. Shortly after they married, she gave birth to a son. "I was expected to settle down with this baby. And I loved him dearly, I really loved him dearly, but I had no idea what to do with this child. And I was twenty-one years old and I didn't, I didn't know how to deal with it. And I knew I didn't want to be there anymore. I didn't, I didn't want to play house. I didn't want to be a mother . . . and I would just say well, I didn't have a mother growing up. I don't know how to be a mother. Also, I was very frightened when my son was born because I remembered how I had felt when my mom died. And I was frightened that the same thing would happen to me and I didn't want to be close to him. You know, something was going on in me that I said 'I just can't do this. I'm gonna hurt this child and I don't want to hurt this child. I don't want to hurt him so I don't want to do this.' I told my husband I was moving out and he said, 'Well, you're taking him.' And I said, 'Well, that's the other thing, I'm leaving him with you.' And it was probably the hardest decision I ever made, but I think it was the right one. I do. I knew I could trust his father."

After she left her husband and child, Sarah traveled around the country, picking up odd jobs to support herself. When she was in her late twenties, she moved back to her family home and worked for her father in his business. That lasted for only a year. Again she picked herself up and moved around, until she met her second husband. They lived together for nearly ten years before they married, four years before our meeting. They had a four-year-old son to whom she devoted herself, striving to emulate her image of her own good, loving mother. In contrast to her earlier fears about her inability to be a mother, Sarah now views motherhood as a special opportunity to bring her closer to her mother.

"She would always be there to say my prayers at night. Always there if I had a nightmare. Always. I'll never forget that. And I do the same with my little boy . . . things like that, they do come back. They really, really do, you know, and I'll sit with my little boy at night until he falls asleep and some people say, 'Oh, you have to make him more independent,' and I'll just stomp my feet and say, 'Look, my mom sat with me when I was young and that's what I'm going to do for him.' It's gotten more important for me over the years to find out who my mom was. OK, and if I am like her, well, maybe I can finish her story, you know, she just got cut off, you know, so maybe I can develop it a little bit more." By imagining herself as continuing her mother's story, Sarah is able to keep her mother as a part of her everyday life. Sarah lost both her mother and her sense of herself for so long and at relatively the same moment. The process of repairing the series of disruptions in her life came together for her at roughly the same age her mother had been when she died. By finding and integrating more of her "self," she also incorporated her mother's life into her own.

Sarah keeps her mother with her in other ways, too. "Sometimes I talk to her. Sometimes I'll be with my son at night. And we always say a little prayer together when he goes to bed and then sometimes I sit there with him after and sometimes I'll even talk to her, you know. 'Oh, Mommy, you'd be proud of Evan.' Things like that. What I end up talking to her about are decisions I've made, like when I came to realize that yes, I could be like my mother. That's OK 'cause my mother was a pretty neat person and so it's OK to be like her and it's something to be proud of and yeah, I'm going to work on that and I'll tell her things like that. Whether she hears me or not, I don't know, but sometimes I feel like she's there."

Another way Sarah maintains contact with her mother is by taking good care of her mother's things that were passed down to her. "I have her Bible, and it was given to her by her mother. This, my wedding ring, was also passed down from her mother to her. My ring doesn't fit properly, but I don't take it to the jewelers. I can't give it to them. Her Bible needs rebinding. I don't want to take it to a bookbinder. But I found a book at the library. I'm going to do it myself. I'm gonna rebind it. I'm very careful with her things. I put them away and every once in a while, like at a special time, I'll go in and look through my little treasures."

Sarah's efforts to make peace with her mother's premature death have been eased by her relationship with her mother-in-law, who provides her with some of the caring she lost at a young age. "My mother-in-law is a family person. She raised her family. She's the mother. Her family is what I envisioned a family to be like. That is what this woman is. You have to go to her house for Thanksgiving dinner . . . You don't just not go. You go. We had to go to my parents [her dad and stepmother] one time, because it was like well look, we always come to your house for Thanksgiving. We gotta go there. She said, 'Fine, you'll come over here first for cake and coffee.' And she fed us so much food in the morning, we got to my parents' house, we weren't hungry. She said, 'Now don't do that again next year, you'll be here for Thanksgiving.' So anyway, my son was born. He was born ten days before Thanksgiving and I thought, 'I can't go . . . I have a ten-day-old infant. I'm tired. Can't go.' They brought Thanksgiving dinner to us. This is something my mother would have done, but fortunately now I have a mother-in-law, now I'm part of her family and she treats me lovingly, a bit like a daughter. She brought Thanksgiving dinner. The only thing I did that day was turn on the coffee machine. They cooked the meal, they washed the dishes, they did everything. It was neat, it was just so neat." Although Sarah did not represent her mother-in-law as a substitute mother—a role that generally could not be filled by anyone—she is grateful and appreciative of the stable family life that had eluded her for so long.

One of the creative ways that Sarah has integrated her mother's suicide and found meaning in her life is through her volunteer work in suicide prevention. Although she had trouble cognitively processing her mother's suicide, and to this day remains quite vague about the illness and events that led up to it, she has found a positive way to synthesize her earlier experiences. "This has helped me in a way with my mom's suicide. I worked with students in the junior high level who were thinking about suicide themselves. I worked on the student support team doing suicide prevention. I studied suicide. I learned everything I could about it. So it's like a learning experience. A very painful one. I think it's made me sensitive sometimes to other people when they're hurting because now I want to help, I want to see if there's some . . . you know if I see . . . if I know somebody's hurting I want to help, I want to see whether I can do something. My stepmother, in fact, threatened suicide one time. And I think I made it from Pennsylvania to New Jersey in about an hour and it's about an hour-and-a-half drive. And I was like, 'I'll be right there.' I know a lot of times they're just threats, but as far as I'm concerned, you hear it, you go."

Neil Roberts: Coming Full Circle

Neil Roberts's narrative focused on how his need to come to terms with his mother's premature death—and many other significant early losses—now provided him with a sense of peace and strength as he faced his own impending death from AIDS. Like Bob's and Sarah's, Neil's account does not center on a single major traumatic event—the early death of his mother—but rather outlines a biography punctuated by many critical disruptions. Neil lost his mother, father, sister-in-law, and two close friends all before the age of twenty-five, and with each loss, Neil was confronted with the need to find a means to make sense of it and find a strategy for coping and moving on. Neil's life—perhaps more than that of any other respondent—became a process of coming to terms with death and learning how to talk about it. Now that he was confronting his own death, the process had come full circle. His account shows the various ways he had attempted to apply to himself what he had learned through the loss of others—particularly of his mother.

Neil grew up in a working-class family in the Northeast, the youngest of four children. His mother was diagnosed with breast cancer when Neil was a small child, had a radical mastectomy when Neil was seven, and died in 1956, when Neil was eleven. Neil graduated from college, earned a master's degree, and then became a teacher in inner-city schools for twenty-eight years. Now in his fifties, Neil is retired and lives with John, his partner for the last twenty years.

Neil remembered having a good relationship with his mother. Although he described her as a "taskmaster" who was not effusive with words of love or with hugs and kisses, he has fond memories of their relationship. "Mother was just a wonderful, a warm, wonderful, supportive person who I wish was in my life longer. I always saw my mom as my support and my security. Everybody said I was like my mom's baby. I was spoiled. I could do no wrong." Although he describes her as "babying" him, Neil also spoke of her efforts, as she became increasingly ill, to teach her children basic survival skills so that they would not be dependent on her to take care of them. "Between the time I was seven and the time she died when I was eleven, she made sure that we all knew how to take care of ourselves, including cooking, sewing, ironing, washing, all of the things that you needed to do to survive. I think my mom weaned us off that need [to be taken care of] by the time she died. I think she somehow managed to make it clear to us that we were going to take care of ourselves, and that the mothering concept wasn't needed at that point."

Neil presented a sharp contrast between the support and strength he received from his mother and the difficulty of his relationship with his father. Neil's father, a Scottish-born machinist, expressed disappointment in the lack of "manliness" Neil exhibited as he was growing up. "I'm pretty clear on him expecting me to be more of a man than I was. My relationship with him was always difficult. I mean, I was a sissy in the schoolyard, things like that. I was the creative one. My oldest brother was baseball and all that kind of stuff, and that was what my dad liked. I got a beating because I was playing with the girls in the neighborhood instead of playing with the boys. Which is ironic, the way life turned out."

Neil's account traced how his father's distance, emotional detachment, and inability to communicate with his children resulted in a deep silence about his mother's sickness and death. Her trips in and out of the hospital were never explicitly explained. "Apparently—though we kids were not informed at the time—my mother had an early bout with cancer. Later, when it recurred, she had a radical mastectomy, which I guess was common in those days—1952. I had no idea. I was just told that Mom went to the hospital and when she came home she couldn't use her arm and stuff, and so we had to be careful and behave ourselves."

After his mother died, his father maintained his distance from his children and avoided any discussion of his wife's death. "It was never discussed. You got up tomorrow morning and you did what you had to do. I don't remember my dad hugging me and saying, 'I'm sorry that Mom died.' He never did that. It was 'Don't cry,' you know, move forward. And no acknowledgment of that hurt or that abandonment or that pain, just none of that." The loss of his mother was terribly difficult for Neil; he felt that his primary support system had collapsed, and he was left with little to replace it. His father's preoccupation with appropriate "masculine" behavior prevented Neil from grieving publicly and heightened his feelings of isolation. "After she died it was even more so, I just felt very alone. I was very isolated, and we weren't allowed to talk about our feelings. We didn't have feelings, you just put one foot in front of the other, and you did what you had to do, but you didn't talk about your feelings. I remember crying and crying and accepting that my mom was never coming back, and I knew that I couldn't tell my dad that I was home alone crying. That was not masculine, that was not toughing it out." Neil's sense of distance from his father worsened after the death of his mother. "After she died, I think he really abandoned us and left us to our own devices for growing up. Particularly like on weekends and stuff when he would go away with his girlfriend."

His father's emotional detachment and Neil's resulting sense of aloneness led him to develop an emotional self-reliance. Not only was he able to do practical tasks for himself, but he and his siblings "learned to be self-sufficient and take care of ourselves and not rely on anybody else. We all survived, but we didn't survive together, we survived as individuals."

Neil's emotional isolation was compounded both by his personal sense of difference from his peers (his emerging attraction to males, with all of its attendant fears and sense of stigma) and his family's lack of conformity with the normative model. All respondents described how difficult it was, after their mothers' deaths, to live in a "deviant" family, and how hard they tried to minimize and normalize their differences from their peers. Neil described how he experienced the normal adolescent pressure to conform: "It was just, you know, you had the scarlet letter on you that your mom had died. That was just another difference and I already had several differences to deal with." His desire to achieve some acceptance by his peers and not be totally marginalized, together with his father's demand that he not grieve publicly (if at all), led Neil to develop a strategy of normalizing and attempting to minimize the "devastation" of his loss. He tried to cultivate a positive view of his mother's death, remembering that the last time he saw his mother in the hospital, she cast her impending death in a positive light, saying, " 'Remember, I'll be better off the next time you see me.' And that was her way of letting me know that she knew she was going to die and that it was a natural process, and it was going to be OK with her. I remember realizing that her suffering was over."

Attempting to represent his loss in a positive light was a way of minimizing his difference from his peers and of trying to lighten his burden of deviance and shame. His attempt to normalize what was clearly an unusual family situation led Neil to exaggerate the self-reliance his mother had cultivated into a sense of emotional independence and distance that grew as he faced further losses. Within a few years of his mother's death, his father, too, passed away. He died of a heart attack when Neil was a junior in high school. Although Neil's sister and his maternal grandmother both made attempts to become caregivers in Neil's life—perhaps his sister more in the pragmatic sense and his grandmother more in the emotional sense—Neil grew up feeling that he could rely only on himself. "Some of the relatives tried to fill in a little bit and stuff like that, but I think the sense of loss and the sense of 'I'm in this by myself' is what got me where I am today, that sense that you can't rely on other people, you really can't count on anybody else because you never know what will happen."

In the following two decades Neil faced the deaths of four other close friends and relatives. The emotional reserve and distance he had cultivated after the death of his mother grew deeper. As the closest people in his life passed away, he became more and more unwilling to share himself with people who he felt were sure to leave him. "I had to be very careful whom I loved because everyone I loved leaves somehow. My first year teaching there was a young woman, and she and her husband were killed in an accident and we had gotten really close because we were both brand-new teachers, and then she passed away. And then I transferred to another school and another teacher and I got very close. She came down with cancer and passed away. So I was like twenty-five, twenty-six years old and realizing that the people that I get very close to die. And that was a very difficult period to understand what was really going on. I think that that sense of death and people dying, when it happens a lot, you protect yourself and you become immune to some of your feelings. And I think that's what happened in my twenties. I really protected myself from more hurt and sadness."

When he was in his late twenties, the cumulative impact of all these losses led Neil to seek the help of a therapist. At the same time, he began his relationship with John, one that was still flourishing some twenty years later when I met Neil. The process of therapy, in combination with his falling in love and working hard to make the relationship work, began a period of personal development in which Neil came to see the disadvantages of his earlier approach of denial and emotional distance. For many years, Neil's independent and self-reliant approach enabled him to pull through his mother's and others' deaths, but it prevented him from openly grieving or even speaking about these events. In therapy he learned a new mode of coping: by recognizing, accepting, and integrating his feelings, he felt he was better able to establish a satisfactory life. "The process of therapy helped me get through the worst of the negative feelings provoked by so many close ones dying. It also helped me to admit to myself that it's OK to feel I would have wanted my parents around a little longer; that I did not have to deny these feelings in order to fit in. The therapist taught me that recognizing and acknowledging my feelings would help me to accept these horrible situations with a greater sense of peace and equanimity.

"For so many years I claimed that my mother's death didn't affect me at all, that it had absolutely no effect on me, none whatsoever. And the reality is, of course it has affected me from day one. Therapy has helped me to see that and provided me with a way of still being OK with it. It helped me to look at life and say this loss was indeed probably the most critical event of my life, but it was one event, and I have since been able to adjust. And so the other deaths got reinterpreted as I learned to integrate this primal one." His earlier mode of thinking about his mother's death and other deaths became dysfunctional and appeared flawed when he found a language through which he could express his pain without getting stuck in it.

Since then, Neil has developed a personal spirituality that maintains his sense of his mother's presence in his life and has helped him to evolve a more positive approach to death. "I just think all the people that have been in our lives are present. I think that their energy is with us. I think the role of mother is so important to us that when we lose our mom, we feel that something is missing. And it is. It is missing, but maybe if we can connect with her spirit it's not all gone. I think that right after she died I certainly felt abandoned and all, but I think that I've come to accept that it is just a process of living. I've just finished reading *The Return to Love* by Marian Williamson. The part of the book about death really kind of said succinctly what I've been working toward for so many years: the sense that the material is just a shell and when we are finished with our body, our spirit goes on to another energy, another space, whatever. Like a lobster sheds, we're just shedding and off to another adventure. And my mom's been on a long adventure, and I don't know that my dad is with her. I think I'll run into all the spirits, though, and I'm looking forward to most, although not all, of them." Because Neil believes in the enduring existence of his mother's spirit, as well as the spirits of the other loved ones he has lost, he is able to approach the losses he's suffered over the years much more positively and with a stronger, more open sense of self.

"We can't go through life without loving, we can't go through life without caring, and if we lose the people we do care about, we accept it and maintain the memories. The process for me was recognizing that I need people in my life that I care about. So I'm not afraid anymore. I was afraid for a long time, and I'm glad I had help in changing that." His narrative revealed that he had adjusted to being able to feel deep emotions and close connections with others without automatically associating those feelings with the deaths of loved ones and his fear of abandonment. Through therapy he found a language that helped him move beyond his extended period of social liminality.

Neil related that the process of coming to terms with the deaths of his mother and his other loved ones assumed an even greater significance for him now that he was facing his own death. The energy he devoted to understanding and accepting death as a part of life made him feel more prepared to accept his own fate. "I have a psychic, intuitive ability that I rely on, and since I've been diagnosed as [HIV-]positive that's become more important to me, so that I'm at peace and not afraid to die. I don't want to, but if it happens, it happens, and I think the process of dealing with my mom and dad's death have allowed me to get to that point. You know, that I'm not going to fight it, I mean, I'm fighting to live, but I'm not going to fight the dying process at all. I'm very glad to live as long as I have, and that comes from a sense of peace about my mom and dad."

Neil's earlier experiences with death have thus helped

him integrate his own death into his ongoing life story. Additionally, he relies on the way his mother dealt with death as a model. "Looking at death, looking at the process of dying and realizing how courageous my mother was in all of this is just, you know, I'm not afraid. She wasn't, why should I be? I think the lessons that she taught have stood very well the test of time: just live life, make the best of what you have." The premature deaths of his parents have aided Neil's acceptance of his own death in another way, too. Since both of his parents died young, he always believed that he would, too. Thus he stated that he felt he had lived longer than he had expected to. "I was in a very serious automobile accident when I was twenty-one or -two, and by all rights I should have been killed, I mean it was a head-on collision on the Ohio Turnpike. So I've always figured the last x number of years have been a bonus. And what I've found, and I think it's probably as much a process of growing older, is that I'm just enjoying the peace that I can surround myself with and all of that. I think that's really neat. And I realized that I've lived longer than my mom, not quite as long as my dad, he died at fifty-two. But I'm in that age range; I just always figured I was going to die young. And that probably is going to be the case. But so far, so good."

As he evaluated the meaning of his own life, Neil reflected on what his parents, had they not died young, might have meant in his present life. He is confident that his mother would have been proud of who he has become. "How would she look at my life? I think it is how I look at my life, that I have been fairly successful in being a good person. And what more is there? I have often thought of how I would deal with her or how I would talk to them as adults, whatever, but I have never thought about how my life would have been different, because that's the past, not the present. I mean, I've thought how would I ever, ever talk to them about my relationship with John. But I also know I wouldn't be the person I am today if I hadn't had those other critical experiences."

Neil's story is that of a person who has spent most of his life coming to terms with the processes of grieving and death. He expressed his sense that our interview was another stage in the evolution of his approach to living and dying. "These issues cycle in and out. Now it is time for me to look at all those issues again. And so I was delighted to see your ad requesting interviewees on the subject of motherloss. It was timed perfectly in my process of reevaluating where I am. And the process is to me fascinating, that every time it comes up, you see it from a different angle. And you know, I'm doing OK. Seeds that were planted were good seeds. I have really been very lucky."

PART III

Reading the Narratives

8

Elements of Biographical Disruption

In seeking a language and a framework in which to narrate their stories of motherloss, most of my respondents were keenly aware of the lack of a ready-made language and scripts that would help them construct these stories. They were unable to draw upon a story line provided by their religious traditions or other institutional affiliations; rather, they struggled to create a coherent story in their own terms. A notable feature of the narratives of motherloss I heard was the failure of institutional religion to help individuals come to terms with the premature deaths of their mothers. When we realize that Americans are reported to be the most highly religious of all industrialized populations[1] and that religion is believed to provide metanarratives—theodicies—that help us make sense of life and death, it is surprising that the religious institutions and communities in which many respondents had grown up did not serve as sources of comfort or meaning when their mothers died. In fact, several interviewees, among them Sheryl, Sid, Sarah, and Bob,

were quite explicit in saying that their mother's premature death led them to question their religion and even to
abandon it. One interviewee, Rachel Morgenstern, a
thirty-nine-year-old single woman, said that if the death
of her mother had any impact on her, it weakened her
belief in God.

There are some exceptions: Darlene, of course, and I
am thinking particularly of Winifred Romano, a sixty-
five-year-old woman involved in a romantic relationship
who, several years after her mother's suicide, entered a
convent (she left the convent in her fifties). In her narrative she portrays this decision as one she had made before her mother's death, but she still affirms that the older
nuns were wonderful role models and mother substitutes.
"I had a lot of other mothers in the community, the novice
mistress, we used to call her Mother, and there were
mother generals and one of them used to always grab us
and give us a big hug, she really was very loving. I guess
that I probably would have suffered more if I had not had
that." Three other people also mentioned the strength
they continued to derive from their religious traditions;
one Catholic man said that his mother's death had actually strengthened his faith.

Several respondents made clear that at the time of their
mother's death, members of their religious communities
were very helpful to them, bringing them food and making sure the family was doing all right. So as far as community support was concerned, many of those whose
families were involved in religious traditions felt that
these communities were there for them, at least immediately after the mother died. But in terms of helping
them cognitively and emotionally to deal with the meaning of their loss, religion had let them down. The disruption of their mother's premature death taught them that

God is not always fair and just to the good, undermining the Jewish and Christian truths that most American children learn early in life. That these individuals can speak about rejecting their religion, and in fact feel compelled to include that repudiation as part of their life stories, is a significant indication of the current status of religion in the lives of many middle-class Americans.

Religion took on the semblance of a self-evident meaning system for very few interviewees; it was a facet of life—perhaps a cultural identity—but it did not provide an overarching structure through which to view the world. Scholars of religion have suggested that in recent decades people have been viewing their relationship to religion not as an inherited set of beliefs and values but rather as the grounds upon which to formulate and experiment with identities and preferences.[2] Secularization theorists have long noted that religious identity is typically privatized and compartmentalized in contemporary U.S. society. If it is not relevant to most spheres of everyday life, then it is not surprising that it could not help my respondents to find a language or structure of belief and ritual that could help them transcend their liminal state. If religion is not generally relevant to the daily rhythms of people's lives—although it can be and is for many people—then religious affiliation and belief do not self-evidently supply a framework in which people can talk about, evaluate, and make meaning out of their experiences, including the death of loved ones.

In the absence of religious or other metanarratives and the silence in which their motherloss was shrouded, my respondents had to struggle to create narratives that helped them make sense of the disruption and weave it into a coherent sense of self. Silence plays an important part in this attempt to reorder, because part of the fundamental sense of disorder is that their mother's death was hidden, made secret, even lied about, and so my interviewees had no script to draw upon to help them cope. Some major transitions in life, such as undergoing a religious conversion or becoming a member of a twelve-step program, provide a script in which to articulate and establish the transition. Premature motherloss, however, is a nonnormative transition—individuals are not prepared for it, and there is no ready language in which to make sense of it. The people around you do not help you find this language; the discomfort of death renders them silent as well. Silences are a way of normalizing through denial. The nonnormative nature of the disruption of motherloss means that each individual struggles to finds her or his own way to repair the disrupted biography and create a narrative that establishes a coherent sense of identity.

The diversity of my respondents' accounts attests to the lack of a readily available script; the accounts themselves demonstrate some of the various ways in which my respondents sought to create a consistent life story that integrated the disruption of motherloss and helped them establish a continuous identity. But despite the variety of forms and language, it is apparent that each narrative plays with and integrates specific themes and patterns. That certain key elements appear and reappear across my sixty interviews illustrates the ways the larger social context shapes people's representations of their individual lives. For example, fifty-seven of my sixty interviewees highlighted the silences that kept them from knowing about their mother's illness or from discussing her death. These silences further removed their mothers from them by denying them the opportunity to maintain their mothers' presence in their everyday conversations and lives, and provide strong evidence of the profound impact of the American denial of death. Similarly, that nearly all respondents generally represented their mothers in idealized terms reveals the power of the cultural constructions of motherhood and the institutional separation of male and female spheres that underlie and reinforce our cultural images.

The central narrative elements in these accounts of motherloss can be roughly grouped into elements of disruption—the focus of this chapter—and elements of repair, which are highlighted in Chapter 9. I emphasize, however, that this mode of organizing these chapters does not imply a strict bifurcation between the processes of biographical disruption and repair. Just as the narratives themselves spiral and circle through time and notions of identity, they also weave in and out of thematic units. For heuristic purposes, it is important to create distinctions between themes, but those distinctions are only convenient and descriptive categories. In presenting these key narrative elements, I show both the commonalities and the differences as they were shaped by gender, age, and social class.

Disrupted Routines

A great disruption in household routine accompanied the mother's illness (if she died after a long illness) or followed her death. Since the mothers of my respondents typically performed the routine tasks that kept their homes and families functioning smoothly, their inability to perform their roles created a noticeable void in their households. Respondents reported on the various ways their families sought to redistribute the mother's tasks in order to ensure the continuity of home life. The large majority reported that these attempts did go smoothly, in that the housework generally got done in some fashion.

At least four strategies for taking over the mother's duties emerged from the narratives: a housekeeper was employed; the child (or children) took over many of the mother's tasks; relatives came in to help; the family struggled along haphazardly from day to day. Over a third of my respondents reported that a housekeeper was brought in to take over the practical tasks the mother could no longer accomplish. Most of these people said that the housekeeper came in from one to three or four days a week; only a few reported having live-in help. Although the use of a housekeeper was a strategy more often adopted by middle-class families, some working-class families also brought in hired help.

In many households, whether or not a housekeeper was employed, children, particularly daughters, were expected to take over aspects of the mother's role; extreme instances of this approach were highlighted in the narratives of Tina and Darlene. Relatives provided occasional help, and in a few instances an aunt arrived to live in the household, either before or after the mother's death. Most families adopted some combination of these strategies when the mother became ill and continued with it after her death.

Silences

The silencing of all discussion about the mother's illness and impending death, as well as most conversations about her after she died, was a key feature of nearly every narrative I heard. These silences crossed gender and class lines. Age, however, did make some difference. My three youngest interviewees, whose mothers had died in the

late 1980s or 1990s, said that their families had been relatively open about the mother's illness and death. They
speculated that their families' ability to discuss the situation was probably influenced by the growing openness
in our society about the processes of death and dying,
grief and mourning.

Slightly over half of my interviewees told me that their
mothers had died of cancer. Most of these people told me
that they were kept totally uninformed about the nature
of their mother's illness—cancer was simply unnameable
at the time that they were growing up. Some of my respondents said that the doctors who treated their mothers
lied to them about what was wrong. For example, Deborah Curtis, a forty-eight-year-old middle-class woman,
said that the doctor had told her father but not her
mother that she had leukemia, leading the mother and
the children to think she was simply anemic. Susan John-
son, a thirty-seven-year-old full-time mother, reported (as
did Tina Martinelli) that the doctor had trivialized her
mother's symptoms, a phenomenon reported in many
studies of gender and health care.[3] When his mother went
into the hospital, Henry Bigelow, a forty-four-year-old
businessman who had grown up in a working-class family, was told that there was something wrong with her
knee and that she would be OK, even though she had been
ill for two years. He had no idea that her condition was
serious until she died in the hospital.

These silences mystified the children. They saw that
something was wrong, but they were never informed
about the seriousness of their mother's condition. Several
people told me that they felt their parents were trying, in
their own way, to protect them from pain. Sarah Mulligan
pointed out that her father tried to "shield" the kids, as if
to say, "They're just kids, don't tell them anything." San-

dra Barry, a thirty-six-year-old mother, narrated how she would sneak around the house trying to eavesdrop on adults' conversations about her mom's illness.

In three of the six cases of suicide, all of which followed periods of depression, the silences that followed were particularly deep: the children were not told the actual cause of their mother's death until years later. This is not surprising, given the stigma attached to mental illness in our society. As we saw in Sarah Mulligan's narrative, her mother's chronic depression and frequent hospitalizations were normalized and silenced. Phil and Tommy Greene did not learn the actual cause of their mother's death until they were in college. Because her depression was never explained to him as an illness, Phil said, her loss was even more confusing to him as a child.

Aside from the three youngest respondents, two others reported having some slight awareness of their mother's long-term illness when it was ongoing. It is notable that these respondents had become caretakers for their mothers. The silences around their mother's illness were less profound in these cases, because the children were attentive to what the mother was going through every day. Katherine Bennett, a forty-five-year-old mental health professional, described how her mother talked extensively with her (aged fourteen) and her sister (aged ten) about her breast cancer and actually showed them the lump in her breast when she was first diagnosed. Kathy reported that she changed her mother's bandages and had other caretaking responsibilities that necessitated some awareness and understanding of her mother's illness. She felt that her knowledge of her mother's condition was unusual and told me that her family was atypically open to discussing a wide variety of topics, including issues related to bodies and sexuality; her mother's openness about her cancer made sense in that context. Like Ellie Collins, Sammy Dickenson, a twenty-seven-year-old biracial African American, reported that his mother had a degenerative muscle disease that required him as well as his father and brother to care for her on a daily basis. Sammy helped his mother with basic things such as eating, bathing, and going to the bathroom.

My respondents' narratives highlighted the continuity of silences and mystification both before, at the time of, and after their mothers died. A large number of respondents who were "shielded" from their mothers' illnesses explained that they were shocked to hear that their mothers had died. As we saw in Sheryl Smith's narrative, concealment of the mother's illness sometimes led the child to feel a sense of betrayal, having been told that everything would be OK. My interviewees' narratives reflected the personal consequences of our culture's general avoidance of death talk. Euphemisms were frequently employed when children were informed that their mothers had died. Respondents reported being told that their mothers had "gone to sleep in the ground," had "gone to heaven," or simply were "gone." Several respondents told me that actually, they were never directly told that their mothers had died. Juan Rosaldo, a thirty-five-year-old manager, told me that he did not find out that his mother had died until several days later; one woman told me that she found out from a friend in school.

The silencing of the child's grief was also very common, an experience conditioned by their fathers' cues as well as by the general cultural ethos of being strong and moving on. Several respondents said that they never saw their fathers cry; they felt that their fathers' behavior modeled the appropriate form of grieving for them. Christine Albert, a single twenty-nine-year-old professional woman, reported that she felt she had to "be brave," as did many other respondents, who sensed that they were rewarded for being stoic. Reflecting on the implicit messages that he learned from his father, Paul Renear described his own reaction to his mother's death: "You don't talk about the past, you just deal with the future. That's done. It's over. Here's what we're going to do now." Paul reported that this emphasis on moving on and not dwelling on the past became integrated into his general philosophy of life.

The silences described in most of these narratives were commonly linked with a sense of shame. The efforts made by the father and other adults to normalize household life meant that the illness and death of the mother and the sense of deep loss that followed were abnormalities that must be shrouded. Sarah Mulligan said she did not want to talk with anyone about her grief as a child because she was afraid people would think she was "nuts" or having "bad thoughts." Rita Madrigal, a thirty-nine-year-old single woman, specifically connected the silences with a sense of guilt and embarrassment: "I think the shame came from the fact that it was hidden. There was shame that she had cancer and there was shame that she was dying, so that's why I felt the way I did, like there was something wrong with her being sick and something wrong with her dying—that it is something that you're ashamed of. And I don't feel good about that now, because it was nothing to be ashamed of, it wasn't her fault. It certainly wasn't my fault."

Given the cultural equation of masculinity with strength and stoicism, I had somewhat expected that my male interviewees would report more pressure to stifle the expression of their grief than the women did. Neil Roberts's narrative highlights the tension between him and his father, who discouraged Neil from crying because it was not a "masculine" form of expression. Nevertheless, as we saw in Sheryl Smith's narrative, both women and men generally reported equally powerful pressures to suppress their feelings of pain and loss. One possible reason is that the fathers were typically of a generation in which men were not socialized to be aware of or express their emotions. Since the emotional management of the family was a task delegated to the mother, her children lost their primary model for dealing with emotions when they lost her. Many of the narratives showed that the fathers were unable to deal with the emotional impact of the death of their wives, nor did they know how to ease their children's pain. Some respondents told me that their fathers' failure to grieve openly led them to question how their dads had actually felt about their dead wives.

The Early End of Childhood

When our social structural arrangements as well as our cultural ideology place the mother in the center of her children's world, it is not surprising that the large majority of my respondents reported that their world was shattered by their mother's death. In his description of his close bond with his mother, Marty Lucente, a fifty-year-old divorced contractor, stated that when his mom died, his "whole world disappeared." Similar statements were made by many others: "My world ended"; "The family fell apart"; "I lost my center."

The void that was so often depicted in these narratives left my respondents with an overwhelming sense of aloneness as well as a lack of emotional support. Sheryl Smith expressed a deep sense of isolation after the death of her mother and a profound feeling of betrayal when her mother's friends failed to keep their promises to help her. Henry Bigelow said that since he always sought his mother's advice as a child, after she died there was "nobody there to listen." Numerous respondents, such as Sid Jacoby, felt that they lost their self-esteem and no longer felt loved. Julia Nivens, aged sixty-five, reported that she had had a happy life until she was thirteen, when her mother died; at that point she no longer had any role model or source of guidance in her life. Harold Campbell, a political scientist in his fifties, identified the same issue: "I kind of grew up by myself basically because there was nobody home. There was no direction." In a powerful expression of the lack of attention to his feelings and reality after his mother died, Harvey Franklin, an upper-middle-class married father and grandfather, aged fifty-seven, stated, "You know, I was treated . . . now that I think of it, not as a child, but the way you might think about a dog that lost its master—let the dog be sad for a while and it will get better."

The loss of caring and disruption of the basic family structure usually required a renegotiation of the child's role. Many of my respondents said that their lives were split in two when their mother died and their childhood was cut short. They were required to relinquish some childhood privileges and take on new adult responsibilities. Several respondents' narratives noted the contradictory nature of their childhood's premature end: their early motherloss both compelled them to grow up too fast and took away their opportunity to develop a mature approach to relationships. Sammy Dickenson felt that his childhood ended early when he took on the responsibility of caring for himself as well as for his mother during her illness. Having taken on many adult obligations, he resented it when adults continued to perceive him as a kid.

In describing the tensions that arose around their rapidly ending childhoods, respondents reported that their families had failed to provide them with the stable family structure that allows children to grow up in a "normal" way. They felt that by losing a normative family, they had, in a sense, lost their birthright. According to the ideology of the nuclear family, children grow up best in a safe and supportive family in which they are permitted to absorb adult responsibilities gradually, at a pace appropriate to their developmental stage. Whether they felt they grew up too fast or never had a chance to grow up, most of my respondents felt that their loss of caring prevented them from going through these "normal" stages of childhood, adolescence, and transition into adulthood.

The women's narratives in particular reflected the common notion that a child cannot grow up normally without her mother. Echoing the social construction of the mother as the most important female figure in a young woman's life, the majority of the women whom I interviewed believed they were missing an essential part of what they needed in order to become a woman. We saw earlier in Ellie Collins's narrative that she felt angry that she could not have a "normal" mother-daughter relationship and that she lost "the female" in her life. In fact, most of the women told me that to some extent, the lack of their mother's guidance left them feeling that they did not know how to be "feminine"—how to dress attractively, apply makeup, cope with menstruation, have romantic relationships, bear and raise children. These women felt that their fathers had no idea about how to cope with their daughters' emerging femininity and sexuality.

It was quite common for my respondents to describe a sense of stigma and alienation when they returned to school after their mother's death. Neil Roberts described his classmates' reactions to his loss as "negative sympa-

thy"; he didn't want that kind of attention because it sin-
gled him out as deviant. Nancy Rosenberg, a widowed
sixty-seven-year-old mother of two grown daughters,
reported that after her mother's death, friends were constantly asking about her mother, unaware that she had
died. Not wanting anyone to "make a fuss" over her,
Nancy would respond, "She's OK." My interviewees reported that it made them uncomfortable when their peers
or teachers offered sympathy because it exacerbated their
feelings of difference and embarrassment. Winifred Romano told that when she went back to school, a nun
pointed her out as "the kid who lost her mom."

All of my respondents highlighted the difficulties
caused by their feelings of alienation during their adolescence, a time when everyone just wants to fit in with the
crowd. As Rita Madrigal said, "At fourteen and fifteen you
want to be like everybody else. I felt like I had this mark
on my head. Like 'Dead Mother.' And for people who
didn't know, I would never tell them. I didn't say I had a
mother but I never mentioned her. Someone once said to
me, 'Oh, but you seem so normal,' and I thought that was
the weirdest statement. Well, of course I'm normal, this
thing happened that changes you, but it was the kind of
thing you just never talked about. In terms of fitting in
with the crowd, you just didn't talk about it." The shame
associated with being different compounded the shattering of the child's world.

It is striking that these portrayals of the child's devastation do not show any distinct patterns between gender,
age, and class groupings. The similarities among the narratives demonstrate that at the time my respondents were
growing up, the nuclear family ideal was dominant and
pervasive, as was the American denial of death. Darlene
Jackson's narrative was unusual in her portrayal of a fam-

ily structure in which the mother's caretaker role was not exclusive. While it is clear how much Darlene loved her mother, her loss did not lead to the complete shattering of Darlene's world. Unlike many others, who reported that they and their siblings simply coped on their own, Darlene emphasized how her siblings stuck together and supported one another through the hard times. The family cohesiveness that Darlene described may be attributable to her large, extended family with many children to care for and adult relatives who were a steady presence.

The lost mothers of their childhood are represented in my respondents' accounts in idealized terms. Nearly all of the narratives depicted a mother who, overall, fulfilled the cultural model of motherhood. My interviewees used strong, superlative terms to depict their mothers; Sheryl's mother was "beatific" and a "Madonna," and another woman's mother was a "beautiful prom queen." Even Carl Diamond, whose narrative followed a different script, idealized his mother's voluptuous beauty and physical presence. It was quite common for respondents to attribute the positive stereotypical images of femininity to their dead mothers—they were described as gentle, loving, much loved, nurturing, sociable, wise, strong, ever present, and often self-sacrificing. These mothers were portrayed as the emotional center of their households, the glue that had held the family together. Her death, therefore, made respondents feel as if their families, and their young lives, had fallen apart.

Since my respondents also portrayed their mothers as their primary sources of guidance and as the persons who affirmed their sense of self-worth, they typically described themselves as "lost" without her. At the beginning of our interview, I provided Henry Bigelow (like all my respondents) with a general description of the purpose of my research. Responding with enthusiasm and appreciation for my project, Henry matter-of-factly described the importance of the maternal role.

"You know we all like to leave our mark, and doing something for your parents I think is wonderful. And especially mom, they're the ones who are the backbone of the family, they're the ones who keep things together, and they are a very important part of our lives. If you don't have them when you're growing up, I mean that makes it even worse. Because you need a role model from both your parents, but your mother is the one who is the most impressionable. She's the one who instills you with all of those values."

Although some interviewees also portrayed characteristics of their mothers they perceived as negative, such as being overly strict or having a nasty temper, their tendency nevertheless to idealize these moms speaks to the power of cultural stereotypes as well as to respondents' desire to hold on to the best possible memories and images. Juan Rosaldo, for example, used such words as "sacred," "divine," and "perfect" in his depiction of his mother, although he had also described her as harsh and even cruel. Holding on to these idealized representations made it impossible for them to feel that anyone else could ever live up to or adequately replace their lost mothers. As one man said, "You just can't replace what a mother does."

Replacing Lost Caring in Childhood

Most of my respondents reported that their fathers had made various—generally unsuccessful—attempts to replace the child's lost caring and to maintain the household's functions. The resources that the father drew upon were often shaped by the family's social class and by the social and kin networks to which the family belonged. In many of the middle-class and upper-middle-class families, the father hired a housekeeper to help with cooking, cleaning, and other tasks around the house. Many fathers relied on the help of relatives, such as aunts, uncles, and grandparents, as well as neighbors and friends of the family. Some children, such Ben Adler and Sarah Mulligan, were sent away to live with relatives or family friends for significant lengths of time. A large number of my respondents learned to care for their own needs as well as the needs of their siblings. Except for a few extreme cases in which the effects of poverty were compounded by total abandonment, the narratives indicated that the practical matters of household life were taken care of in one way or another. Respondents made clear, however, that although their fathers usually managed to provide for their children materially, they were unable to care for them emotionally.

A few distinct patterns emerged from these narratives about fathers' attempts to care for their children. The majority of respondents reported that their fathers were so overwhelmed by their own sense of loss that they were unable to comfort their children. Sheryl Smith and a few others reported that their fathers coped by immersing themselves in their work, leaving their kids to fend for themselves. A few respondents had seen their father cry about his wife's death, but these expressions of his feelings did not make him any more likely to be emotionally available to his children. About a fourth of my interviewees said that their father expressed his grief in powerful bursts of anger, often directed at the motherless kids.

Some of these narratives included incidents of the father's neglect or abuse of his children. At the extreme, a few respondents ended up in foster homes or orphanages when their father failed to look after them. Several people represented their fathers as emotional wrecks who drank to excess, then became either maudlin or verbally abusive. While my respondents described various ways in which their dads reacted to their loss, the large majority reported that their fathers were unable to meet their children's emotional needs or replace the warmth and affection they had lost. Nevertheless, a few dads were portrayed as wonderfully supportive men who did their best to fill in the emotional gap the children felt after their mothers died. These narratives depicted fathers who tried very hard to become more involved in their kids' lives. The Greene brothers both told me that immediately after their mother's death, their dad placed his children at the center of his life, leaving work early every day in order to be home with his children for dinner. Julia Nivens said that her father's caring became very important for her sense of stability while she was growing up.

A large number of respondents talked about the roles of their extended family members, usually aunts, in attempting to replace the caring the children had lost. Some people, especially women, described their aunts as offering comfort and advice, and as helping them to learn about "female things." Many of the respondents, however, both male and female, expressed a deep ambivalence toward their aunts, some of whom had said quite openly that they did not want to become substitute mothers. Besides, as these narratives made clear, respondents felt that no one could adequately replace their lost mothers. A few respondents who were cared for by their relatives described feeling quite unsafe in their new situations. Recall Sarah Mulligan, who reported that after she was sent to live with her aunt and uncle, she was frightened by her uncle's alcoholism, his nasty temper, and his attempts to abuse her. A few men reported feeling resentful of their aunts' domineering ways and their misguided attempts to erase the children's mothers from their memories. That so many of my respondents expressed resentment and fear of the relatives who were caring for them underlines their strong feeling that the mother is the only person who can adequately maintain and preserve the child's emotional well-being.

The view of surrogate mothers as inadequate emerged even more forcefully in accounts of stepmothers. Ben Adler was quite typical in perceiving his dad's new wife as forcefully and insistently trying to erase his dead mother's presence from the household and from his mind. Many respondents told of stepmothers who removed all of the mother's pictures, acted harshly, and were overly controlling of the children's lives. Several respondents described how they and their siblings made up hateful names for their stepmother or refused to recognize her name at all, as Ben Adler and his sister did when they referred to their stepmother as X. Stepmothers were seen as simply unable to do what "real" mothers did for their children.

A few respondents, however, told relatively positive stepmother stories. As we have seen, Ellie liked her young and hip stepmom quite a bit, although she emphasized that she did not think of her as a mom but rather as her father's wife and her friend. Some of these respondents were glad for the sense of normality provided by an adult woman's presence in the household. But even those respondents who felt that their father's remarriage helped their family to achieve a semblance of normality generally represented the second wife as inferior to their "real" mothers.

As they narrated their transition into adulthood, several respondents said that their premature loss of maternal caring had hindered them in their schooling and in their careers. Although a few men felt that their mother's death had limited their educational options, this experience was reported more frequently by my female respondents. As we saw earlier, Tina was held back from going to college because she was pressured to remain the caretaker for her father. It is striking how she talks about her sister, who ended up getting a scholarship to an Ivy League university and then stayed on in the community where she had gone to school. Tina contrasted her own options, which were very much shaped by her gender and social class, with those that her sister was fortunate enough to have had. Some women said that their fathers encouraged them to get married and have children rather than to pursue a career. Although Sandra Barry told me that her father did encourage her to go to college, he was more concerned about her finding a suitable mate than about her educational and professional achievement. She strongly believed that just as her mother had worked hard to place Sandra's older brother in the best college program for him, she would have done the same for Sandra had she lived long enough. In this sense, we can see how children felt that their mother's death had a bearing on their options as they made the transition into adulthood in distinctly gendered ways.

Reverberating Losses

My respondents' depictions of the profound biographical disruption that followed their mothers' deaths illustrate the various and complex ways in which this loss reverberated throughout their lives. Two of the persistent effects of loss that were highlighted in many interviews were lingering problems with intimacy and struggles with depression. It is simplistic to say that these issues were caused by the premature deaths of their mothers. Most members of our society experience, at least to some extent and at some times in their lives, difficulties in establishing and maintaining intimate relationships. Similarly, depression is clearly not confined to people who have lost their mothers. Nevertheless, since respondents often connected their efforts to deal with these issues— and many other difficulties in their lives—with the experience of motherloss, they warrant some discussion.

Anxiety about intimate relationships, including the fear of abandonment and rejection, is one of the chronic conditions of our times. Because geographical mobility is such a prominent feature of contemporary U.S. society, many people feel little sense of attachment to the place where they live. At least once in their lives, and often more frequently, people move away from their family, community, and familiar surroundings. The resultant sense of isolation and alienation contributes to difficulties in getting close to people. Certainly this general state is one of the factors in the "triumph of the therapeutic" in our society.[4] But this issue was articulated with particular power and poignancy by my interviewees, most of whom wondered how they could trust others and feel confident and secure in relationships after experiencing the death of the most formative relationship of their childhood.

More than two-thirds of the women I interviewed indicated that they linked their problems with intimacy and getting close to others with their mother's death. Some of them reported that their need to become independent at such a young age made it difficult for them to integrate their lives with others'. Some respondents, such as Rita Madrigal told me that their fear of loss led them to avoid intimacy and commitment. Others indicated that this early loss had made them feel overly dependent on others. Ellie Collins, for instance, mentioned that she feels she needs her friends more than they need her. At one extreme was a college-educated working-class woman who felt so cheated of a "normal" model of womanhood (her mother was an alcoholic and died of alcohol-related causes) that she felt completely unable to deal with relationships and had chosen a life of celibacy. At the other end of the continuum were those women who said that although they had had serious problems with intimacy, they had been able to work through many of those problems and were involved in good relationships at the time of the interview.

Most of the women fell somewhere in between these extremes, stating that they wanted and needed love and intimacy, but feared that if they let themselves care deeply about someone else, they might be abandoned. In addition, they worried about doing something wrong in relationships and being responsible for their own abandonment. In general, social class did not seem to shape their representation of their relationships, but age did— this concern was expressed much more frequently by women in their thirties, forties, and fifties than by those in their sixties and seventies.

The men described similar difficulty in getting close to others and maintaining intimate relationships. Over half of the men made explicit connections between their mother's death and their lingering difficulties with emotional closeness. Their responses articulated many of the same issues described by the women. For example, Sid's narrative emphasized his fear of abandonment and lack of trust in women. As he said, "If you let yourself get close to women, they'll leave you." Juan Rosaldo similarly reported that the loss of his mother's love made him particularly ready to feel abandoned. When his wife is not physically affectionate with him, he perceives her as rejecting him, an issue he has struggled with in therapy.

Depression, as I assured Bob, is more common in individuals who have suffered an early traumatic loss than it is in the general population. Psychologists and psychiatrists have been linking emotional experiences with bodily and chemical reactions that may in fact encode a susceptibility to depression in a person's physical being. Not surprisingly, many respondents described struggles with depressive episodes; several reported experiencing a long-term depression that had been helped by medication.

Twelve female respondents (slightly over a third of the women, with not much variation by age or social class) explicitly connected their experiences of depression with the death of their mother. Although the very youngest interviewees (two twenty-year-olds and a twenty-three-year-old) did not refer to bouts of depression, a respondent who was twenty-five did. Similarly, the eldest of my interviewees (those aged sixty and above) also did not report feelings of depression after their mothers died. Since these differences are found in only a few respondents, I am uncertain how to interpret them. One of the younger women reported that her family talked often and openly about her mother's illness and death. They did not repress their grief but encouraged each other to express it freely, suggesting the possibility that recent changes in the way we view death (the development of hospices, therapy, support groups) may lead to less repression of the feelings that, unexpressed, emerge as depression. But another woman's experiences do not conform to this idea: Christine Albert, who was twenty-nine when we met, had opportunities to experience and articulate her grief with her family and with the aid of social services, yet her struggles with depression were a prominent feature of her account, and she spoke about the antidepressant medication that had helped her. One possible explanation for the eldest respondents' failure to talk about feeling depressed is that the language and open expression of depression were more stigmatized and thus less available to them in their youth than they were for the younger respondents.

Lisa Rapaport told me that when she was in college and in her twenties, she masked her depression by self-medicating with recreational drugs. She was the only person who talked about substance abuse as a possible means of coping with depression. Two respondents, one whose mother committed suicide—Sarah Mulligan—and another whose mother ultimately died of alcohol abuse reported that they were so afraid of becoming like their mothers that they left the husbands they had married when they were young, and left their babies too.

In accord with the general findings about gender and depression in the U.S. population, fewer men—only six of the thirty male interviewees—than women reported struggling with depression as a result of their mother's death. Their ages ranged from thirty-five to forty-five and they were from both working-class and middle-class backgrounds. Three of these men explicitly connected their depression with their drug and alcohol abuse. A couple of other men reported drinking large amounts of alcohol, but they did not connect their drinking with feelings of depression.

These narratives reveal that a mother's premature

death is experienced as a major disruptive event that creates reverberations that linger throughout the lives of the children they leave behind. Nevertheless, respondents' accounts do not stop at detailing the disruptions caused by motherloss; they tell also of the various ways these people sought wholeness and attempted, through their narratives, to repair their disrupted biographies.

9

Elements of
Biographical Repair

Narratives are works in progress as well as depictions of lives in progress. The project of biographical repair is a lifelong process. Throughout our lives we construct stories that attempt to establish coherent, linear biographies out of the ordered—and disordered—events that characterize our lives. The narrative production of identity involves accounting for disruptions as well as fashioning solutions. My interviewees' accounts of mother-loss featured several common patterns of repair that correlated with—and attempted to resolve—the particular elements of disruption that resulted from premature maternal death. In order to counter the silences and loss of mothers' caring activities and presence that were highlighted in their accounts, respondents went on to tell of their attempts to break the silences, replace lost caring, and maintain their mothers' symbolic presence in their lives.

Breaking Silences

The pain involved in breaking the silence surrounding a mother's death can be enormous, but the continued pain and sense of tragic loss that is internalized when one is unable to break the silence is even more devastating. My interviewees described a variety of approaches to breaking silence and discovering a language and metaphor through which they could articulate their experiences of motherloss; their narratives reflected the approaches they have found most useful and meaningful. Carl's narrative, for instance, echoed the structure of Freudian analysis, while Ellie's revealed that the good fortune of having an open and communicative father enabled her to construct a narrative premised on open grieving and talk about the pain of her mother's death.

Over half of my respondents (slightly more women than men, and across the range of social classes) described the process of therapy as one way in which they were able, with the encouragement of therapists and the narrative language they provided, to come to terms with their experiences of motherloss. Since the therapeutic modality often encourages people to search for those deeply buried and repressed incidents that might be thwarting them in their current lives, therapy encouraged respondents to see that their silences about motherloss prevented them from adequately grieving. Sheryl Smith's narrative provides dramatic evidence of the way therapy helped her to grieve fully and openly. Respondents reported that once their therapists helped them to recognize and then release these emotions of pain and sadness—even though it was often years after their mothers had died—they were freed to make sense of this disruptive event and weave it into their coherent narratives of identity. Several respondents reported that their experiences in therapy helped them to deal better with their problems with intimacy and fear of rejection. Mark Rills, a forty-four-year-old businessman who was the father of two sons, was explicit about how helpful therapy was for him: "I firmly believe that if it weren't for therapy I would still be closed in terms of my feelings. Luckily I got help and changed that. I firmly believe that if it weren't for that, I don't know if I ever would have gotten married or if it would have been the right person or if it ever would have lasted." Other interviewees related that therapy helped them uncover memories of their mothers and thus reestablish connections with them in everyday life. A few respondents said, as Sarah Mulligan did, that the process helped them to recognize their tendency to idealize their late mothers and to refashion their conceptions in a more realistic form.

The interview situation itself, by providing people with an opportunity to narrate motherloss and the ways in which they made sense of it, became a means of breaking silences. Certainly the story some interviewees told was a version of one they had learned to tell at some earlier point, perhaps in therapy or in the context of meaningful relationships they had had. Many others claimed that the interview was the first time they were able to talk about their experiences of motherloss, since they had felt silenced in their earlier attempts to discuss their dead mothers. Whatever the case, the very telling of their narratives to me in this context provided all respondents with an opportunity to arrive at new forms of expression and self-integration. This was a key factor, I think, in people's willingness to talk with me about this situation.

The majority of women and men respondents, across

age and social class lines, told me that the process of being interviewed had helped them to think and talk about their mother's death. Many said that the interview helped to trigger memories they hadn't thought of for years. By offering respondents a forum for telling their stories and establishing a cohesive narrative about the disruption of motherloss and the ways they had sought to repair it, the interview enabled them to construct accounts that pulled in distant memories and set them in dialogue with their present lives, or, as one woman said, to "pull things together." Several people explicitly stated that through the very telling of their stories they were able to see linkages and connections that they had not seen before. Marty Lucente asked for a pad of paper, saying, "I want to write these connections down—I've never thought of some of these things and I want to be able to think about them later." The narrative construction of identity through the interview provided a context in which people could construct a sense of self in which past, present, and future were more smoothly integrated.

Of course, an account created in an interview, or in any other setting, is a representation of the meaning of events in a particular context. A few interviewees were aware of the constructed nature of narratives. The clearest articulation of this perception was by Peter Burke, who, as I mentioned in Chapter 5, was very conscious of the selectivity and "slant" of his representations.

Both women and men expressed concern that their reports of their experiences should seem "normal" and resonate with those of my other interviewees. Interestingly, slightly more men than women explicitly stated that the interview process was very meaningful and helpful to them. This may seem surprising, since in general I found that the women were somewhat more comfortable than the men in talking about their motherloss experiences, as was reflected, for example, in my significantly greater ease in recruiting women interviewees than men. One possible reason that men were more likely to articulate their positive experience with the interview process is precisely that they were less likely than women to feel that it was safe and OK for them to release their deep emotions about this experience in their everyday lives.

Fewer than half of my respondents reported that at some point they sought to talk about their mothers with other people in their lives. Age was a factor here; the older interviewees reported that many of the people who had known their mothers had passed away and so there were few people available for such conversations. Several women and men who had young children emphasized the importance of talking to their children about the grand-mothers they did not know. Mark Rills told me, "Sue [his wife] and I have pictures of my mother out in our house and I have gone through this whole thing with my older son for the past two or three years. He knows my mother as 'Nanna.' When he would see the picture of my mother on my desk he would say, 'Who's that?' and so I've ex-plained it to him."

Respondents often reported that when they were young it was very difficult to break their family's silences and discuss motherloss with their siblings. As adults, how-ever, several engaged in such conversations and used them as a way to reconstruct memories or their late mother. Christine Albert told me that as an adult in search of a greater understanding of her mother's life, she deliberately asked an uncle for information that would help her put her mother in perspective. Christine and the others she spoke with had so idealized her mother that Christine sought to learn whether her mother had had any negative qualities. That way Christine might be less anxious about living up to her mother's image. Both women and men who had an opportunity to discuss their mothers found some consolation in conversation. Nevertheless, nearly half of my respondents said that they had not talked about their mothers with anyone, except, in some cases, with a therapist.

Replacing Lost Caring

Many of my respondents made clear that they were often thrust into taking over some aspects of the mother's caretaking role at a young age. Many women and some men described having to take over household duties such as laundry, cleaning, and cooking, tasks they did not relish and did not feel prepared to do. Both Tina's and Darlene's narratives revealed that some daughters, especially in working-class families, were called upon to take on the caretaker role in its entirety. Darlene's transition to the maternal role was smooth and enabled her to replace lost care by caring for others when she was still very young; Tina did not feel nearly as comfortable in her role. Most of my interviewees did not fully take on the caretaking role until they were much older, at which point it became for them a meaningful way of establishing continuity and in some way replacing the caring they had lost.

More than half of the women and men I interviewed described the formation of families of their own as an important step in establishing biographical continuity. By directly participating in the advancement of the chain of generations, they were able to continue and reproduce the maternal caretaking that had been so important to them as young children. Most of the women who had children were very articulate—more so than the men—

about how important having children was to their enact-
ment of their gender identity and to the desire to become
connected to their mothers. The process of becoming the
mother has helped many of them to mend the rupture in
their lives and to feel more at peace with their loss and
with themselves.

It is important to specify that only seventeen of the
women I interviewed had children, whereas twenty-three
of the men were fathers. Age is likely to account for a
large part of this difference: my sample of men included
only one man under thirty, whereas five of the women
were under thirty, and all of them expressed a desire to
have children in the future. In addition, because women
are socialized to identify with their mothers, a few of the
women deliberately avoided having children as a way to
avoid this identification. Sheryl Smith, as we saw, chose
to lavish her affection on her dogs and friends; she did
not want to marry and risk the abandonment she associates with counting on others. Also, she feared that she
herself would become ill and die, thus leaving her children in the same awful situation she had been in. Both
women who gave up the children they had had when they
were young had been too worried about their own mental
health to feel able to rear and care for a child.

Like Sheryl, I, too, made a conscious choice not to have
children, a decision that was linked to a variety of factors.
For one, early motherloss impressed upon me the idea
that mothers die. Of course I know that this is not necessarily the case, but to me dying meant more than going
to one's grave. I had been precocious as a child, and from
a young age I knew in my gut that my father was dominant and that my mother lacked power in our household.
I felt that by becoming a mother, a woman loses some of
her individual time, space, and freedom, which for me

represented a form of dying. When I was still very young I decided that I would be primarily a career woman. At that time, in the early 1960s, motherhood and career were seen as incompatible options. In addition, my mother's death left me in an extremely unhappy household—my father, who never planned to be the caretaker of three children under the age of fifteen, released the full force of his pain and anger about losing his beautiful wife on his children. Not only were we silent about our mother and her death, but ours was a household in which little conversation took place at all. I spent my adolescence longing to escape this situation, and I left there with a gut feeling that families can be very difficult and painful for their members and that I would avoid creating one of my own. It is important to note, however, that an unhappy adolescence has no one single affect on a person's future life. Although Sheryl and I avoided reproducing families of our own, many other interviewees consciously chose to have families at least partly as a way to redo their past and create happier families than the ones they grew up in.

The men who had children were less likely than the women to self-reflexively connect their choice to be parents with their desire to achieve continuity with their mother and to take over where she had left off. Their emphasis was more on the sense of stability they achieved by having families of their own. Women talked about being there for their children because their mother wasn't there for them, and they know the kind of pain that absence caused. As Lisa Rapaport told me, "I've chosen to stay home with my children. I'm lucky we can afford it. They're young once and I want to cherish every single moment with them. That is one thing I learned from the loss of my mother. That nothing is permanent and you have to enjoy every day with your children while you can." When motherless women became mothers, their experiences of their mother's death gained new relevance. Their new status occasioned reflection about their experiences of being mothered as well as how they wanted to shape their own mothering of their children.

Many interviewees (both those with and those without children) described their practice of caring for other people in their lives as another way of restoring the caring they had lost so prematurely. Although cultivating a caring personality is not unique to those who are motherless, respondents often explicitly connected their attempts to take care of others to the loss of caring in their own lives. Since I myself am keenly aware of the profound impact the loss of my mother's nurturing had on my life and chose not to have children of my own, I seek to be highly attentive to and caring of my students, especially when they are facing difficult family situations. Both women and men, across age and social class categories, described the value they placed on being a caring person who helps others. Several respondents described how they developed very close friendships; friends became the loving, nurturing families they had lost. About a third of my interviewees spoke about being particularly helpful to people who were in difficult situations and in need of extra support; they knew too well what that was like. Some mentioned caring for younger siblings after the mother's death as one way of continuing the feeling of caring in their lives. Sheryl Smith, as we saw, dotes on and takes great care of her dogs, a practice she instituted shortly after her mother died.

It was clear that for these interviewees, caring for others was a very important means of biographical repair, and I was fascinated by the variety of ways people envisioned and practiced caring. For example, my younger brother, Mark, who was totally helpless when, at age nine, he woke up one morning to find his mother dead, has since studied emergency medical techniques and become a member of a volunteer ambulance corps in his community. His regular job is manager of an ambulance care company. When I asked him if he saw any connections between these adult choices and our mother's early death, he clearly agreed.

In an example that took me by surprise, a set of twins, the Legassis, who were by far the hardest living of all my respondents—they described growing up in dire poverty and being sexually molested as children, and one of them had just been released from prison after serving a term for sexual abuse—concluded their interview by stressing how important it is for them to be helpful to others. After all, they know all too well how it feels to be left helpless. And in this way they try to carry on their mother's values of goodness and warmth. Like several other respondents, they told me that they agreed to be interviewed because they hoped that by publicizing the consequences and pain of early motherloss, this book might help others to cope.

Since mothers represent the female gender and femininity to their young children, it is not surprising that many of the men, who clearly did not get enough mothering as children, sought wives who embodied their lost mothers' best traits. Several men stated that their wives or girlfriends physically resembled the mothers they had lost. About half of the men explicitly stated that they were looking for a maternal figure in their marriages or significant relationships. Ben Adler described how he deliberately sought "motherly" women as wives, and specified that by "motherly" he meant resembling his own mother. In fact, he felt that his first two marriages had failed because those wives were not maternal and nurturing enough toward him or their children. These men sought women they could depend on emotionally—the type of woman who was at the center of their representations of their own mother, and who embodied the cultural model of "woman" as the emotional center of the household. For men, establishing long-term relationships with motherly women was an important way of replacing the essential caring they had lost and thus a means of repairing their disrupted biographies.

The women respondents were much less likely to talk about replacing the caring they had lost by finding motherly, nurturing partners. Conventional gender socialization trains women to identify with their mothers and to seek partners who will fulfill the complementary "masculine" role. The cultural stereotype that connects women with nurturing and caring is so powerful that when I turned to my computer's thesaurus (in a 1997 program) for an alternative word for "nurturing," the synonym provided was "like a woman." The alternative words offered were "feminine, female, ladylike, effeminate, womanish, womanly, gentle."

Nevertheless, these stereotypes are not accepted by all people, and a few of the women whose mothers had died reported that although they did not necessarily consciously seek nurturing men, their partners were indeed quite gentle, caring, and supportive. Madeline Perri, a forty-two-year-old full-time mother of a son, told me that her husband is a substitute mom for her and that he taught her to cook. Similarly, I have observed that although I am fiercely protective of my independence, I select men who tend to be gentle and nurturing, and who, at least in some ways, put me at the center of their worlds—they are there for me as a mom might have been.

My first husband had told me on our very first date, before he knew much about my own life story, that he "mothers" people. I found that peculiar and asked him why he did so. "I don't know," he said, "I just do." In retrospect, it was not surprising that I married him at the age of twenty-four, eleven years after my mother died and five years after leaving my father's home.

Nearly all respondents felt that no matter what, they would never be able to replace the maternal caring they had lost. Despite diligent searching for someone to give them the total care and devotion that they imagined their mothers would have provided, maternal love and nurturing were still expressed as irreplaceable. One of the Legassi twins told me, "I'm looking for love, that's the way I would go. Although our foster parents were quite good to us and cared for us deeply, they could not love us like our mother had. We wanted our mother's nurturing and care, which we could not get."

Nearly half of the men and just over one-third of the women told me that their mother's premature death led them to develop a sense of self-reliance and independence at a young age, a strength that has served them well throughout their lives. Several women, however, felt that their independence was a mixed blessing—while it has helped them achieve some measure of career success and stability, it has also made it harder for them to become interdependent with partners. Their accounts of their mixed feelings about their strength and self-reliance reveal the power of narrative to absorb complexities and tensions. Although we generally do strive to present ourselves as consistent, narratives, because they offer an open space to represent and work out our life stories, are not free of contradiction and inconsistency. People can actually learn how to feel comfortable with their inconsistencies through the language they use to delineate their life stories. Some of the same women who talked about being independent and "tough" also talked about feeling depressed, wanting someone to care about them, wishing their mothers were around. These seemingly opposing impulses need not be seen as irreconcilable; people often have varied and multiple perceptions of themselves. To erase all inconsistency from one's life story is to create a story that does not actually engage with what it means to go about the project of living and making meaning out of life.

The men expressed less ambiguity and a clearer sense of pride in their independence. Several described themselves as "self-made." Paul proudly told me that he can do anything he wants any time he wants, all by himself! Marty Lucente, who was brought up as an only child, emphasized how he learned early on to take care of and do for himself. "I was forced to be very independent and I think that's great because I did things that I would probably never have attempted otherwise."

Through the variety of ways my respondents said they tried to replace the caring they had lost, we can see that diverse formulas work for different people, or even for the same person at distinct points in time. For some, the most consistent and successful approach was represented in the comment: "My loss of caring when I was much younger has led me to seek out people who will care about me. I want to replace the caring I lost." For others, the connection between lost caring and independence was more strongly emphasized: "My loss of caring when I was much younger has led me to feel very independent and self-reliant. Because I had the experience of not being cared for and nurtured in a maternal way, I know I am capable of relying on myself." The two approaches are not mutually exclusive, however; life history narratives of individuals are always in process and are flexible enough to embrace the multiple choices and modes of expression through which we make sense of our lives.

Maintaining the Mother's Symbolic Presence

Given the fluidity of many forms of contemporary religious expression, my interviewees were able to construct creatively many ways of maintaining the symbolic presence of their mothers in their lives. Some of these forms drew directly upon the religious traditions in which they had been raised, such as the Jewish ritual of annual cemetery visits described by Carl; others were individual modes of gathering up pieces and strands from many traditions to fashion a personal bricolage of rituals and practices.

Symbolic representations and acts are often crucial to the preservation of a memory, feeling, or experience. The practices through which respondents remember mothers who were live presences only in their childhood depend on creative symbolization. Just as my interviewees found that the process of arriving at a language through which to narrate motherloss was both liberating—since language breaks the stifling silence about death and grief—and creative, the use of symbolic representations similarly enables them to develop, express, and maintain their ongoing connection with their dead mothers. Symbols, in a very powerful way, enable individuals to move between different levels of experience and reality. While it is overly simplistic to say that symbols directly connect the individual to the past or to memories, the dynamic use of symbols helps the individual to recreate, revise, and enact the memory of the dead mothers they are evoking. Like language, symbols simultaneously represent and create. The symbolic ways my interviewees summoned up their mother's presence—I think of the man who sewed a piece of his mother's bridal veil into his wedding yarmulke and the people who converse with their mothers at their graves—are multilayered and complex, but they helped them reestablish a relationship that was meaningful to them.

At least two-thirds of my respondents expressed a need to maintain their mother's presence in their lives. While the women emphasized this need slightly more than the men, most of my respondents, with some variations by age, gender, and social class, described their strategies for maintaining an ongoing relationship with their mothers.

One distinct age-specific pattern that took form among the women did not appear among the men. It was especially common for women in their thirties and forties to discuss their mother's presence in the context of marriage, pregnancy, and raising their own children. Many of these women clearly stated that becoming mothers and raising children was a continuation of their relationship with their own mothers. The life cycle events around pregnancy and raising children evoked a kind of cyclical interaction with their mothers. While many of the men emphasized the importance of having their own families, they did not make such a distinct connection between their parenting and their mothers' symbolic presence in their lives. In contrast, most of the women who were in their sixties and seventies said that they did not especially try to maintain their mothers' presence in their lives. Nancy Rosenberg explained that at sixty-seven she does not think about her mom much because her mother has been gone for such a long time. Julia Nivens, too, said that she had thought about her mom more when she and her children were younger than she did later in life. In contrast, most of the women who were rearing young children reported that they thought about—and missed— their mothers more than ever before as they gave birth and watched their children grow up.

Like the women who were over sixty, the women in their early twenties were also less likely to emphasize their efforts to maintain their mothers' symbolic presence in their lives. However, unlike the women in the older age group, several of these women seemed to make overt attempts to avoid thinking about their mothers. It is striking that these women were extremely concerned with being "normal," a concern that may partly be a function of being young adults. Having had only a few years in which to cope with their losses, a few devoted their efforts more to minimizing the impact of this disruptive event as they made the transition into their social worlds as adults.

While the women's responses to questions about symbolic presence followed distinct age-specific patterns, the men's responses showed no correlation with age. Perhaps differences in gender identification influence the respondents' perceptions of their relationships with their mothers as they go through different stages in their lives. I am not taking an essentialist view of gender or suggesting that women are automatically bonded to their mothers simply by having children. I think, rather, that the commonality in their embodied experiences and behavior led these women to identify with their mothers as mothers. They felt that becoming mothers themselves helped them to understand their mothers' experiences.

Women who did not have children also attempted to maintain their mothers' symbolic presence. We saw that Sheryl Smith was attached to her mother's belongings, cherished photographs of her mother, and highlighted the various ways in which she resembled her mother. I, too, have increasingly and consciously sought to retain a sense of my mother in my life by placing her photos in my living room, cherishing the jewelry I inherited from her, and, most important, writing this book. Christine Albert and others described their mothers' abiding presence as providing someone with whom they can talk on a regular basis.

Intertwined with issues of gender are socioeconomic factors that also influenced the way some respondents expressed their symbolic relationships with their mothers. In both Darlene's and Tina's narratives we saw that class conditions influenced their roles as replacement mothers for their siblings and caretakers for their fathers. The continuation of these roles through adulthood was one way these respondents integrated motherloss into their lives. Before her mother's death, Darlene had already been in a caretaker role; she experiences herself as contiguous with her mom. Similarly, Tina became so completely the mother in her household that her narrative made no mention of whether she consciously sought to maintain her mother's symbolic presence in her life.

The men's strategies for maintaining their mothers' symbolic presence in their lives were not clearly shaped by class or age characteristics. As we saw, several of the men's narratives echoed those of the women who reported that their own families were one means through which they sustained a sense of their mothers in their adult lives. Mark Rills reported that he recently had started bringing his older child to the cemetery to show him his mother's grave and to talk with him about death. Although he does not feel strongly about organized religion, he feels spiritually connected with his mother by raising his kids Jewish. Juan Rosaldo talked about how important it was to him to have open communication with his daughter about death and to teach her to respect the dead. While teaching their children about death was a means of breaking silences, it was also a way for these men to maintain an ongoing relationship with their mother. By communicating with their children about her death, these respondents sought to establish their late mother as a presence in their children's lives as well as their own.

My respondents described a wide variety of strategies to sustain an ongoing sense of relationship with their mother. Many people emphasized the importance of keeping their mother's personal belongings or photos in their homes. Mark Rills, who had sewn a piece of his mother's wedding veil into the yarmulke he wore at his wedding, also spoke of his delight at being able to use his mother's fine linens and silver when he entertained. Frank McCourt, at sixty-five, still has his mother's christening outfit and childhood toys; he enjoys taking out her photos and sharing them with his children and grandchildren. Sarah Mulligan, as we saw, described her worries about getting her mom's wedding ring and Bible fixed; they were so important to her that she was afraid to leave them at a shop. Sheryl Smith had her mother's favorite holiday skirt hanging on her bedroom wall.

Another way in which respondents maintained their mothers' presence was by creating sacred practices—adapted from their religious traditions or from other traditions, or made up—that evoked their mother's presence, thereby achieving a sense of continuity in their lives. Many people visited their mother's grave regularly, using that as a time to think about her or pray to her. Mary French, a woman in her seventies, lives across the street from the cemetery where her mother is buried; she feels it is her duty to visit regularly and to pray and talk to her mother. Carl Diamond described his long-term practice of lighting a cigarette every time he visited his mother's grave; as he watched the smoke rise, he felt in communication with his mother, who had been a smoker herself. Although he felt that this practice was "ghoulish," he continued it for many years because it helped him feel more connected to her.

Carrying out religious rituals they had learned in their youth was another means of maintaining connections with their mothers in the present. Several of the Jewish respondents reported observing the custom of visiting their mothers' graves right before the high holidays in the fall. Some said that participating in memorial observances, such as sending in annual notices to the newspaper, or the Jewish practice of saying the prayer in commemoration of the dead on several holidays during the year, gave them an opportunity to think about their moms. Sid Jacoby mentioned that he continues to have Sabbath meals with his family as a way of maintaining something special from his childhood. Walter Devlin, age sixty, reported that he continued to go to mass despite his religious ambivalence; it was a practice that had mattered greatly to his mother and thus a means for him to continue his relationship with her.

Although many respondents said that they did not feel any particular connection with their mother by visiting her grave or carrying out traditional religious practices, they invented their own traditions that helped them remember their mother and ritually mark their ongoing connections with her. Every year on Mother's Day, Rachel Morgenstern got together with her motherless friends to celebrate what they called Dead Mother's Day. They marked the occasion, she said, by shopping for bathing suits (a difficult exercise for many women, given their internalized notions about body image), going to a bad movie, or getting drunk. Sheryl Smith, like her mother, had a practice of writing short stories that she never finished. Henry Bigelow was planning on singing a song with his church choir that his mother had really liked and dedicating it to her. Juan Rosaldo told me that he regularly reads his mother's letters and listens to music that she loved, both strategies for establishing her presence in his everyday life.

About a fourth of my respondents found it helpful to converse with their mothers on an ongoing basis. Harry Stevenson, age fifty-five, said that when he talks with his mother, she helps him figure things out, as if he had her voice in his head saying, "You have to go home and work on this thing and here's an idea." Bob McPherson mentioned that when he visits his mother's grave, he sometimes asks her, "When are you going to come get me?" Katherine Bennett told me that she regularly talks with her mother while jogging; she feels she gets advice from her mom when she needs it. Several respondents stated explicitly that they saw their mothers as guiding spirits in their lives, essences they could rely on during difficult times.

While several respondents described their mothers as continuing sources of guidance and wisdom, many emphasized other types of spiritual connections with their mothers. Neil Roberts saw his mother as his "angel"; he talked about her as an energy that was always with him. Katherine Bennett told me she sees her mother's death not as a loss but as a "difference," a change in their relationship, which nevertheless can continue through a spiritual connection. Diane Jardine, a divorced woman in her fifties, reported that her mother's presence is with her all the time: "There is not a day that goes by without my thinking about her . . . everything ends up connecting with her."

Henry Bigelow stated that his mother is his guardian angel; she helped him survive major accidents in which he might otherwise have died. A few respondents, such as Darlene Jackson, described visions of their mother's ghost. Despite the general absence of organized religion in most of my respondents' lives, many described with a great deal of certainty the spiritual dimension of their sense of connection and relationship with their mothers. Their sense of their mothers as actively present in their lives helps them repair their disrupted biographies and establish continuity between their past and present lives.

Another common means by which respondents maintained their mother's presence in their adult lives was by emphasizing their resemblance to her. In effect, they were claiming that their mother, although no longer physically present, nevertheless lived on through them. My interviewees sought to carry on their mother's best qualities and values, in particular her compassion, warmth, ability to relate to and be caring of others, and righteousness. Katherine played out her mother's great compassion through working in a helping profession. Similarly, Paul Renear, the self-made divorced man I referred to earlier, told me that he carries on his mother's goodness and humanity by doing charity work and being a "people person." Several women and men told me that their mothers were the moral role models in their lives, providing a standard against which they continually measured themselves. Sammy Dickenson told me that although he does not share his mother's Christian fundamentalist beliefs, he continues to uphold and respect the strong moral values she instilled in him when he was a child. He felt that these ethical sensibilities prevented him from getting involved in the use of drugs, despite significant peer pressure to do so. Despite his differences with her means of expressing her faith, he identifies with her in his search for "truth" and "ideals," a personal journey that he frequently emphasized in his interview.

The common tendency to idealize their mothers made it difficult for some of my respondents to feel that they could live up to their mothers and thus have their mothers live on through them. Sid Jacoby emphasized his strong, omnipresent sense of inadequacy; he was not sure that his mother would have been proud of the person he had become. Christine Albert told me that her mom had always been portrayed as perfect, and she worried that she could never live up to her image. While some of the women expressed a desire to be as pretty as their mothers were, many respondents strove to embody the fine traits they attributed to their mothers, such as discipline, intelligence, good organizational skills, creativity, and strength.

Through the process of narrating these stories of disruption and repair, my respondents had an opportunity to recreate their sense of themselves by integrating their past, present, and future lives. While our culture offers few ready-made scripts or a language for making meaning of motherloss, interviewees' narratives showed many striking similarities in how they articulated and made sense of the disruption and reintegration of their lives. Since mothers are culturally constructed as essential to their children and families, their early death represents such a threat to the stability of their children's social worlds that it has been literally inconceivable. These narratives were spoken out of the pervasive silences surrounding this event and reflected my interviewees' struggles both to find the terms to narrate their stories and to come to terms with motherloss in their lives.

10

Coming to Terms with Motherloss

I could not live in any of the
worlds offered to me. . . . I believe
one writes because one has to
create a world in which one
can live.

Anaïs Nin, In Favor
of the Sensitive Man

Part of the process of coming to terms with motherloss
is moving beyond cultural and institutional silences in
the face of death and finding the terms in which to tell
this story. Constructing narratives of this disruptive event
and locating it in the context of an ongoing, continuous
biography helps those who have suffered such a loss to
move beyond the state of linguistic disquietude that typically results from the silencing of important life events.
Articulating—and thus reexperiencing—motherloss provides a way to order and categorize this disruption and
weave it into a coherent narrative of identity. By speaking
the account into being, one not only tells the story but
reshapes and reconfigures one's sense of self in the process.

In writing this book, I have had to come to terms with
my own motherloss. From a deeply buried, taboo subject

in my mind—as well as in the life of my family—the loss of my mother at a young age has emerged as a central feature in my narrative construction of self. No longer will I ever pretend that "it's no big deal" that my mother died when I was thirteen, or that I simply overcame it and went on to live a successful life. Instead, I recognize the ambiguities in my story. Indeed I did persevere and make a life for myself that works, but this early loss nevertheless continues to reverberate through my life, making me particularly sensitive to the death of other people close to me, fearful about rejection, as well as fiercely independent and self-reliant. I often wonder what my mother would think of me as an adult and of the choices I've made, which were quite different from hers. Like many women of her generation, she left college to marry and raise a family; in contrast, I chose to stay in academic settings and not to have children. How would she respond to my having spent five years delving into the meanings of motherloss in my life as well as in sixty other lives?

My reconstruction of my identity through the co-creation of and immersion in narratives of motherloss affects not only me but also my interactions with other significant people in my life. For example, by writing this book and breaking my family's long-held taboo about my mother's death, I have been instrumental in bringing my brothers, whom I have periodically pestered with questions, to see how silent we actually have been. During my first few years of work on this project, my younger brother, Mark, expressed his discomfort by frequently asking, "Are you still writing books about dead people?" His coming to terms with my project, as revealed by the pride with which he mentioned it in a public forum, suggests that he may be engaged in the process of integrating his own experiences of motherloss.

In Chapter 1 I told of recurring dreams about my mother during the years I worked on this book. In those dreams I was a child whose mother had suddenly reappeared from the world of the dead, and I confronted her about her failure to properly feed us, her children, and me in particular. As I began working on the conclusion to this book, I had another dream about my mother. This one was particularly vivid. In it, I was standing as an adult with my mother. I told her that I was writing a book about people whose mothers died when they were growing up. She looked terribly pained and sad, and she began to fade out into a skeleton, and then she was gone. But in a moment she reappeared and was there with me again, and we silently looked at each other in mutual acknowledgment. Although my mother is obviously not alive and we never had a chance to establish an adult relationship, the process of writing this book has changed my relationship with her. No longer am I the child who has lost her mother, but an adult who has worked hard to come to terms with her loss.

Nearly all of my respondents, at the end of our interviews, expressed how glad they were for the chance to discuss motherloss, an important subject they normally avoided in order to protect themselves and others from the pain it evoked. They found the conversation healing in some way; the opportunity to break long-held silences and speak their contradictions and inconsistencies into a coherent narrative was psychically comforting and peaceful.

In researching and writing narratives of motherloss, I have become deeply aware of the transformative potential of social science. Reconstructing my own narrative of identity has changed me; my work with respondents in co-creating their accounts of motherloss has had an impact on my life as well as on theirs. The telling of lives always transforms those lives.[1] I hope that ultimately this kind of work can contribute to the reconfiguration of the discipline of sociology and to the rethinking of some of our social and cultural institutions and norms.

This work is situated within the ongoing conversation among anthropological and sociological ethnographers about the linkages between the various human sciences and the need to enrich the social sciences by the incorporation of methods and perspectives from the humanities.[2] The fascination with narratives and the growing awareness that people's words reveal not only the structures of human experience but the molding of those experiences by social and cultural factors is one outgrowth of the trend to broaden the definition and relevance of the social sciences. Since humans understand and constitute their lives through the stories they tell, narratives provide a useful way of understanding human experiences. They reveal the many ways we construct sense and meaning of the various complex and ambiguous elements of our lives.

As early as 1970 Alvin Gouldner promoted a reflexive approach to sociology that rested on an acknowledgment that "there is no knowledge of the world that is not a knowledge of our own experience with it and our relation to it." Instead of seeking a distanced, objective "truth" about the social world apart from its knowers, reflexive sociology challenges us to understand that social scientists are inevitably part of what we study and of the "knowledge" we derive from our research. "The knower's knowing of himself—of who, what, and where he is—on the one hand, and of others and their social worlds, on the other, are two sides of a single process."[3]

My own relationship to this project and my modes of

seeking and "producing" knowledge have been informed by the theoretical models of reflexive sociology and the exemplary work of those who have sought to integrate this paradigm within their scholarly work. One of my goals in this project has been to contribute to others' efforts to break down the artificial boundaries between the human disciplines and to transcend limited conventional and scientistic understandings of human life. The relevance of this work to people's efforts to comprehend and make sense of experiences of loss would have been weaker if I had expunged all references to my own experiences with motherloss from this work. One aim of this book has been to reveal the various ways in which meaning is attached to human experiences of loss. By revealing my own attempts to break silences and come to terms with emotional pain, I have indicated one pathway to understanding the experiences of others and of culture and loss. There is a power in thinking itself as a practice of everyday life. Intellectual honesty, I am certain, comes from honesty with and about oneself.

Telling lives is not devoid of analysis or theory; rather narrative weaves the analysis into the very telling of the story. Analysis is revealed in the modes and language in which experiences and reflections are represented. In this work I seek to contribute to the developing tradition of social scientists whose analytic insights are developed in interaction with lived experience as it is narrated by the people whose lives we seek to understand. This work presents multiple voices and ways of reading my respondents' narratives. Through the very language I have used to represent their representations I have hoped not only to inform my readers of the "facts" of the experience of motherloss but also to evoke their empathic feelings. The validity of this work lies in its ability to evoke in my readers the feeling that the experiences represented in it are authentic, believable, and possible and that they are useful in helping others to understand and make meaning out of their own experiences.[4]

Transgressing disciplinary boundaries, breaking silences, and evoking deep feelings, however, can sometimes be uncomfortable for people who, reared in U.S. mainstream culture, prefer to keep the private and public separate, and resist the insertion of emotions into academic discourse. Although our cultural attitudes toward death are slowly changing, telling stories of motherloss still produces discomfort and resistance to the expression of loss and pain. As Sally Cline wrote, "Choosing to write about death is choosing to be looked upon as a freak. . . . Choosing to talk about writing about death is choosing to swim against the stream. It is asking to be silenced."[5] During the years I worked on this book, I found that in meeting new people and discussing what we do, my mere mention of the topic of this book could become a conversation stopper. If, in our society in general, death is taboo and grieving is unseemly, then perhaps by associating myself so deeply with this subject I was breaking social norms and making people uncomfortable.

This book aims to change society by challenging our cultural taboos about death as well as our particular social constructions of motherhood. The image of Mother as embodied in the institution of Motherhood and as articulated in my respondents' narratives is generally so idealized that no one could live up to it. My respondents' representations typically portrayed mothers who were unconditionally loving, all-nurturing, and always "there" at the center of their young lives. A few of my respondents recognized that they were presenting an idealized image of their mothers; they had learned in therapy that we often idealize the people and relationships we have lost. As I listened to my respondents describe their mothers, I tried to discern which aspects of their narratives were idealized and which were not. Such a distinction, however, was nearly impossible; even those respondents who acknowledged that their depictions were idealistic were adamant in maintaining that their mothers had ultimately been beatific and marvelous. What place could such a distinction have in a narrative of motherloss? If the mother figure had been filled out with greater realism—if more respondents had detailed incidents of spankings and conflict—would that have helped ease their feelings of loss and made them feel that their mothers were not, in fact, irreplaceable? For these narrators, who were deprived of the opportunity to develop mature relationships with their mothers, these idealized cultural constructions provide a ready model in which to frame their depictions of the mothers they lost. Further, by inserting the institutionalized version of Mother into their accounts, they found it easier to normalize their biographies, to minimize their sense of deviance. In addition, all accounts we tell become facts in and of themselves, to the listener as well as the speaker. Mainly, our accounts are related to reality, but they surely cannot reproduce it. In describing their mothers as possessing those ideal traits of Motherhood, respondents were able to smoothly fill the gap between what they had experienced and remembered and what they needed to tell about.

My study reveals that the ongoing ideology of the gendered division of labor—that women are responsible for the emotional maintenance of the family—creates a crisis situation when mothers are no longer available, for whatever reason. Several years ago the *New York Times Magazine* featured a story, "Christy Chooses a Mother," which described how a young girl and her mother searched for an appropriate mother substitute to take care of Christy after her mother's impending death from AIDS. Just when they thought they had found a suitable replacement and had developed a relationship with the "new mom" and her son, the potential new mother revealed—in Christy's mother's eyes—an ongoing favoritism for her son over Christy. And so the search continued. Although Christy and her mother sought a substitute—thinking one *could* be found and thus that a mother could be replaced—their experiences underlined the argument of this book, that when motherhood is socially constructed as an exclusive and intensive role, mothers wind up being impossible to replace.

This particular formulation of motherhood can be dangerous—for the mothers who find their multiple roles very challenging as well as for the families that are left behind when the mother is lost. This narrow vision of gender and family roles, enshrined in our cultural ideology and reinforced through social structures, asserts that only one person in one particular social role is capable of—and truly suited for—the emotional care of children. The division of labor in the nuclear family remains so circumscribed that not only is it impossible for a person in a different category (an aunt, a father, a friend) to take the mother's place; no one at all can do so. How, then, can individual families or we as a society formulate workable solutions for situations in which the mother is no longer present? The changes required to alleviate this situation are fundamental and far-reaching. They involve a redefinition of gender so that both females and males can embody a wider range of human qualities and a reorganization of work and other social institutions so that women's and men's participation in public roles will no longer be limited by conventional assumptions about family roles. The involvement of multiple adults in the care and nurture of children would also alleviate the pressures on individual mothers and on disrupted families, such as those we have met in this book.

Interview Guide

I. General Background Questions

1. Tell me something about your background. (Use as prompts: Where you grew up, your education, marital status, occupation, parents' education and occupation, siblings, etc.)

II. Initial Loss and Years Afterward

2. Tell me, in as much detail as you can, what happened when your mother died. What were the circumstances leading up to her death?

3. How old were you when your mom died? How old was she?

4. How was her death handled in your family? How, precisely, were you told about her death? Was it discussed much? If she had been ill prior to her death, had that been discussed? Were you aware of what was happening to her? Were you prepared in any way for your mother's death?

5. Did you go to therapy after she died? [*If yes*] Was it helpful? Tell me about it in detail. [*If no*] Do you have any thoughts about whether that might have been useful?

6. Tell me as much as you can about what happened in the next days, weeks, and months.
7. What was it like to go back to school?
8. Did you have any dreams/nightmares/physical symptoms as a response to your mother's death?
9. How did household tasks get taken care of?
10. Did any relatives fill in? What about family friends?
11. Did you and your siblings help each other through?
12. Were there any special friends or their families who were important to you at this point?
13. Was there anyone who became (in any way) a substitute mother?
14. Did you learn to self-mother in any ways?
15. Did/do you experience any anger with regard to your mother's death? Any guilt?
16. Did family finances change as a result of your mother's death?
17. Did you have pictures of your mom out in your house?

III. Family Life Prior to Loss

Here probe for additional information on nature of family life when person was growing up. Who was involved in the family constellation? What were the relationships like among siblings, between parents, between interviewee and each parent, etc.?

IV. Relationship with Mom in Particular

18. Tell me, in as much detail as you can, what your mother was like. (Probes: What did she look like? What was her personality? Likes and dislikes? Favorite activities? Interests?)
19. What sorts of things would you do with your mother?
20. How would you describe your relationship with your mother? (Probe: Were you close? Were there tensions? Describe.)
21. Tell me a story about a day you spent with your mother. Can you think of other such stories to tell?

22. What did you like best about your mother? Least?
23. Were there things you liked to talk to her about? Were there things you deliberately avoided discussing with her?
24. Did you and she argue about anything?
25. Since her death, have you spoken with family friends or relatives about her? How did they describe her? What sorts of things have you learned from these discussions?
26. Do you resemble your mom in any way? (Probes: Looks, personality traits, interests, likes and dislikes, etc.)

V. Relationship with Father

27. Tell me about your relationship with your father prior to your mom's death. How, if at all, did that relationship change after her death?
28. What was your father like when you were growing up? (Probe: Get rich details here, such as what did he look like? What was his personality? Likes and dislikes? Favorite activities? Interests?) Did he change after your mother's death?
29. Do you resemble your dad in any way? (Probe for specifics.)
30. What was your father's involvement in your life as you were growing up? Did that change after your mother's death?
31. Tell me a story about something you did with your dad.
32. How did your father respond to your mother's death?
33. Did he give you and your siblings any guidance or clues about how to respond?
34. Did your father remarry?
35. (*If yes*) Tell me as much as you can about the circumstances of his remarriage. When and how did he meet his new wife? What was she like? Did she have children of her own? How were these new children integrated into the household? Did you get along with them? How did her (and her children's) presence affect household dynamics and daily life in your family?

VI. Relationships with Other Family Members Before and After Mother's Death

36. Were you close to your siblings? Describe.
37. Did your mother's death affect your relationship with your siblings? How?
38. If you had younger siblings, did you feel a need to take care of them after your mother's death?
39. Were there other relatives involved in your life as you were growing up? (Probe: Get a detailed account of the ways in which they might have been helpful to the children and dad; if they took over any household tasks; if they played any emotional roles, etc.) What about family friends? (Again, probe for details.) Did these relationships change after your mother's death? Please specify.
40. After your mother died, would you and your siblings and your dad talk about her? With whom, in particular, did these conversations take place, and what was their nature?
41. Do you currently talk about your mother with your dad or his wife or your siblings? (Probe as to why or why not, and what these conversations are about, who initiates them, etc.)
42. Is there anyone else with whom you currently talk about your mom? Tell me something about these conversations.

VII. Religion

43. Was religion important in your family's life prior to your mother's death? Describe in detail.
44. Did religion play a role in the rituals surrounding her death and in the mourning period? Tell me about the rituals observed. What did they mean to you? Did you find them helpful?
45. What roles, in particular, did the leader and members of the religious community play? Did any of them come around to help your family? In what ways?
46. Do you and your family believe in an afterlife? In heaven and hell?

47. Do you think you will be reunited with your mom after your own death?

48. Did your mother's death in any way affect your religious feelings, beliefs, and attitudes?

49. Do you ever feel your mother's presence in your life now? Tell me in some detail about the circumstances in which you can feel her presence. Do they involve any activities on your part or that you do with others? Do you have any particular rituals for invoking her presence? Do you talk to her? Pray? Communicate in any other ways?

VIII. Life Story After Mother's Death

50. Tell me about your life since your mother's death. (Here probe for the broad outlines—education, dating, marriage, jobs, what the person has done, where she or he has been, etc.—and then ask for lots of particulars.)

51. When you were growing up, after your mother died, who helped you with things such as homework and relationships, [*for women*] first bra and menstrual period?

52. When did you begin dating?

53. With whom did you talk about dating? If your mom had been alive, do you think you might have spoken with her?

54. Do you dream about your mother? Tell me about some of those dreams.

55. Are friendships important to you? In what ways?

56. Tell me about your intimate relationships. (Probe for some details.) Do you feel that they have been affected in any way because of your mother's death?

57. Do you have children?

58. Was your decision to have (or not to have) children in any way affected by your mother's death? Please elaborate.

59. Are there any ways in which your mother's early death affects your interactions with your children and the ways you have chosen to raise them?

60. How do you feel that your mother's illness has affected you? Affected the course of your life?

61. Can you think of ways your life might have been different if your mother had not died when you were young?
62. Do you think there were any positive outcomes for you from your mother's premature death?
63. When do you think of your mom?
64. Do you miss her? At any times in particular?
65. Do you visit your mother's grave? Is there any pattern to these visits?
66. Do you observe any rituals of observance in church or synagogue? On your own, or with friends or relatives?
67. Do you have any of your mother's things? How do you feel about them?
68. Do you think your mother would be proud of the woman/man you have become? Tell me about this.
69. Can you think of any more stories about your mom you want to tell me?
70. Have you ever written anything about your mother? (*If yes*) Would you be willing to show it to me?
71. Do you have any pictures of your mother, and of your mother and yourself, that you would like to show me?

IX. Representations of Motherhood and Family

72. This next question calls for free association. Please tell me the first thing that comes to mind when you think of: Mother. Family.
73. Is there anything else important to you that we did not cover?
74. What was it like to be interviewed about this subject?

Notes

Chapter 1. The Researcher and the Researched

1. Bury, 1982; Becker, 1997.
2. Behar, 1993, 1996; Geertz, 1988; Wolf, 1992.
3. Harris, 1996.
4. Ellis, 1995.
5. Edelman, 1994.
6. Personal communications.
7. Chodorow, 1978; Gilligan, 1982; Hays, 1996; Tannen, 1990.
8. Although by 1970 over 50 percent of all mothers were in paid employment, our social structures, culture, and policies have still not caught up with this reality in respect to the constraints and negative images that haunt the "working mother."
9. For example, see Stack, 1974; Burke, 1994; and essays in Coll et al., 1998.
10. Lawless, 1993; Oakley, 1992.
11. De Vault, 1991.

Chapter 2. Narrating Motherloss
as Biographical Disruption

1. In 1994 Hope Edelman published a groundbreaking book, *Motherless Daughters,* which examines the narratives of women of all ages who lost their mothers at some point in their lives. This book differs from hers in several significant respects: (1) I have included an equal number of men in my sample because I am interested in the gendered ways that motherloss is represented; (2) I have focused my study on motherloss at a particular period of life, early adolescence, so that my narratives will be comparable on that dimension across respondents; (3) the interpretive framework of *Motherless Daughters* is drawn from psychology and speaks in terms of developmental stages; this book focuses its analytic lens on the ways in which the social context—the structural division of labor by gender and our cultural ideologies of gender—shapes the narratives people tell about motherloss.

2. Hays, 1996.

3. Becker, 1973.

4. I think here of President Jimmy Carter's attempt to convene a White House conference on the family, only to find that the participants could not agree on what a family is.

5. For a greatly more elaborated version of this brief account I present here, see, among others, Ryan, 1975; Hays, 1996; Coltrane, 1996; Ehrenreich and English, 1978; Degler, 1980; and Lasch, 1977.

6. Ryan, 1975, p. 76.

7. Ehrenreich and English, 1978, p. 3.

8. Lasch, 1977; Welter, 1966.

9. Hays, 1996.

10. Parsons et al., 1955.

11. Garey, 1999.

12. De Vault, 1991, p. 30.

13. Gordon, 1996, p. xxii.

14. See Fulton, 1965; Kastenbaum and Aisenberg, 1972; Kübler-Ross, 1969; Sudnow, 1967; Weisman, 1972.

15. Charmaz, 1980, p. 78.
16. Cline, 1997, p. 19.
17. Ariès, 1974.
18. Gorer, 1984.
19. Ariès et al., 1974, p. 151.
20. The sociologist Kathy Charmaz, for instance, tells of various cultural studies that describe the public general acceptance of death in Chinese culture and the Hindu approach to death as "deliverance" (1980, pp. 86–87).
21. Ariès, 1974, p. 12.
22. Charmaz, 1980, p. 87.
23. Stephenson, 1985, p. 32.
24. Kaufman and Raphael, 1996, p. 4.
25. Tillich, 1952, p. 110.
26. Mishler, 1989.
27. Dubos, 1987, p. 157; Charmaz, 1980, p. 102.
28. Ariès, 1974, pp. 88–89.
29. Sontag, 1978, pp. 8, 9.
30. Charmaz, 1980, p. 271.
31. Ibid., pp. 282–283.
32. Stephenson, 1985, p. 33.
33. Cline, 1997, p. 59.
34. Ariès, 1974, pp. 89–90.
35. Giddens, 1991, pp. 203–204.
36. Spock and Parker, 1992, p. 534.
37. Laurel Richardson has defined a collective story as one that "tells the experience of a sociologically constructed category of people in the context of larger sociocultural and historical forces. The sociological protagonist is a collective one. I think of similarly situated individuals who may or may not be aware of their life affinities as coparticipants in a collective story" (1997, p. 14).
38. Miller, 1996, p. 159.
39. Gordon, 1996, p. 26.
40. Rosenwald and Ochberg, 1992, pp. 4–5.
41. Ibid., pp. 3–4.
42. Ibid., p. 5.

43. Ibid., p. 271.

44. Clifford and Marcus, 1986; Marcus and Fischer, 1986; Richardson, 1997; Gouldner, 1970; Reinharz, 1983; Stacey, 1998.

45. Richardson, 1997, p. 6.

46. See Turner, 1967.

47. Rosenwald and Ochberg, 1992, p. 62.

48. Ibid., pp. ix, 9, 6.

49. Richardson, 1997, pp. 58–59.

50. Gordon, 1996, p. xx.

51. Miller, 1996, p. 2.

52. Gornick, 1996, p. 5.

53. Rieff, 1987.

54. Quoted in Rhiel and Suchoff, 1996, p. 181.

55. Miller, 1996, pp. ix–x.

56. Gordon, 1996, p. 5.

57. Becker, 1997.

58. Abu-Lughod, 1993.

Chapter 3. An Archetypal Narrative

1. All names in this book are pseudonyms; to protect the anonymity of my respondents, I have also changed some identifying characteristics. I have not, however, changed any of the basic elements of my respondents' stories.

2. Chodorow, 1978; Miller, 1976; Degler, 1980; De Vault, 1991.

3. Hall, 1997. Karen McCarthy Brown and I organized a conference called "Religion Outside the Institutions" that was sponsored by the Center for the Study of American Religion at Princeton University and held there in June 1998.

Chapter 4. The Myth of the Perfect Mother

1. Many more than three interviewees—in fact, over half of them—had fathers who remarried while the children were at home. Only three, however, reported positive relationships with their stepmothers.

2. Ruddick, 1989.
3. Garey, 1999.
4. Di Leonardo, 1987.
5. De Vault, 1991.

Chapter 5. A Different Script

1. Cline, 1997, p. 246.
2. Fine, 1997, discusses the stigma and taboo about suicide.
3. See Tabouret-Keller, 1997.

Chapter 7. Reverberating Losses

1. Becker, 1997, pp. 177, 190.
2. Other authors who write about parental death similarly trace a pattern of reverberating losses. See, for example, Edelman, 1994, and Harris, 1996.
3. Ruddick, 1989.
4. Lloyd, 1980, p. 529.
5. Bifulco, Harris, and Brown, 1992, p. 433.
6. Finkelstein, 1988, p. 3.
7. The ethical issue of how much information to reveal to interviewees has been discussed in the social science literature. The feminist sociologist Ann Oakley (1992) deliberately broke the mainstream professional code of researcher neutrality in her study of pregnancy and motherhood. She found that her interviewees, young pregnant women, lacked important and basic knowledge about birthing and motherhood, and she consciously made a decision that she should provide them with whatever information she could rather than deliberately withhold information that could be helpful to them.
8. Kramer, 1993.
9. Charmaz, 1980; Cline, 1997.

Chapter 8. Elements of Biographical Disruption

1. Luckmann, 1967.
2. Bellah et al., 1985; Berger, 1969.

3. Carr, Freund, and Somani, 1995.
4. Rieff, 1987.

Chapter 10. Coming to Terms with Motherloss

1. Ellis, 1995, p. 316
2. See, for example, Clifford and Marcus, 1985; Ellis, 1995; Marcus and Fischer, 1986; Richardson, 1997; Stacey, 1998.
3. Gouldner, 1970, p. 493.
4. Ellis, 1995, p. 318
5. Cline, 1997, p. 14

References

Abu-Lughod, Lila. 1993. *Writing Women's Worlds: Bedouin Stories.* Berkeley: University of California Press.

Ariès, Philippe. 1974. *Western Attitudes Toward Death: From the Middle Ages to the Present.* Baltimore: Johns Hopkins University Press.

Ariès, Philippe, et al., eds. 1974. *Death in America.* Philadelphia: University of Pennsylvania Press.

Becker, Ernest. 1973. *The Denial of Death.* New York: Free Press.

Becker, Gay. 1997. *Disrupted Lives: How People Create Meaning in a Chaotic World.* Berkeley: University of California Press.

Behar, Ruth. 1993. *Translated Woman: Crossing the Border with Esperanza's Story.* Boston: Beacon Press.

———. 1996. *The Vulnerable Observer: Anthropology That Breaks Your Heart.* Boston: Beacon Press.

Bellah, Robert N., Richard Madsen, William M. Sullivan, Ann Swidler, and Steven M. Tipton. 1985. *Habits of the Heart: Individualism and Commitment in American Life.* Berkeley: University of California Press.

Berger, Peter L. 1969. *The Sacred Canopy: Elements of a Soci-*

ological Theory of Religion. Garden City, N.Y.: Anchor/Doubleday.

Bifulco, Antonia, Tirrill Harris, and George Brown. 1992. "Mourning or Early Inadequate Care? Reexamining the Relationship of Maternal Loss in Childhood with Adult Depression and Anxiety." *Development and Psychopathology* 4: 433–449.

Burke, Phyllis. 1994. *Family Values: A Lesbian Mother's Fight for Her Son.* New York: Vintage.

Bury, Michael. 1982. "Chronic Illness as Biographical Disruption." *Sociology of Health and Illness* 4, 2 (July): 167–182.

Carr, Phyllis L., Karen M. Freund, and Sujata Somani, eds. 1995. *The Medical Care of Women.* Philadelphia: Saunders.

Charmaz, Kathy. 1980. *The Social Reality of Death: Death in Contemporary America.* Reading, Mass.: Addison-Wesley.

Chodorow, Nancy. 1978. *The Reproduction of Mothering: Psychoanalysis and the Sociology of Gender.* Berkeley: University of California Press.

Clifford, James, and George E. Marcus, eds. 1986. *Writing Culture: The Poetics and Politics of Ethnography.* Berkeley: University of California Press.

Cline, Sally. 1997. *Lifting the Taboo: Women, Death, and Dying.* New York: New York University Press.

Coll, Cynthia Garcia, Janet L. Surrey, and Kathy Weingarten, eds. 1998. *Mothering Against the Odds.* New York: Guilford Press.

Coltrane, Scott. 1996. *Family Man: Fatherhood, Housework, and Gender Equity.* New York: Oxford University Press.

Corea, Gena. 1977. *The Hidden Malpractice: How American Medicine Treats Women as Patients and Professionals.* New York: Morrow.

Degler, Carl N. 1980. *At Odds: Women and the Family in America from the Revolution to the Present.* New York: Oxford University Press.

De Vault, Marjorie L. 1991. *Feeding the Family: The Social Organization of Caring as Gendered Work.* Chicago: University of Chicago Press.

Di Leonardo, Micaela. 1987. "The Female World of Cards and Holidays: Women, Families, and the Work of Kinship." *Signs: Journal of Women in Culture and Society* 12, 3: 440–453.

Dubos, René. 1987. *Mirage of Health: Utopias, Progress, and Biological Change*. New Brunswick: Rutgers University Press.

Edelman, Hope. 1994. *Motherless Daughters: The Legacy of Loss*. Reading, Mass.: Addison-Wesley.

Ehrenreich, Barbara, and Deirdre English. 1978. *For Her Own Good: 150 Years of the Experts' Advice to Women*. Garden City, N.Y.: Anchor/Doubleday.

Ellis, Carolyn. 1995. *Final Negotiations: A Story of Love, Loss, and Chronic Illness*. Philadelphia: Temple University Press.

Festinger, Leon. 1957. *A Theory of Cognitive Dissonance*. Stanford: Stanford University Press.

Fine, Carla. 1997. *No Time to Say Goodbye: Surviving the Suicide of a Loved One*. New York: Bantam Doubleday Dell.

Finkelstein, Harris. 1988. "The Long-Term Effects of Early Parent Death: A Review." *Journal of Clinical Psychology* 44 (January): 3–9.

Fulton, Robert. 1965. *Death and Identity*. New York: Wiley.

Garey, Anita Ilta. 1999. *Weaving Work and Motherhood*. Philadelphia: Temple University Press.

Geertz, Clifford. 1988. *Works and Lives: The Anthropologist as Author*. Stanford: Stanford University Press.

Giddens, Anthony. 1991. *Modernity and Self-Identity: Self and Society in the Late Modern Age*. Stanford: Stanford University Press.

Gilligan, Carol. 1982. *In a Different Voice: Psychological Theory and Women's Development*. Cambridge: Harvard University Press.

Gordon, Mary. 1996. *The Shadow Man*. New York: Random House.

Gorer, Geoffrey. 1984. "The Pornography of Death." In *Death: Current Perspectives*, ed. Edwin Schneidman, pp. 26–30. Palo Alto: Mayfield.

Gornick, Vivian. 1996. "Why Memoir Now?" *Women's Review of Books* 13, *10–11* (July): 5.

Gouldner, Alvin. 1970. *The Coming Crisis of Western Sociology.* New York: Avon.

Hall, David D., ed. 1997. *Lived Religion in America: Toward a History of Practice.* Princeton: Princeton University Press.

Harris, Maxine. 1996. *The Loss That Is Forever: The Lifelong Impact of the Early Death of a Mother or Father.* New York: Penguin.

Hays, Sharon. 1996. *The Cultural Contradictions of Motherhood.* New Haven: Yale University Press.

Hochschild, Arlie. 1989. *The Second Shift: Working Parents and the Revolution at Home.* New York: Viking.

Jarrell, Randall, trans. 1972. *Snow-White and the Seven Dwarfs: A Tale from the Brothers Grimm.* New York: Farrar, Straus, & Giroux.

Kahn, Robbie Pfeufer. 1995. *Bearing Meaning: The Language of Birth.* Urbana: University of Illinois Press.

Kastenbaum, Robert, and Ruth Aisenberg. 1972. *The Psychology of Death.* New York: Springer.

Kaufman, Gershon, and Lev Raphael. 1996. *Coming Out of Shame: Transforming Gay and Lesbian Lives.* New York: Doubleday.

Kramer, Peter D. 1993. *Listening to Prozac.* New York: Viking.

Kübler-Ross, Elisabeth. 1969. *On Death and Dying.* New York: Macmillan.

Lasch, Christopher. 1977. *Haven in a Heartless World: The Family Besieged.* New York: Basic Books.

Lawless, Elaine J. 1993. *Holy Women, Wholly Women: Sharing Ministries of Wholeness Through Life Stories and Reciprocal Ethnography.* Philadelphia: University of Pennsylvania Press.

Lloyd, Camille. 1980. "Life Events and Depressive Disorder Reviewed." *Archives of General Psychiatry* 37 (May): 529–535.

Luckmann, Thomas. 1967. *The Invisible Religion: The Problem of Religion in Modern Society.* New York: Macmillan.

Marcus, George E., and Michael M. J. Fischer. 1986. *Anthro-*

pology as Cultural Critique: An Experimental Moment in the Human Sciences. Chicago: University of Chicago Press.

Miller, Jean Baker. 1976. *Toward a New Psychology of Women.* Boston: Beacon Press.

Miller, Nancy K. 1996. *Bequest & Betrayal: Memoirs of a Parent's Death.* New York: Oxford University Press.

Mishler, Elliot G. 1989. "Critical Perspectives on the Biomedical Model." In *Perspectives in Medical Sociology,* ed. Phil Brown, pp. 153–166. Prospect Heights, Ill.: Waveland Press.

Oakley, Ann. 1992. *Social Support and Motherhood: The Natural History of a Research Project.* Oxford: Blackwell.

Parsons, Talcott, and Robert F. Bales, with James Olds et al. 1955. *Family, Socialization, and Interaction Process.* Glencoe, Ill.: Free Press.

Raine, Nancy Venable. 1998. *After Silence: Rape & My Journey Back.* New York: Crown.

Reinharz, Shulamit. 1983. "Experiential Analysis: A Contribution to Feminist Research." In *Theories of Women's Studies,* ed. Gloria Bowles and Renate Duelli Klein, pp. 162–191. London: Routledge & Kegan Paul.

Rhiel, Mary, and David Suchoff, eds. 1996. *The Seductions of Biography.* New York: Routledge.

Rich, Adrienne. 1976. *Of Woman Born: Motherhood as Experience and Institution.* New York: Norton.

Richardson, Laurel. 1997. *Fields of Play: Constructing an Academic Life.* New Brunswick: Rutgers University Press.

Rieff, Philip. 1987. *The Triumph of the Therapeutic: Uses of Faith After Freud.* Chicago: University of Chicago Press.

Rosenwald, George C., and Richard L. Ochberg, eds. 1992. *Storied Lives: The Cultural Politics of Self-Understanding.* New Haven: Yale University Press.

Ruddick, Sara. 1989. *Maternal Thinking: Toward a Politics of Peace.* Boston: Beacon Press.

Ryan, Mary P. 1975. *Womanhood in America: From Colonial Times to the Present.* New York: New Viewpoints.

Sontag, Susan. 1978. *Illness as Metaphor.* New York: Farrar, Straus, & Giroux.

Spock, Benjamin, and Steven Parker. 1992. *Dr. Spock's Baby and Child Care.* New York: Pocket Books.

Stacey, Judith. 1998. *Brave New Families: Stories of Domestic Upheaval in Late-Twentieth-Century America.* Berkeley: University of California Press.

Stack, Carol B. 1974. *All Our Kin: Strategies for Survival in a Black Community.* New York: Harper & Row.

Stephenson, John. 1985. *Death, Grief, and Mourning: Individual and Social Realities.* New York: Free Press.

Sudnow, David. 1967. *Passing On: The Social Organization of Dying.* Englewood Cliffs, N.J.: Prentice-Hall.

Tabouret-Keller, Andrée. 1997. "Language and Identity." In *The Handbook of Sociolinguistics,* ed. Florian Coulmas, pp. 315–326. Oxford: Blackwell.

Tannen, Deborah. 1990. *You Just Don't Understand: Women and Men in Conversation.* New York: Morrow.

Tillich, Paul. 1952. *The Courage to Be.* New Haven: Yale University Press.

Turner, Victor. 1967. *The Forest of Symbols: Aspects of Ndembu Ritual.* Ithaca, N.Y.: Cornell University Press.

Weisman, Avery D. 1972. *On Dying and Denying: A Psychiatric Study of Terminality.* New York: Behavioral Publications.

Welter, Barbara. 1966. "The Cult of True Womanhood, 1820–1860." *American Quarterly* 18 (Summer): 151–174.

Wolf, Margery. 1992. *A Thrice-Told Tale: Feminism, Postmodernism, and Ethnographic Responsibility.* Stanford: Stanford University Press.

Index

Index: Carol Roberts
Text: 11/14 Aster
Display: Frutiger and Aster
Composition: Binghamton Valley Composition
Printing and binding: Maple-Vail Book Manufacturing Group